Court Delay and Human Rights Remedies

This book brings legal and academic perspective to the theory and practice surrounding the right to a fair hearing within a reasonable time. This field of rights has been somewhat neglected academically, a fact which jars with the sheer volume of case law budding from this single, simple, fundamental right, bearing testimony to the widespread concern with delay in judicial proceedings which transcends the boundaries of states or legal systems.

The work provides a blueprint for analysing the effectiveness of legal remedies across entire legal systems, as well as in any given individual case. The first part focuses on deriving legal principles from the body of jurisprudence of the European Court of Human Rights in Strasbourg, while the second part contains illustrations of the practical application of such principles.

The content constitutes essential reading for students, academics, lawyers, judges, practitioners and all those who wish to understand the issue of delay in judicial proceedings, and the legal context of available remedies. The author aims to raise awareness about the human rights issues which come into play when delivery of justice is delayed, and to provide both an academic and practical reference.

Dr Caroline Savvidis holds a Doctor of Laws degree and is the managing partner of BN&P Advocates, a law firm with a global focus on the resolution of family office issues and the improvement of private and public efficiency in governance and regulation. Dr Savvidis has researched and written extensively on the topic of human rights and legal remedies for court delay; she is a guest lecturer at various universities, and regularly presents at international conferences on issues relating to cross-border regulation, constitutional and human rights law.

This thought-provoking introduction to the study of court delay and human rights remedies provides in-depth analyses of relevant legal issues in the contexts of the European Court of Human Rights and Malta, and serves as a guide to the study of court proceedings and human rights protection from a novel angle. It is written in a lively, accessible and enlightening manner. It contains much that will be invaluable to both the scholars and practitioners in the field of international human rights law, offering dynamic insights into the study of human rights protection and making a significant contribution to the subject. The writing allows the readers to delve deeper.

Professor Shen Wei, *Shanghai Jiao Tong University, China*

The problem of excessive judicial delays continues to plague many legal systems in Europe and it has given rise to a phenomenal volume of cases before the Strasbourg court. Caroline Savvidis's study of this long-neglected problem is an impressive, insightful contribution which will be of the greatest interest to students, practitioners and governmental reformers.

Professor Vernon Valentine Palmer, *Tulane Law School, USA*

Court Delay and Human Rights Remedies

Enforcing the Right to a Fair Hearing
'Within a Reasonable Time'

Caroline Savvidis

LONDON AND NEW YORK

First published 2016
by Routledge
2 Park Square, Milton Park, Abingdon, Oxon OX14 4RN

and by Routledge
711 Third Avenue, New York, NY 10017

First issued in paperback 2018

Routledge is an imprint of the Taylor & Francis Group, an informa business

© 2016 Caroline Savvidis

The right of Caroline Savvidis to be identified as author of this work has been asserted by him/her in accordance with sections 77 and 78 of the Copyright, Designs and Patents Act 1988.

All rights reserved. No part of this book may be reprinted or reproduced or utilised in any form or by any electronic, mechanical, or other means, now known or hereafter invented, including photocopying and recording, or in any information storage or retrieval system, without permission in writing from the publishers.

Trademark notice: Product or corporate names may be trademarks or registered trademarks, and are used only for identification and explanation without intent to infringe.

British Library Cataloguing in Publication Data
A catalogue record for this book is available from the British Library

Library of Congress Cataloging-in-Publication Data
Savvidis, Caroline.
 Court delay and human rights remedies: enforcing the right to a fair hearing 'within a reasonable time' / by Caroline Savvidis.
  pages cm
 Based on author's thesis (doctoral—University of Malta, 2010), issued under title: The right to a fair hearing within a reasonable time.
 Includes bibliographical references and index.
 ISBN 978-1-4724-6416-3 (hardback)
 1. Speedy trial–Europe. 2. European Court of Human Rights.
 3. Speedy trial–Malta. I. Title.
 KJC3832.S63S28 2015
 345.24'075—dc23
 2015025307

ISBN 13: 978-1-138-60654-8 (pbk)
ISBN 13: 978-1-4724-6416-3 (hbk)

Typeset in Bembo
by Apex CoVantage, LLC

To my family

Contents

Statutes	x
Judgments	xxvii
Abbreviations	xlvi
Foreword	xlvii
Preface	li
Acknowledgements	lii

Introduction   1

Aims and Parameters of Research 1
The Strasbourg Pot Calling the National Kettles Black? A Vicious Circle 5
Subsidiarity – The Need for Effective Remedies at a National Level to Uphold Convention Rights 5

1 Preliminary Pleas and Fundamental Concepts Relevant to Length-of-Proceedings Cases Brought Before the European Court of Human Rights   8

Chapter Introduction 8
Chapter 1 – Section 1 – Article 35(1) Exhaustion of (Effective) Domestic Remedies 9
Chapter 1 – Section 2 – Article 34 Loss of Victim Status – Incompatibility Ratione Personae 14

2 Guidance Drawn from Judgments of the European Court of Human Rights; the Relevance and Utility of ECHR Articles 6 and 13 to Length-of-Proceedings Cases   22

Chapter Introduction 22
Chapter 2 – Section 1 – The Strasbourg Court's Method of Examination 23

Chapter 2 – Section 2 – Article 13: General Observations 35
Chapter 2 – Section 3 – Case Study Based on the Legal System of Italy: The Scordino-Type Cases 37
Chapter 2 – Section 4 – How does the European Court Calculate the Quantum of Compensation under Article 41? 39

3 Case Study Based on the Legal System of Malta, Part I: Human Rights Remedies for Delay   53

Chapter Introduction 53
Chapter 3 – Section 1 – Analysis of Violations Found by the European Court against Malta Resulting From Divergences in the Interpretation and Application of the Convention 55
Chapter 3 – Section 2 – Overview of the Length-of-Proceedings Case Law of Malta and the Interpretation and Application of Convention Provisions by the Local Courts 56
Chapter 3 – Section 3 – Should the Courts of Constitutional Jurisdiction in Malta Decline Jurisdiction on the Basis that Adequate Means of Redress Exist Under Ordinary Law? 76

4 Case Study Based on the Legal System of Malta, Part II: Remedies for Delay Within Ordinary Law   83

Chapter Introduction 83
Chapter 4 – Section 1 – No Redress against Private Parties Can Be Sought Through Constitutional Action 84
Chapter 4 – Section 2 – Ordinary Remedies are Not Prejudiced by and Do Not Prejudice Constitutional Remedies 85
Chapter 4 – Section 3 – What Ordinary Remedies Exist for Delay in Judicial Proceedings? 85
Chapter 4 – Section 4 – Ordinary Remedies for Delay in Judicial Proceedings – The Action for Damages in Tort 86

5 Case Study Based on the Legal System of Malta, Part III: Conclusions   95

Conclusion   105

Appendix A – Statistics Demonstrating the Volume of Length-of-Proceedings Violations Found by the Strasbourg Court, Expressed as a Percentage of Total Convention Violations   109

*Appendix B – Length-of-Proceedings Violations Expressed as
  a Percentage of Overall Violations per State, 1999–2008* 112
Bibliography 114
Index 119

Statutes

This table sets out in full the articles cited within the text, for ease of reference. The articles found hereunder do not represent the entirety of the relevant legal instruments. The original or updated legislative acts can be found on the website of the respective issuing body or by following the links provided.

International Instruments

Convention for the Protection of Human Rights and Fundamental Freedoms

(European Convention on Human Rights as amended by Protocols No. 11 and No. 14) Full instrument available at: <http://www.echr.coe.int/Documents/Convention_ENG.pdf>

...

Article 1
Obligation to respect Human Rights

The High Contracting Parties shall secure to everyone within their jurisdiction the rights and freedoms defined in Section I of this Convention.

Article 2
Right to life

1. Everyone's right to life shall be protected by law. No one shall be deprived of his life intentionally save in the execution of a sentence of a court following his conviction of a crime for which this penalty is provided by law.
2. Deprivation of life shall not be regarded as inflicted in contravention of this Article when it results from the use of force which is no more than absolutely necessary:

    (a) in defence of any person from unlawful violence;

(b) in order to effect a lawful arrest or to prevent the escape of a person lawfully detained;
(c) in action lawfully taken for the purpose of quelling a riot or insurrection.

...

Article 5
Right to liberty and security

1 Everyone has the right to liberty and security of person. No one shall be deprived of his liberty save in the following cases and in accordance with a procedure prescribed by law:

(a) the lawful detention of a person after conviction by a competent court;
(b) the lawful arrest or detention of a person for noncompliance with the lawful order of a court or in order to secure the fulfilment of any obligation prescribed by law;
(c) the lawful arrest or detention of a person effected for the purpose of bringing him before the competent legal authority on reasonable suspicion of having committed an offence or when it is reasonably considered necessary to prevent his committing an offence or fleeing after having done so;
(d) the detention of a minor by lawful order for the purpose of educational supervision or his lawful detention for the purpose of bringing him before the competent legal authority;
(e) the lawful detention of persons for the prevention of the spreading of infectious diseases, of persons of unsound mind, alcoholics or drug addicts or vagrants;
(f) the lawful arrest or detention of a person to prevent his effecting an unauthorised entry into the country or of a person against whom action is being taken with a view to deportation or extradition.

2 Everyone who is arrested shall be informed promptly, in a language which he understands, of the reasons for his arrest and of any charge against him.

3 Everyone arrested or detained in accordance with the provisions of paragraph 1 (c) of this Article shall be brought promptly before a judge or other officer authorised by law to exercise judicial power and shall be entitled to trial within a reasonable time or to release pending trial. Release may be conditioned by guarantees to appear for trial.

4 Everyone who is deprived of his liberty by arrest or detention shall be entitled to take proceedings by which the lawfulness of his detention shall be decided speedily by a court and his release ordered if the detention is not lawful.

5 Everyone who has been the victim of arrest or detention in contravention of the provisions of this Article shall have an enforceable right to compensation.

Article 6
Right to a fair trial

1. In the determination of his civil rights and obligations or of any criminal charge against him, everyone is entitled to a fair and public hearing within a reasonable time by an independent and impartial tribunal established by law. Judgment shall be pronounced publicly but the press and public may be excluded from all or part of the trial in the interests of morals, public order or national security in a democratic society, where the interests of juveniles or the protection of the private life of the parties so require, or to the extent strictly necessary in the opinion of the court in special circumstances where publicity would prejudice the interests of justice.
2. Everyone charged with a criminal offence shall be presumed innocent until proved guilty according to law.
3. Everyone charged with a criminal offence has the following minimum rights:
   (a) to be informed promptly, in a language which he understands and in detail, of the nature and cause of the accusation against him;
   (b) to have adequate time and facilities for the preparation of his defence;
   (c) to defend himself in person or through legal assistance of his own choosing or, if he has not sufficient means to pay for legal assistance, to be given it free when the interests of justice so require;
   (d) to examine or have examined witnesses against him and to obtain the attendance and examination of witnesses on his behalf under the same conditions as witnesses against him;
   (e) to have the free assistance of an interpreter if he cannot understand or speak the language used in court.

...

Article 8
Right to respect for private and family life

1. Everyone has the right to respect for his private and family life, his home and his correspondence.
2. There shall be no interference by a public authority with the exercise of this right except such as is in accordance with the law and is necessary in a democratic society in the interests of national security, public safety or the economic wellbeing of the country, for the prevention of disorder or crime, for the protection of health or morals, or for the protection of the rights and freedoms of others.

...

Article 10
Freedom of expression

1. Everyone has the right to freedom of expression. This right shall include freedom to hold opinions and to receive and impart information and ideas

without interference by public authority and regardless of frontiers. This Article shall not prevent States from requiring the licensing of broadcasting, television or cinema enterprises.

2   The exercise of these freedoms, since it carries with it duties and responsibilities, may be subject to such formalities, conditions, restrictions or penalties as are prescribed by law and are necessary in a democratic society, in the interests of national security, territorial integrity or public safety, for the prevention of disorder or crime, for the protection of health or morals, for the protection of the reputation or rights of others, for preventing the disclosure of information received in confidence, or for maintaining the authority and impartiality of the judiciary.

...

Article 12
Right to marry

Men and women of marriageable age have the right to marry and to found a family, according to the national laws governing the exercise of this right.

...

Article 13
Right to an effective remedy

Everyone whose rights and freedoms as set forth in this Convention are violated shall have an effective remedy before a national authority notwithstanding that the violation has been committed by persons acting in an official capacity.

...

Article 34
Individual applications

The Court may receive applications from any person, non-governmental organisation or group of individuals claiming to be the victim of a violation by one of the High Contracting Parties of the rights set forth in the Convention or the protocols thereto. The High Contracting Parties undertake not to hinder in any way the effective exercise of this right.

Article 35
Admissibility criteria

1   The Court may only deal with the matter after all domestic remedies have been exhausted, according to the generally recognised rules of international law, and within a period of six months from the date on which the final decision was taken.

2 The Court shall not deal with any application submitted under Article 34 that

   (a) is anonymous; or
   (b) is substantially the same as a matter that has already been examined by the Court or has already been submitted to another procedure of international investigation or settlement and contains no relevant new information.

3 The Court shall declare inadmissible any individual application submitted under Article 34 if it considers that:

   (a) the application is incompatible with the provisions of the Convention or the Protocols thereto, manifestly ill-founded, or an abuse of the right of individual application; or
   (b) the applicant has not suffered a significant disadvantage, unless respect for human rights as defined in the Convention and the Protocols thereto requires an examination of the application on the merits and provided that no case may be rejected on this ground which has not been duly considered by a domestic tribunal.

4 The Court shall reject any application which it considers inadmissible under this Article. It may do so at any stage of the proceedings.

...

Article 41
Just satisfaction

If the Court finds that there has been a violation of the Convention or the Protocols thereto, and if the internal law of the High Contracting Party concerned allows only partial reparation to be made, the Court shall, if necessary, afford just satisfaction to the injured party.

...

Article 46
Binding force and execution of judgments

1 The High Contracting Parties undertake to abide by the final judgment of the Court in any case to which they are parties.
2 The final judgment of the Court shall be transmitted to the Committee of Ministers, which shall supervise its execution.
3 If the Committee of Ministers considers that the supervision of the execution of a final judgment is hindered by a problem of interpretation of the judgment, it may refer the matter to the Court for a ruling on the question of interpretation. A referral decision shall require a majority vote of two thirds of the representatives entitled to sit on the Committee.

4 If the Committee of Ministers considers that a High Contracting Party refuses to abide by a final judgment in a case to which it is a party, it may, after serving formal notice on that Party and by decision adopted by a majority vote of two thirds of the representatives entitled to sit on the Committee, refer to the Court the question whether that Party has failed to fulfil its obligation under paragraph 1.
5 If the Court finds a violation of paragraph 1, it shall refer the case to the Committee of Ministers for consideration of the measures to be taken. If the Court finds no violation of paragraph 1, it shall refer the case to the Committee of Ministers, which shall close its examination of the case.

...

Protocol to the Convention for the Protection of Human Rights and Fundamental Freedoms

Paris, 20.III.1952

...

Article 1
Protection of property

Every natural or legal person is entitled to the peaceful enjoyment of his possessions. No one shall be deprived of his possessions except in the public interest and subject to the conditions provided for by law and by the general principles of international law.

The preceding provisions shall not, however, in any way impair the right of a State to enforce such laws as it deems necessary to control the use of property in accordance with the general interest or to secure the payment of taxes or other contributions or penalties.

...

Rules of Court

(1 July 2014, European Court of Human Rights) Full instrument available at: <http://www.echr.coe.int>

Chapter V – Proceedings after the Admission of an Application
Rule 614 – Pilot-judgment procedure

1 The Court may initiate a pilot-judgment procedure and adopt a pilot judgment where the facts of an application reveal in the Contracting Party concerned the existence of a structural or systemic problem or other similar dysfunction which has given rise or may give rise to similar applications.

2 (a) Before initiating a pilot-judgment procedure, the Court shall first seek the views of the parties on whether the application under examination results from the existence of such a problem or dysfunction in the Contracting Party concerned and on the suitability of processing the application in accordance with that procedure.

    (b) A pilot-judgment procedure may be initiated by the Court of its own motion or at the request of one or both parties.

    (c) Any application selected for pilot-judgment treatment shall be processed as a matter of priority in accordance with Rule 41 of the Rules of Court.

3 The Court shall in its pilot judgment identify both the nature of the structural or systemic problem or other dysfunction as established as well as the type of remedial measures which the Contracting Party concerned is required to take at the domestic level by virtue of the operative provisions of the judgment.

4 The Court may direct in the operative provisions of the pilot judgment that the remedial measures referred to in paragraph 3 above be adopted within a specified time, bearing in mind the nature of the measures required and the speed with which the problem which it has identified can be remedied at the domestic level.

5 When adopting a pilot judgment, the Court may reserve the question of just satisfaction either in whole or in part pending the adoption by the respondent Contracting Party of the individual and general measures specified in the pilot judgment.

6 (a) As appropriate, the Court may adjourn the examination of all similar applications pending the adoption of the remedial measures required by virtue of the operative provisions of the pilot judgment.

    (b) The applicants concerned shall be informed in a suitable manner of the decision to adjourn. They shall be notified as appropriate of all relevant developments affecting their cases.

    (c) The Court may at any time examine an adjourned application where the interests of the proper administration of justice so require.

7 Where the parties to the pilot case reach a friendly-settlement agreement, such agreement shall comprise a declaration by the respondent Contracting Party on the implementation of the general measures identified in the pilot judgment as well as the redress to be afforded to other actual or potential applicants.

8 Subject to any decision to the contrary, in the event of the failure of the Contracting Party concerned to comply with the operative provisions of a pilot judgment, the Court shall resume its examination of the applications which have been adjourned in accordance with paragraph 6 above.

9 The Committee of Ministers, the Parliamentary Assembly of the Council of Europe, the Secretary General of the Council of Europe, and the Council of Europe Commissioner for Human Rights shall be informed of the adoption of a pilot judgment as well as of any other judgment in which the

Court draws attention to the existence of a structural or systemic problem in a Contracting Party.
10 Information about the initiation of pilot-judgment procedures, the adoption of pilot judgments and their execution as well as the closure of such procedures shall be published on the Court's website.

Laws of Malta

Full instruments available at: <http://www.justiceservices.gov.mt/LOM.aspx>

Chapter 0 – Constitution

...

Chapter IV

...

Article 39
Provisions to secure protection of law

1 Whenever any person is charged with a criminal offence he shall, unless the charge is withdrawn, be afforded a fair hearing within a reasonable time by an independent and impartial court established by law.
2 Any court or other adjudicating authority prescribed by law for the determination of the existence or the extent of civil rights or obligations shall be independent and impartial; and where proceedings for such a determination are instituted by any person before such a court or other adjudicating authority, the case shall be given a fair hearing within a reasonable time.

...

Article 46
Enforcement of protective provisions

1 Subject to the provisions of sub-articles (6) and (7) of this article, any person who alleges that any of the provisions of articles 33 to 45 (inclusive) of this Constitution has been, is being or is likely to be contravened in relation to him, or such other person as the Civil Court, First Hall, in Malta may appoint at the instance of any person who so alleges, may, without prejudice to any other action with respect to the same matter that is lawfully available, apply to the Civil Court, First Hall, for redress.
2 The Civil Court, First Hall, shall have original jurisdiction to hear and determine any application made by any person in pursuance of sub-article (1) of this article, and may make such orders, issue such writs and give such directions as it may consider appropriate for the purpose of enforcing, or

securing the enforcement of, any of the provisions of the said articles 33 to 45 (inclusive) to the protection of which the person concerned is entitled: Provided that the Court may, if it considers it desirable so to do, decline to exercise its powers under this sub-article in any case where it is satisfied that adequate means of redress for the contravention alleged are or have been available to the person concerned under any other law.

3   If in any proceedings in any court other than the Civil Court, First Hall, or the Constitutional Court any question arises as to the contravention of any of the provisions of the said articles 33 to 45 (inclusive), that court shall refer the question to the Civil Court, First Hall, unless in its opinion the raising of the question is merely frivolous or vexatious; and that court shall give its decision on any question referred to it under this sub-article and, subject to the provisions of sub-article (4) of this article, the court in which the question arose shall dispose of the question in accordance with that decision.

4   Any party to proceedings brought in the Civil Court, First Hall, in pursuance of this article shall have a right of appeal to the Constitutional Court.

5   No appeal shall lie from any determination under this article that any application or the raising of any question is merely frivolous or vexatious.

6   Provision may be made by or under an Act of Parliament for conferring upon the Civil Court, First Hall, such powers in addition to those conferred by this article as are necessary or desirable for the purpose of enabling the Court more effectively to exercise the jurisdiction conferred upon it by this article.

7   Rules of Court making provision with respect to the practice and procedure of the Courts of Malta for the purposes of this article may be made by the person or authority for the time being having power to make rules of court with respect to the practice and procedure of those Courts, and shall be designed to secure that the procedure shall be by application and that the hearing shall be as expeditious as possible.

...

Chapter 12 – Code of Organisation and Civil Procedure

...

Book Second – Part I – Title II

...

Article 154
Proceedings by sworn application

1   The procedure by sworn application is considered to institute a cause, when the court issues or gives an order to a party to appear before it on

the day and at the hour appointed, in order to show cause why the claim contained in the sworn application should not be allowed.
2 In the appointment of such day allowance shall be made for the time required for the preliminary written procedures of the case to be closed, provided that in urgent cases the court may appoint a day for the trial of the case before the close of the preliminary written procedures.

...

Book Second – Part I – Title IV and V

...

Article 181B
Judicial representation of Government

1 The judicial representation of the Government in judicial acts and actions shall vest in the head of the government department in whose charge the matter in dispute falls:

...

2 The Attorney General shall represent Government in all judicial acts and actions which owing to the nature of the claim may not be directed against one or more heads of other government departments.

...

Article 194
Posting up of cause list

1 The registrar shall cause a list of the causes which are to be tried at a particular sitting to be posted up at the side of the entrance of the court room where the causes are to be heard at least one hour before the case is to be heard, saving urgent cases referred to in article 154(2).
2 The list shall bear the date on which it is posted up as aforesaid and shall be signed by the registrar.
3 The list shall be deemed to be posted up, according to the regulations, on the date which it bears and at the time of the closing of the registry.

...

Court Practice and Procedure and Good Order Rules

Legal Notice 279 of 2008, Subsidiary Legislation 12.09

...

Part I – Court Practice and Procedure concerning Constitutional Matters

...

Article 6
Expeditious hearing and disposal of hearing

Once a case has been set down for hearing the court shall ensure that, consistently with the due and proper administration of justice, the hearing and disposal of the case shall be expeditious, and the hearing of the cause shall as far as possible continue to be heard on consecutive days, and, where this is not possible, on dates close to one another.

...

Part III – Court Practice and Procedure concerning Drawing up of Lists, Hearings to be Held by Appointment, Adjournment of Causes and Conduct of Proceedings

...

Article 9
Causes to be heard, etc., in chronological order

1 In making the list referred to in article 194 of the Code, the Registrar, Civil Court and Tribunals, or the Registrar, Gozo Courts and Tribunals, as the case may be, shall act in accordance with such instructions as may be given to him by the court, which shall ensure that, as far as possible, causes shall be heard and decided in the chronological order of the date of filing of the act with which the cause was introduced in the registry of the court. Not all causes ready for hearing shall be inserted in the list, but only as many as the Judge or Magistrate, as the case may be, considers he can deal with in any particular sitting: Provided that, without prejudice to anything contained in any other law, priority shall be given in setting a cause for hearing and in the hearing thereof to-

   (i) cases of retrial;
   (ii) spoliation suits referred to in article 791 of the Code;
   (iii) cases of contempt of court;
   (iv) appeals from decisions of the Civil Court (Family Section);
   (v) cases dealing with recognition and enforcement of foreign judgments;
   (vi) arbitration cases; and
   (vii) cases which of their nature require to be treated with greater expeditiousness.

2   Witnesses summoned for a particular sitting shall, as far as possible, be heard at such sitting.
3   The hearing of a cause, whether at pre-trial or trial stage, or other procedure shall, as far as possible, be by appointment for a given time as determined by the court or by the judicial assistant, as the case may be.
4   Where several causes or other procedures are to be heard during the course of any sitting, the court or the judicial assistant shall stagger the said causes or procedures at reasonable intervals to ensure that the parties, and witnesses if any, are not required to attend at the same time.

Article 10
Adjournment of causes

1   A cause may be adjourned in exceptional circumstances only if the court is satisfied that such circumstances exist and so states in the decree ordering the adjournment specifying those circumstances, and only on an application filed by the party requesting the adjournment not later than fifteen working days before the day due for hearing or, if the cause of the adjournment arises after the expiration of the said time limit, as soon as practicable thereafter; and the application shall specify in detail the circumstances justifying the request and shall be confirmed on oath by the applicant or, if the applicant is absent from Malta or is otherwise unable to confirm the application in person, such fact shall be stated in the application.
2   The following may be deemed to be exceptional circumstances for the purposes of the foregoing sub-rule:
    (a) the temporary illness of counsel;
    (b) the agreement between the parties to refer the cause to arbitration or mediation; and
    (c) any other exceptional circumstances which the court considers to be serious and sufficient.
3   In every case the circumstances justifying the request and concession of an adjournment shall be recorded in the acts of the proceedings.

Article 11
Conduct of proceedings

1   Evidence in a cause shall be heard either directly by the court or by means of an affidavit except in those cases where the nature of the case requires proof by a technical referee, who shall as far as possible assist the court when the evidence is heard by it *viva voce*, and where a need arises such evidence may be heard by the referee, also with the assistance of a legal referee or a judicial assistant, in a sitting fixed for the purpose.
2   Where no pre-trial hearing has taken place, the court shall on the first sitting of a cause ensure that the disputed issues of fact and of law in the

cause are identified and recorded in the acts of the proceedings, and that the parties shall indicate and record in the acts of the proceedings the specific object of each witness indicated by them according to article 561 of the Code, also to ensure, among other things, the proper application of article 558 of the said Code.

3 During the first sitting of each case the court shall-

(a) either fix a date or consecutive dates for the hearing of all the witnesses of the parties up to the adjournment of the cause for judgment, and where it is not possible to fix consecutive dates, to fix dates which are as near as possible to one another, in order to reach the same objective; or

(b) if the parties agree (to a request made by one of the parties) that all evidence be produced by means of affidavits (or when the court is unable to fix a date for the hearing of evidence *viva voce*), the court shall order specific periods during which each party is to produce all its evidence by means of an affidavit, and shall subsequently fix the date when the cross examination of the witnesses who had made an affidavit shall be heard, if such cross examination is requested.

4 The terms referred in sub-rule (3) may be extended by the court for valid and serious reasons which shall be indicated in the order granting the extension.

5 Where a witness refuses to co-operate with any of the parties and refuses to make an affidavit, such party shall file an application as is referred to in article 173(2) of the Code, in sufficient time so that such witness shall appear and give evidence before the judicial assistant in accordance with the said article.

Article 12
Appointment of legal referees shall be restricted

1 The appointment of legal referees shall be restricted to special and particular cases where a real necessity arises because the cause requires specialised knowledge in a particular field of law. On any such appointment the court shall indicate clearly and precisely in the decree the reasons and justification for such an appointment.

2 In cases where such legal referees are appointed, evidence shall be produced by means of a sworn statement (affidavit) or otherwise as the court may direct and within such time as shall be stated in the decree appointing the referees. The court may in each case order the legal referee to report to it on such dates as indicated by the court, so that the court shall be in a position to ascertain that its orders have been complied with. The court shall fix a date for the definitive filing of the report.

...

Chapter 16 – Civil Code

...

Book Second – Part II – Title IV – Sub-Title II

...

Article 1030
Proper use of one's right

Any person who makes use, within the proper limits, of a right competent to him, shall not be liable for any damage which may result therefrom.

Article 1031
Liability for damage caused through one's fault

Every person, however, shall be liable for the damage which occurs through his fault.

Article 1032
When a person is deemed to be in fault

1 A person shall be deemed to be in fault if, in his own acts, he does not use the prudence, diligence, and attention of a bonus paterfamilias.
2 No person shall, in the absence of an express provision of the law, be liable for any damage caused by want of prudence, diligence, or attention in a higher degree.

Article 1033
Culpable negligence

Any person who, with or without intent to injure, voluntarily or through negligence, imprudence, or want of attention, is guilty of any act or omission constituting a breach of the duty imposed by law, shall be liable for any damage resulting therefrom.

...

Article 1045
Measure of damages

1 The damage which is to be made good by the person responsible in accordance with the foregoing provisions shall consist in the actual loss which the act shall have directly caused to the injured party, in the expenses which the latter may have been compelled to incur in consequence of the damage, in the loss of actual wages or other earnings, and in the loss of

future earnings arising from any permanent incapacity, total or partial, which the act may have caused.
2. The sum to be awarded in respect of such incapacity shall be assessed by the court, having regard to the circumstances of the case, and, particularly, to the nature and degree of incapacity caused, and to the condition of the injured party.

...

Article 1047
Where damage consists in depriving person of use of his own money

1. The damage which consists in depriving a person of the use of his own money, shall be made good by the payment of interest at the rate of eight per cent a year.
2. If, however, the party causing the damage has acted maliciously, the court may, according to circumstances, grant also to the injured party compensation for any other damage sustained by him, including every loss of earnings, if it is shown that the party causing the damage, by depriving the party injured of the use of his own money, had particularly the intention of causing him such other damage, or if such damage is the immediate and direct consequence of the injured party having been so deprived of the use of his own money.
3. The sum to be awarded in respect of such loss of earnings shall be assessed by the court having regard to the circumstances of the case.

...

Chapter 319 – European Convention Act

...

Article 3
Enforcement of Convention

1. The Human Rights and Fundamental Freedoms shall be, and be enforceable as, part of the Law of Malta.

...

Article 4
Procedure for enforcement of Human Rights and Fundamental Freedoms

1. Any person who alleges that any of the Human Rights and Fundamental Freedoms, has been, is being or is likely to be contravened in relation to him, or such other person as the Civil Court, First Hall, in Malta may appoint at the instance of any person who so alleges, may, without prejudice to any other action with respect to the same matter that is lawfully available, apply to the Civil Court, First Hall, for redress.

2   The Civil Court, First Hall, shall have original jurisdiction to hear and determine any application made by any person in pursuance of subarticle (1), and may make such orders, issue such writs and give such directions as it may consider appropriate for the purpose of enforcing, or securing the enforcement, of the Human Rights and Fundamental Freedoms to the enjoyment of which the person concerned is entitled: Provided that the court may, if it considers it desirable so to do, decline to exercise its powers under this subarticle in any case where it is satisfied that adequate means of redress for the contravention alleged are or have been available to the person concerned under any other ordinary law.

3   If any proceedings in any court other than the Civil Court, First Hall, or the Constitutional Court any question arises as to the contravention of any of the Human Rights and Fundamental Freedoms, that court shall refer the question to the Civil Court, First Hall, unless in its opinion the raising of the question is merely frivolous or vexatious; and that court shall give its decision on any question referred to it under this subarticle and, subject to the provisions of subarticle (4), the court in which the question arose shall dispose of the question in accordance with that decision.

4   Any party to proceedings brought in the Civil Court, First Hall, in pursuance of this article shall have a right of appeal to the Constitutional Court.

5   No appeal shall lie from any determination under this article that any application or the raising of any question is merely frivolous or vexatious.

6   The Rules of Court made in accordance with article 46(7) of the Constitution as in force from time to time shall apply *mutatis mutandis* to the practice and procedure of the courts for the purpose of this article as if the proceedings made under this article were proceedings made under article 46 of the Constitution.

7   Where it is alleged that any of the Human Rights and Fundamental Freedoms and any of the provisions of articles 33 to 45 (inclusive) of the Constitution has been, is being or is likely to be contravened, the demand for redress or the reference to the Civil Court, First Hall, in accordance with article 46 of the Constitution and this article may be made in the same application or reference.

8   Where an application for redress or any reference to the Civil Court, First Hall, made after the 30th April, 1987 is made exclusively either under article 46 of the Constitution or under this article and is still pending before the Civil Court, First Hall, or the Constitutional Court, the court may examine whether or not the facts complained of are in violation of the corresponding Human Rights and Fundamental Freedoms, in the first case, or of the corresponding Fundamental Rights and Freedoms of the Individual enforceable under the Constitution, in the second case; and if the court so finds it may order accordingly the redress it may deem appropriate under any of the aforesaid laws.

...

Article 5
Right of Individual Petition

No person shall be hindered in the exercise of his right to petition the Secretary-General of the Council of Europe in accordance with the provisions of Article 25 of the Convention and of all the Articles of the said Convention related thereto.

Article 6
Enforcement of the decisions of the European Court of Human Rights

1. Any judgment of the European Court of Human Rights to which a declaration made by the Government of Malta in accordance with Article 46 of the Convention applies, may be enforced by the Constitutional Court in Malta, in the same manner as judgments delivered by that court and enforceable by it, upon an application filed in the Constitutional Court and served on the Attorney General containing a demand that the enforcement of such judgment be ordered.
2. Before adjudging upon any such demand the Constitutional Court shall examine if the judgment of the European Court of Human Rights sought to be enforced, is one to which a declaration as is referred to in subarticle (1) applies.
3. The Constitutional Court shall order the enforcement of a judgment referred to in this article if it finds that such judgment is one to which a declaration referred to in subarticle (2) applies.

...

First Schedule

...

Article 6

1. In the determination of his civil rights and obligations or of any criminal charge against him, everyone is entitled to a fair and public hearing within a reasonable time by an independent and impartial tribunal established by law.

...

Article 13

Everyone whose rights and freedoms as set forth in this Convention are violated shall have an effective remedy before a national authority notwithstanding that the violation has been committed by persons acting in an official capacity.

...

Judgments[1]

European Court of Human Rights, Strasbourg

A.P. v Italy [GC], (App no. 35265/97) (28 July 1999)
Abdoella v the Netherlands, (App no. 12728/87) (25 November 1992) Series A no. 248-A
Abdolkhani and Karimnia v Turkey, (App no. 30471/08) (22 September 2009)
Abdulaziz, Cabales and Balkandali v the United Kingdom, (App nos 9214/80, 9473/81 and 9474/81) (28 May 1985) Series A no. 94
Adamović v Serbia, (App no. 41703/06) (2 October 2012)
Agrokompleks v Ukraine (just satisfaction), (App no. 23465/03) (25 July 2013)
Agrokompleks v Ukraine, (App no. 23465/03) (6 October 2011)
Akdivar and Others v Turkey, (App no. 21893/93) (16 September 1996) 1996-IV
Akhan v Turkey, (App no. 34448/08) (31 May 2012)
Aksoy v Turkey, (App no. 21987/93) (18 December 1996) 1996-VI
Aleksandr Novikov v Russia, (App no. 7087/04) (11 July 2013)
Alexandre v Portugal, (App no. 33197/09) (20 November 2012)
Amat-G Ltd and Mebaghishvili v Georgia, (App no. 2507/03) ECHR 2005-VIII
Andrášik and Others v Slovakia (dec.), (App nos 57984/00, 60237/00, 60242/00, 60679/00, 60680/00, 68563/01 and 60226/00) ECHR 2002-IX
Andreucci v Italy, (App no. 12955/87) (27 February 1992) Series A no. 228-G
Angelucci v Italy, (App no. 12666/87) (19 February 1991) Series A no. 196-C
Antoni v the Czech Republic, (App no. 18010/06) (25 November 2010)
Apicella v Italy [GC], (App no. 64890/01) (29 March 2006)
Apicella v Italy, (App no. 64890/01) (10 November 2004)
Ardelean v Romania, (App no. 28766/04) (30 October 2012)
Armando Iannelli v Italy, (App no. 24818/03) (12 February 2013)
Arvanitaki-Roboti and Others v Greece [GC], (App no. 27278/03) (15 February 2008)
Arvanitaki-Roboti and Others v Greece, (App no. 27278/03) (18 May 2006)
Associação de Investidores do Hotel Apartamento Neptuno v Portugal, (App no. 46336/09) (16 April 2013)
Association of the Victims of S.C. Rompetrol S.A. and S.C. Geomin S.A. and Others v Romania, (App no. 24133/03) (25 June 2013)
Ateş Mimarlık Mühendislik A.Ş v Turkey, (App no. 33275/05) (25 September 2012)

Aydan v Turkey, (App no. 16281/10) (12 March 2013)
Aysu v Turkey, (App no. 44021/07) (13 March 2012)
Azzopardi v Malta, (App no. 28177/12) (6 November 2014)
Baggetta v Italy, (App no. 10256/83) (25 June 1987) Series A no. 119
Bąk v Poland, (App no. 7870/04) (16 January 2007) ECHR 2007-II (extracts)
Bako v Slovakia (dec.), (App no. 60227/00) (15 March 2005)
Barišič v Slovenia, (App no. 32600/05) (18 October 2012)
Barna v Hungary (no. 2), (App no. 35364/09) (25 March 2014)
Barta and Drajkó v Hungary, (App no. 35729/12) (17 December 2013)
Bartha v Hungary, (App no. 33486/07) (25 March 2014)
Batmaz v Turkey, (App no. 714/08) (18 February 2014)
Beck v Norway, (App no. 26390/95) (26 June 2001)
Beggs v the United Kingdom, (App no. 25133/06) (6 November 2012)
Beguš v Slovenia, (App no. 25634/05) (15 December 2011)
Belinger v Slovenia, (App no. 42320/98) (13 June 2002)
Belperio and Ciarmoli v Italy, (App no. 7932/04) (21 December 2010)
Benkő and Soósné Benkő v Hungary, (App no. 17596/12) (8 July 2014)
Berhani v Albania, (App no. 847/05) (27 May 2010)
Berretta and Ciarcia v Italy, (App nos 37904/03 and 11334/04) (7 December 2010)
Bertin-Mourot v France, (App no. 36343/97) (2 August 2000)
Berü v Turkey, (App no. 47304/07) (11 January 2011)
Bezzina Wettinger and Others v Malta, (App no. 15091/06) (8 April 2008)
Billi v Italy, (App no. 15118/89) (26 February 1993) Series A no. 257-G
Bilyy v Ukraine, (App no. 14475/03) (21 October 2010)
Bjelič v Slovenia, (App no. 50719/06) (18 October 2012)
Blaga v Romania, (App no. 54443/10) (1 July 2014)
Boca v Belgium, (App no. 50615/99) (15 November 2002) ECHR 2002-IX
Bock v Germany, (App no. 11118/84) (29 March 1989) Series A no. 150
Boddaert v Belgium, (App no. 12919/87) (12 October 1992) Series A no. 235-D
Bor v Hungary, (App no. 50474/08) (18 June 2013)
Borgese v Italy, (App no. 12870/87) (26 February 1992) Series A no. 228-B
Borisenko v Ukraine, (App no. 25725/02) (12 January 2012)
Borobar and Others v Romania, (App no. 5663/04) (29 January 2013)
Borodin v Russia, (App no. 41867/04) (6 November 2012)
Bosnigeanu and Others v Romania, (App nos 56861/08 and 33 others) (4 November 2014)
Bottazzi v Italy [GC], (App no. 34884/97) ECHR 1999-V
Boucke v Montenegro, (App no. 26945/06) (21 February 2012)
Broniowski v Poland (dec.) [GC], (App no. 31443/96) (28 September 2005) ECHR 2002-X
Brusco v Italy (dec.), (App no. 69789/01) (6 December 2001) ECHR 2001-IX
Bubláková v Slovakia, (App no. 17763/07) (15 February 2011)
Buchholz v Germany, (App no. 7759/77) (6 May 1981) Series A no. 42
Buj v Croatia, (App no. 24661/02) (1 June 2006)
Buldakov v Russia, (App no. 23294/05) (19 July 2011)

Burdov v Russia (no. 2), (App no. 33509/04) (15 January 2009)
Burdov v Russia, (App no. 59498/00) ECHR 2002-III
C.P. and Others v France, (App no. 36009/97) (1 August 2000)
Caldas Ramirez de Arrellano v Spain (dec.), (App no. 68874/01) ECHR 2003-I (extracts)
Calleja v Malta, (App no. 75274/01) (7 April 2005)
Caloc v France, (App no. 33951/96) (20 July 2000) ECHR 2000-IX
Capuano v Italy, (App no. 9381/81) (25 June 1987) Series A no. 119
Çarkçı v Turkey (no. 2), (App no. 28451/08) (14 October 2014)
Çatal v Turkey, (App no. 26808/08) (17 April 2012)
Cazenave de la Roche v France, (App no. 25549/94) (9 June 1998) 1998-III
Çelikalp v Turkey, (App no. 51259/07) (18 December 2012)
Cengiz Kılıç v Turkey, (App no. 16192/06) (6 December 2011)
Central Mediterranean Development Corporation Limited v Malta, (App no. 35829/03) (24 October 2006)
Cerin v Croatia, (App no. 54727/00) (15 November 2001)
Chahal v the United Kingdom, (App no. 22414/93) (15 November 1996) 1996-V
Charzyński v Poland (dec.), (App no. 15212/03) ECHR 2005-V
Chuykina v Ukraine, (App no. 28924/04) (13 January 2011)
Chyżyński v Poland, (App no. 32287/09) (24 July 2012)
Ciğerhun Öner v Turkey (no. 2), (App no. 2858/07) (23 November 2010)
Cocchiarella v Italy [GC], (App no. 64886/01) (29 March 2006) ECHR 2006-V
Cocchiarella v Italy, (App no. 64886/01) (10 November 2004)
Coëme and Others v Belgium, (App nos 32492/96, 32547/96, 32548/96, 33209/96 and 33210/96) ECHR 2000-VII
Comingersoll S.A. v Portugal [GC], (App no. 35382/97) (6 April 2000) ECHR 2000-IV
Constantin Florea v Romania, (App no. 21534/05) (19 June 2012)
Cooperativa Parco Cuma v Italy, (App no. 12145/86) (27 February 1992) Series A no. 231-E
Covezzi and Morselli v Italy, (App no. 52763/99) (9 May 2003)
Csiki v Romania, (App no. 11273/05) (5 July 2011)
D.M.T. and D.K.I. v Bulgaria, (App no. 29476/06) (24 July 2012)
D.P. v Poland, (App no. 34221/96) (20 January 2004)
Dachar v France, (App no. 42338/98) (10 October 2000)
Dadiani and Machabeli v Georgia, (App no. 8252/08) (12 June 2012)
Dalia v France, (App no. 26102/95) (19 February 1998) 1998-I
Danijel Pečnik v Slovenia, (App no. 44135/06) (18 October 2012)
Danilo Kovačič v Slovenia, (App no. 24376/08) (18 April 2013)
Davies v the United Kingdom, (App no. 42007/98) (16 July 2002)
De Clerck v Belgium, (App no. 34316/02) (25 September 2007)
De Hohenzollern (of Romania) v Romania, (App no. 18811/02) (27 May 2010)
De Ieso v Italy, (App no. 34383/02) (24 April 2012)
De Micheli v Italy, (App no. 12775/87) (26 February 1993) Series A no. 257-D
Debono v Malta, (App no. 34539/02) (7 February 2006)
Deguara Caruana Gatto and Others v Malta, (App no. 14796/11) (9 July 2013)

Delle Cave and Corrado v Italy, (App no. 14626/03) (5 June 2007) ECHR 2007-VI
Deumeland v Germany, (App no. 9384/81) (29 May 1986) Series A no. 100
Deweer v Belgium, (App no. 6903/75) (27 February 1980) Series A no. 35
Dewicka v Poland, (App no. 38670/97) (4 April 2000)
Deyanov v Bulgaria, (App no. 2930/04) (30 September 2010)
Di Cola v Italy, (App no. 44897/98) (15 December 2005)
Diana v Italy, (App no. 11898/85) (27 February 1992) Series A no. 229-A
Dimitrov and Hamanov v Bulgaria, (App nos 48059/06 and 2708/09) (10 May 2011)
Dinç and Others v Turkey, (App no. 34098/05) (13 November 2014)
Di Sante v Italy (dec.), (App no. 56079/00) (24 June 2004)
Dobbertin v France, (App no. 13089/87) (25 February 1993) Series A no. 256-D
Domingos Marques Ribeiro Maçarico v Portugal, (App no. 12363/10) (17 January 2012)
Doran v Ireland, (App no. 50389/99) (31 July 2003) ECHR 2003-X (extracts)
Doustaly v France, (App no. 26256/95) (23 April 1998) 1998-II
Dudgeon v the United Kingdom, (App no. 7525/76) (22 October 1981) Series A no. 45
E.M.B. v Romania, (App no. 4488/03) (13 November 2012)
Eastaway v the United Kingdom, (App no. 74976/01) (20 July 2004)
Eckle v Germany, (App no. 8130/78) (15 July 1982) Series A no. 51
Ekdal and Others v Turkey, (App no. 6990/04) (25 January 2011)
Emel Boyraz v Turkey, (App no. 61960/08) (2 December 2014)
Enculescu v Romania, (App no. 20789/07) (19 November 2013)
Enver Kaplan v Turkey, (App no. 40343/08) (25 June 2013)
Erfar-Avef v Greece, (App no. 31150/09) (27 March 2014)
Ergezen v Turkey, (App no. 73359/10) (8 April 2014)
Eriksson v Sweden, (App no. 60437/08) (12 April 2012)
Ernestina Zullo v Italy [GC], (App no. 64897/01) (29 March 2006)
Ernestina Zullo v Italy, (App no. 64897/01) (10 November 2004)
Esposito v Italy, (App no. 35771/03) (27 November 2007)
Etcheveste and Bidart v France, (App nos 44797/98 and 44798/98) (21 March 2002)
F.L. v Italy, (App no. 25639/94) (20 December 2001)
Fatih Taş v Turkey, (App no. 36635/08) (5 April 2011)
Fedina v Ukraine, (App no. 17185/02) (2 September 2010)
Fehr and Lauterburg v Switzerland (dec.), (App nos 708/02 and 1095/02) (21 June 2005)
Fergadioti-Rizaki v Greece, (App no. 27353/09) (18 April 2013)
Fernández-Molina González and Others v Spain, (App nos 64359/01 and others) ECHR 2002-IX (extracts)
Ferreira Alves v Portugal (no. 6), (App no. 46436/06 and 55676/08) (13 April 2010)

Finger v Bulgaria, (App no. 37346/05) (10 May 2011)
Fırat Can v Turkey, (App no. 6644/08) (24 May 2011)
Floarea Pop v Romania, (App no. 63101/00) (6 April 2010)
Flores Cardoso v Portugal, (App no. 2489/09) (29 May 2012)
Földes and Földesné Hajlik v Hungary, (App no. 41463/02) (ECHR 2006-XII)
Follo and Others v Italy, (App nos 28433/03, 28434/03, 28442/03, 28445/03 and 28451/03) (31 January 2012)
Fortunat v Slovenia, (App no. 42977/04) (18 April 2013)
Foti and Others v Italy, (App nos 604/76, 7719/76 and 7781/77) (10 December 1982) Series A no. 56
Foundation Hostel for Students of the Reformed Church and Stanomirescu v Romania, (App nos 2699/03 and 43597/07) (7 January 2014)
Francesco Quattrone v Italy, (App no. 13431/07) (26 November 2013)
Frendo Randon and Others v Malta, (App no. 2226/10) (22 November 2011)
Frydlender v France [GC], (App no. 30979/96) (27 June 2000) ECHR 2000-VII
Funke v France, (App no. 10828/84) (25 February 1993) Series A no. 256-A
G. v Italy, (App no. 12787/87) (27 February 1992) Series A no. 228-F
Gadzhikhanov and Saukov v Russia, (App nos 10511/08 and 5866/09) (31 January 2012)
Gagliano Giorgi v Italy, (App no. 23563/07) (6 March 2012) ECHR 2012 (extracts)
Gama da Costa v Portugal, (App no. 12659/87) (5 March 1990) Commission decision
Gana v Italy, (App no. 13024/87) (27 February 1992) Series A no. 230-H
Gasiņš v Latvia, (App no. 69458/01) (19 April 2011)
Gassner v Austria, (App no. 38314/06) (11 December 2012)
Gast and Popp v Germany, (App no. 29357/95) ECHR 2000-II
Gavula v Ukraine, (App no. 52652/07) (16 May 2013)
Gelli v Italy, (App no. 37752/97) (19 October 1999)
Georgios Papageorgiou v Greece (no. 2), (App no. 21032/08) (15 October 2009)
Georgios Papageorgiou v Greece, (App no. 59506/00) (9 May 2003) ECHR 2003-VI (extracts)
Gera de Petri Testaferrata Bonici Ghaxaq v Malta, (App no. 26771/07) (5 April 2011)
Gera de Petri Testaferrata Bonici Ghaxaq v Malta (just satisfaction), (App no. 26771/07) (3 September 2013)
Gereksar and Others v Turkey, (App nos 34764/05, 34786/05, 34800/05 and 34811/05) (1 February 2011)
Gheorghe v Romania, (App no. 19215/04) (15 March 2007) ECHR 2007-III (extracts)
Giummarra and Others v France (dec.), (App no. 61166/00) (12 June 2001)
Giuseppe Mostacciuolo v Italy (no. 1) [GC], (App no. 64705/01) (29 March 2006)
Giuseppe Mostacciuolo v Italy (no. 1), (App no. 64705/01) (10 November 2004)
Giuseppe Mostacciuolo v Italy (no. 2) [GC], (App no. 65102/01) (29 March 2006)
Giuseppe Mostacciuolo v Italy (no. 2), (App no. 65102/01) (10 November 2004)

Giuseppe Romano v Italy, (App no. 35659/02) (5 March 2013)
Giuseppina and Orestina Procaccini v Italy [GC], (App no. 65075/01) (29 March 2006)
Globa v Ukraine, (App no. 15729/07) (5 July 2012)
Głowacki v Poland, (App no. 1608/08) (30 October 2012)
Glykantzi v Greece, (App no. 40150/09) (30 October 2012)
Göçmen v Turkey, (App no. 72000/01) (17 October 2006)
Gonzalez Marin v Spain (dec.), (App no. 39521/98) ECHR 1999-VII
Gorbatenko v Ukraine, (App no. 25209/06) (28 November 2013)
Gorodnitchev v Russia, (App no. 52058/99) (24 May 2007)
Goroshchenya v Russia, (App no. 38711/03) (22 April 2010)
Gouveia Da Silva Torrado v Portugal (dec.), (App no. 65305/01) (27 March 2003)
Grässer v Germany, (App no. 66491/01) (5 October 2006)
Grigoryan v Armenia, (App no. 3627/06) (10 July 2012)
Grigoryev v Russia, (App no. 22663/06) (23 October 2012)
Grzinčič v Slovenia, (App no. 26867/02) ECHR 2007-V (extracts)
Guincho v Portugal, (App no. 8990/80) (10 July 1984) Series A no. 81
Gulmammadova v Azerbaijan, (App no. 38798/07) (22 April 2010)
Gürceğiz v Turkey, (App no. 11045/07) (15 November 2012)
Gürkan v Turkey, (App no. 1154/04) (29 March 2011)
H. v the United Kingdom, (App no. 9580/81) (8 July 1987) Series A no. 120
H.T. v Germany, (App no. 38073/97) (11 October 2001)
Hábenczius v Hungary, (App no. 44473/06) (21 October 2014)
Hadjikostova v Bulgaria (no. 2), (App no. 44987/98) (22 July 2004)
Hadjikostova v Bulgaria, (App no. 36843/97) (4 December 2003)
Hakan Toktaş v Turkey, (App no. 45336/08) (10 December 2013)
Hall v Austria, (App no. 5455/06) (6 March 2012)
Handölsdalen Sami Village and Others v Sweden, (App no. 39013/04) (30 March 2010)
Handyside v the United Kingdom, (App no. 5493/72) (7 December 1976) Series A no. 24)
Hartman v Czech Republic, (App no. 53341/99) (10 July 2003) ECHR 2003-VIII (extracts)
Hartman v Slovenia, (App no. 42236/05) (18 October 2012)
Hasan Yazıcı v Turkey, (App no. 40877/07) (15 April 2014)
Hasko v Turkey, (App no. 20578/05) (17 January 2012)
Havala v Slovakia, (App no. 47804/99) (12 November 2002)
Hentrich v France, (App no. 13616/88) (22 September 1994) Series A no. 296-A
Henworth v the United Kingdom, (App no. 515/02) (2 November 2004)
Hoffer and Annen v Germany, (App nos 397/07 and 2322/07) (13 January 2011)
Hoholm v Slovakia, (App no. 35632/13) (13 January 2015)
Hokkanen v Finland, (App no. 19823/92) (23 September 1994) Series A no. 299-A
Holzinger v Austria (no. 1), (App no. 23459/94) (30 January 2001) ECHR 2001-I
Horvat v Croatia, (App no. 51585/99) (26 July 2001) ECHR 2001-VIII

Horych v Poland, (App no. 13621/08) (17 April 2012)
Howarth v the United Kingdom, (App no. 38081/97) (21 September 2000)
Hristova and Others v Bulgaria, (App nos 11472/04 and 40590/08) (26 June 2012)
Humen v Poland [GC], (App no. 26614/95) (15 October 1999)
I.A. v France, (App no. 28213/95) (23 September 1998) 1998-VII
I.D. v Romania, (App no. 3271/04) (23 March 2011)
I.J.L. and Others v the United Kingdom, (App nos 29522/95, 30056/96 and 30574/96) ECHR 2000-IX
İbrahim Güler v Turkey, (App no. 1942/08) (15 October 2013)
Idalov v Russia [GC], (App no. 5826/03) (22 May 2012)
İhsan Ay v Turkey, (App no. 34288/04) (21 January 2014)
İletmiş v Turkey, (App no. 29871/96) (6 December 2005) ECHR 2005-XII
Ilijkov v Bulgaria, (App no. 33977/96) (26 July 2001)
Ioannis Anastasiadis and Others v Greece, (App no. 45823/08) (18 April 2013)
István and Ištvánová v Slovakia, (App no. 30189/07) (12 June 2012)
Ivan Panchenko v Ukraine, (App no. 10911/05) (10 December 2009)
Ivanov and Dimitrov v the former Yugoslav Republic of Macedonia, (App no. 46881/06) (21 October 2010)
Jacquie and Ledun v France, (App no. 49493/98) (28 March 2000)
Jafarli and Others v Azerbaijan, (App no. 36079/06) (29 July 2010)
Jama v Slovenia, (App no. 48163/08) (19 July 2012)
Jehovah's Witnesses of Moscow v Russia, (App no. 302/02) (10 June 2010)
Jensen v Denmark, (App no. 48470/99) (20 September 2001) ECHR 2001-X
JGK Statyba Ltd and Guselnikovas v Lithuania, (App no. 3330/12) (5 November 2013)
JGK Statyba Ltd. v Lithuania (just satisfaction), (App no. 3330/12) (27 January 2015)
Julien v France, (App no. 42276/98) (14 November 2002)
Jurijs Dmitrijevs v Latvia, (App no. 37467/04) (2 October 2012)
Kaçiu and Kotorri v Albania, (App nos 33192/07 and 33194/07) (25 June 2013)
Kaić and Others v Croatia, (App no. 22014/04) (17 July 2008)
Kakamoukas and Others v Greece [GC], (App no. 38311/02) (15 February 2008)
Kakamoukas and Others v Greece, (App no. 38311/02) (22 June 2006)
Kalajzic v Croatia, (App no. 15382/04) (28 September 2006) Section I
Kalashnikov v Russia, (App no. 47095/99) ECHR 2002-VI
Kalinkin and Others v Russia, (App nos 16967/10, 37115/08, 52141/09, 57394/09, 57400/09, 2437/10, 3102/10, 12850/10, 13683/10, 19012/10, 19401/10, 20789/10, 22933/10, 25167/10, 26583/10, 26820/10, 26884/10, 28970/10, 29857/10, 49975/10 and 56205/10) (17 April 2012)
Kalinkin and Others v Russia, (App nos 16967/10, 37115/08, 52141/09, 57394/09, 57400/09, 2437/10, 3102/10, 12850/10, 13683/10, 19012/10, 19401/10, 20789/10, 22933/10, 25167/10, 26583/10, 26820/10, 26884/10, 28970/10, 29857/10, 49975/10 and 56205/10) (17 April 2012)
Kangasluoma v Finland, (App no. 48339/99) (20 January 2004)

Kapusız v Turkey, (App no. 4753/07) (7 December 2010)
Karpetas v Greece, (App no. 6086/10) (30 October 2012)
Kashavelov v Bulgaria, (App no. 891/05) (20 January 2011)
Katte Klitsche de la Grange v Italy, (App no. 12539/86) (27 October 1994) Series A no. 293-B
Kaynak and Çokkalender v Turkey, (App no. 34445/08) (31 May 2012)
Kemmache v France (no. 1 and no. 2), (App no. 12325/86 and 14992/89) (27 November 1991) Series A no. 218 135
Kępa v Poland (dec.), (App no. 43978/98) (30 September 2003) Section IV
Khashiyev and Akayeva v Russia, (App nos 57942/00 and 57945/00) (24 February 2005)
Kincses v Hungary, (App no. 66232/10) (27 January 2015)
Kiryakov v Ukraine, (App no. 26124/03) (12 January 2012)
Kiurkchian v Bulgaria, (App no. 44626/98) (24 March 2005)
Kobernik v Ukraine, (App no. 45947/06) (25 July 2013)
Komanickýv Slovakia (no. 6), (App no. 40437/07) (12 June 2012)
König v Germany, (App no. 6232/73) (28 June 1978) Series A no. 27
Kontsevych v Ukraine, (App no. 9089/04) (16 February 2012)
Kopnin and Others v Russia, (App no. 2746/05) (28 May 2014)
Kormacheva v Russia, (App no. 53084/99) (29 January 2004)
Korosidou v Greece, (App no. 9957/08) (10 February 2011)
Kozlica v Croatia, (App no. 29182/03) (2 November 2006)
Krasuski v Poland, (App no. 61444/00) (14 June 2005) ECHR 2005-V (extracts)
Kravtas v Lithuania, (App no. 12717/06) (18 January 2011)
Krivova v Ukraine, (App no. 25732/05) (9 November 2010)
Kucejová v Slovakia, (App no. 74550/12) (26 November 2013)
Kudła v Poland [GC], (App no. 30210/96) ECHR 2000-XI
Kugler v Austria, (App no. 65631/01) (14 October 2010)
Kuppinger v Germany, (App no. 62198/11) (15 January 2015)
Kurdov and Ivanov v Bulgaria, (App no. 16137/04) (31 May 2011)
Laine v France, (App no. 41476/98) (17 January 2002)
Laino v Italy [GC], (App no. 33158/96) (18 February 1999) ECHR 1999-I
László Magyar v Hungary, (App no. 73593/10) (20 May 2014)
Lavrov v Russia, (App no. 33422/03) (17 January 2012)
Lazariu v Romania, (App no. 31973/03) (13 November 2014)
Le Compte, Van Leuven and De Meyere v Belgium, (App nos 6878/75 and 7238/75) (23 June 1981) Series A no. 43
Lechner and Hess v Austria, (App no. 9316/81) (23 April 1987) Series A no. 118
Ledonne v Italy (no. 1), (App no. 35742/97) (12 May 1999)
Ledonne v Italy (no. 2), (App no. 38414/97) (12 May 1999)
Liadis v Greece, (App no. 16412/02) (Sect. 1) (27 May 2004)
Liġeres v Latvia, (App no. 17/02) (28 June 2011)
Liseytseva and Maslov v Russia, (App nos 39483/05 and 40527/10) (9 October 2014)

Lizanets v Ukraine, (App no. 6725/03) (31 May 2007)
Łobarzewski v Poland, (App no. 77757/01) (25 November 2003)
Lopatin and Medvedskiy v Ukraine, (App nos 2278/03 and 6222/03) (20 May 2010)
Lorenzi, Bernardini and Gritti v Italy, (App no. 13301/87) (27 February 1992) Series A no. 231-G
Louerat v France, (App no. 44964/98) (13 February 2003)
Lukenda v Slovenia, (App no. 23032/02) (6 October 2005) ECHR 2005-X
Luli and Others v Albania, (App nos 64480/09, 64482/09, 12874/10, 56935/10, 3129/12 and 31355/09) (1 April 2014)
Lustig-Prean and Beckett v the United Kingdom, (App nos 31417/96 and 32377/96) (27 September 1999)
Lyubov Stetsenko v Russia, (App no. 26216/07) (17 April 2014)
M.Ö. v Turkey, (App no. 26136/95) (19 May 2005)
Maciariello v Italy, (App no. 12284/86) (27 February 1992) Series A no. 230-A
Mahmut Öz v Turkey, (App no. 6840/08) (3 July 2012)
Makbule Akbaba and Others v Turkey, (App no. 48887/06) (10 July 2012)
Makedonski v Bulgaria, (App no. 36036/04) (20 January 2011)
Malicka Wąsowska v Poland (dec.), (App no. 41413/98) (5 April 2001)
Manieri v Italy, (App no. 12053/86) (27 February 1992) Series A no. 229-D
Manushaqe Puto and Others v Albania (revision), (App nos 604/07, 43628/07, 46684/07 and 34770/09) (4 November 2014)
Manushaqe Puto and Others v Albania, (App nos 604/07, 43628/07, 46684/07 and 34770/09) (31 July 2012)
Manzoni v Italy, (App no. 11804/85) (19 February 1991) Series A no. 195-B
Marian Toma v Romania, (App no. 48372/09) (17 June 2014)
Mariapori v Finland, (App no. 37751/07) (6 July 2010)
Marien v Belgium, (App no. 46046/99) (3 November 2005)
Marpa Zeeland B.V. and Metal Welding B.V. v the Netherlands, (App no. 46300/99) (9 November 2004) ECHR 2004-X (extracts)
Martins and Garcia Alves v Portugal, (App no. 37528/97) (16 November 2000)
Martins Castro and Alves Correia de Castro v Portugal, (App no. 33729/06) (10 June 2008)
Martins Moreira v Portugal, (App no. 11371/85) (26 October 1988) Series A no. 143
Matter v Slovakia, (App no. 31534/96) (5 July 1999)
Matusik v Poland, (App no. 3826/10) (1 October 2013)
Mavitan v Turkey, (App no. 41613/05) (18 January 2011)
McFarlane v Ireland [GC], (App no. 31333/06) (10 September 2010)
Medeni Uğur v Turkey, (App no. 49651/06) (24 January 2012)
Meglič v Slovenia, (App no. 29119/06) (18 April 2013)
Megyeri v Germany, (App no. 13770/88) (12 May 1992) Series A no. 237-A
Mehmet Yolcu v Turkey, (App no. 33200/05) (15 November 2012)
Menshakova v Ukraine, (App no. 377/02) (8 April 2010)

Merit v Ukraine, (App no. 66561/01) (30 March 2004)
Messochoritis v Greece, (App no. 41867/98) (12 April 2001)
Metaxas v Greece, (App no. 8415/02) (27 May 2004)
Mežnarič v Slovenia, (App no. 41416/06) (18 April 2013)
Michalak v Poland, (App no. 16864/02) (18 September 2007)
Michelioudakis v Greece, (App no. 54447/10) (3 April 2012)
Międzyzakładowa Organizacja Związkowa NSZZ Solidarność de Świdnica v Poland, (App no. 13505/08) (28 February 2012)
Mifsud v France [GC], (App no. 57220/00) (11 September 2002) ECHR 2002-VIII
Mikhail Grishin v Russia, (App no. 14807/08) (24 July 2012)
Mikulić v Croatia, (App no. 53176/99) (7 February 2002) ECHR 2002-I
Milić v Montenegro and Serbia, (App no. 28359/05) (11 December 2012)
Mincheva v Bulgaria, (App no. 21558/03) (2 September 2010)
Mocanu and Others v Romania, (App nos 10865/09, 45886/07 and 32431/08) (13 November 2012)
Moroko v Russia, (App no. 20937/07) (12 June 2008)
Mramor v Slovenia, (App no. 31391/05) (18 January 2011)
Müller-Hartburg v Austria, (App no. 47195/06) (19 February 2013)
Musci v Italy, (App no. 64699/01) (10 November 2004)
Mushta v Ukraine, (App no. 8863/06) (18 November 2010)
Musiał v Poland [GC], (App no. 24557/94) (25 March 1999) ECHR 1999-II
Nalbantski v Bulgaria, (App no. 30943/04) (10 February 2011)
Naumoski v the former Yugoslav Republic of Macedonia (revision), (App no. 25248/05) (5 December 2013)
Naumoski v the former Yugoslav Republic of Macedonia, (App no. 25248/05) (27 November 2012)
Neumeister v Austria, (App no. 1936/63) (27 June 1968) Series A no. 8
Nibbio v Italy, (App no. 12854/87) (26 February 1992) Series A no. 228-A
Niculescu-Dellakeza v Romania, (App no. 5393/04) (26 March 2013)
Niederböster v Germany, (App no. 39547/98) (27 February 2003) ECHR 2003-IV (extracts)
Niedzwiecki v Germany, (App no. 58453/00) (25 October 2005)
Nikolov and Others v Bulgaria, (App nos 44184/05, 22250/06 and 37182/07) (21 February 2012)
Niskasaari and Others v Finland, (App no. 37520/07) (6 July 2010)
Novo and Silva v Portugal, (App no. 53615/08) (25 September 2012)
Novović v Montenegro and Serbia, (App no. 13210/05) (23 October 2012)
Nuutinen v Finland, (App no. 32842/96) (27 June 2000) ECHR 2000-VIII
Nuvoli v Italy, (App no. 41424/98) (16 May 2002)
Obermeier v Austria, (App no. 11761/85 and 11761/85) (28 June 1990) Series A no. 179
Ogražden Ad and Others v the former Yugoslav Republic of Macedonia, (App nos 35630/04, 53442/07 and 42580/09) (29 May 2012)
Olujić v Croatia, (App no. 22330/05) (5 February 2009)
Öneryıldız v Turkey [GC], (App no. 48939/99) (30 November 2004) ECHR 2004-XII

Öneryıldız v Turkey, (App no. 48939/99) (18 June 2002)
Orožim v Slovenia, (App no. 49323/06) (18 April 2013)
Oršuš and Others v Croatia [GC], (App no. 15766/03) (16 March 2010)
Oršuš and Others v Croatia, (App no. 15766/03) (17 July 2008)
Osakovskiy v Ukraine, (App no. 13406/06) (17 July 2014)
Oyal v Turkey, (App no. 4864/05) (23 March 2010)
Pacifico and Others v Italy, (App nos 34389/02, 34390/02, 34392/02 and 34458/02) (15 November 2012)
Palmero v France, (App no. 77362/11) (30 October 2014)
Palmigiano v Italy, (App no. 37507/97) (11 January 2000)
Panetta v Italy, (App no. 38624/07) (15 July 2014)
Panju v Belgium, (App no. 18393/09) (28 October 2014)
Papamichalopoulos and Others v Greece, (App no. 14556/89) (24 June 1993) Series A no. 260-B
Parizov v the former Yugoslav Republic of Macedonia, (App no. 14258/03) (7 February 2008)
Pašić v Slovenia, (App no. 41060/07) (18 April 2013)
Paskal v Ukraine, (App no. 24652/04) (15 September 2011)
Patrianakos v Greece, (App no. 19449/02) (15 July 2004)
Paulino Tomas v Portugal, (App no. 58698/00) (27 March 2003) ECHR 2003-VIII
Pedersen and Baadsgaard v Denmark [GC], (App no. 49017/99) (17 December 2004) ECHR 2004-XI
Pedersen and Baadsgaard v Denmark, (App no. 49017/99) (19 June 2003)
Pejčić v Serbia, (App no. 34799/07) (8 October 2013)
Pelipenko v Russia, (App no. 69037/10) (2 October 2012)
Pélissier and Sassi v France [GC], (App no. 25444/94) (25 March 1999) ECHR 1999-II
Penias and Ortmair v Austria, (App no. 35109/06 and 38112/06) (18 October 2011)
Peter v Germany, (App no. 68919/10) (4 September 2014)
Petr Korolev v Russia, (App no. 38112/04) (21 October 2010)
Petukhov v Ukraine, (App no. 43374/02) (21 October 2010)
Philis v Greece (no. 1), (App nos 12750/87, 13780/88 and 14003/88) (27 August 1991) Series A no. 209
Philis v Greece (no. 2), (App no. 19773/92) (27 June 1997) 1997-IV
Pieniążek v Poland, (App no. 62179/00) (28 September 2004)
Pishchalnikov v Russia, (App no. 7025/04) (24 September 2009)
Plut and Bičanič-Plut v Slovenia, (App no. 7709/06) (18 July 2013)
Podbelšek Bračič v Slovenia, (App no. 42224/04) (18 April 2013)
Poiss v Austria, (App no. 9816/82) (23 April 1987) Series A no. 117
Popandopulo v Russia, (App no. 4512/09) (10 May 2011)
Popovski v the former Yugoslav Republic of Macedonia, (App no. 12316/07) (31 October 2013)
Portington v Greece, (App no. 28523/95) (23 September 1998) 1998-VI
Poyraz v Turkey, (App no. 15966/06) (7 December 2010)
Pretto and Others v Italy, (App no. 7984/77) (8 December 1983) Series A no. 71

Probstmeier v Germany, (App no. 20950/92) (1 July 1997) 1997-IV
Rasiewicz v Slovenia, (App no. 40445/06) (18 October 2012)
Raylyan v Russia, (App no. 22000/03) (15 February 2007)
Reinhardt and Slimane-Kaïd v France, (App nos 23043/93 and 22921/93) (31 March 1998) 1998-II
Rezette v Luxembourg, (App no. 73983/01) (13 July 2004)
Ribič v Slovenia, (App no. 20965/03) (19 October 2010)
Riccardi Pizzati v Italy [GC], (App no. 62361/00) (29 March 2006)
Riccardi Pizzati v Italy, (App no. 62361/00) (10 November 2004)
Riccardi v Romania, (App no. 3048/04) (3 April 2012)
Richard v France, (App no. 33441/96) (22 April 1998) 1998-II
Riđić and Others v Serbia, (App nos 53736/08, 53737/08, 14271/11, 17124/11, 24452/11 and 36515/11) (1 July 2014)
Rifat Demir v Turkey, (App no. 24267/07) (4 June 2013)
Ringeisen v Austria, (App no. 2614/65) (16 July 1971) Series A no. 13
Ristić v Serbia, (App no. 32181/08) (18 January 2011)
Roduit v Switzerland, (App no. 6586/06) (3 September 2013)
Rösslhuber v Austria, (App no. 32869/96) (28 November 2000)
Ruiz-Mateos v Spain, (App no. 12952/87) (23 June 1993) Series A no. 262
Rummi v Estonia, (App no. 63362/09) (15 January 2015)
Rumpf v Germany, (App no. 46344/06) (2 September 2010)
Ruotolo v Italy, (App no. 12460/86) (27 February 1992) Series A no. 230-D
Rytchenko v Russia, (App no. 22266/04) (20 January 2011)
S.C. Bartolo Prod Com SRL and Botomei v Romania, (App no. 16294/03) (21 February 2012)
Sabeur Ben Ali v Malta, (App no. 35892/97) (29 June 2000)
Saliba and Others v Malta (just satisfaction), (App no. 20287/10) (22 January 2013)
Saliba and Others v Malta, (App no. 20287/10) (22 November 2011)
Saliba v Malta, (App no. 4251/02) (8 November 2005)
Samoylovich v Ukraine, (App no. 28969/04) (16 May 2013)
Sarı v Turkey and Denmark, (App no. 21889/93) (8 November 2001)
Sarp Kuray v Turkey, (App no. 23280/09) (24 July 2012)
Sartory v France, (App no. 40589/07) (24 September 2009)
Schaal v Luxembourg, (App no. 51773/99) (18 February 2003)
Schembri and Others v Malta (just satisfaction), (App no. 42583/06) (28 September 2010)
Schembri and Others v Malta, (App no. 42583/06) (10 November 2009)
Scopelliti v Italy, (App no. 15511/89) (23 November 1993) Series A no. 278
Scordino v Italy (no. 1) [GC], (App no. 36813/97) (29 March 2006) ECHR 2006-V
Scordino v Italy (no. 1), (App no. 36813/97) (29 July 2004)
Sedminek v Slovenia, (App no. 9842/07) (24 October 2013)
Selmouni v France [GC], (App no. 25803/94) (28 July 1999) ECHR 1999-V
Sereny v Romania, (App no. 13071/06) (18 June 2013)
Sergey Timofeyev v Russia, (App no. 12111/04) (2 September 2010)

Serrano Contreras v Spain, (App no. 49183/08) (20 March 2012)
Şevket Kürüm and Others v Turkey, (App no. 54113/08) (25 November 2014)
Shahanov v Bulgaria, (App no. 16391/05) (10 January 2012)
Shcherbakov v Russia (no. 2), (App no. 34959/07) (24 October 2013)
Shcherbakov v Russia, (App no. 23939/02) (17 June 2010)
Shenoyev v Russia, (App no. 2563/06) (10 June 2010)
Siermiński v Poland, (App no. 53339/09) (2 December 2014)
Signe v France, (App no. 55875/00) (14 October 2003)
Šilc v Slovenia, (App no. 45936/99) (29 June 2006)
Šilih v Slovenia [GC], (App no. 71463/01) (9 April 2009)
Šilih v Slovenia, (App no. 71463/01) (28 June 2007)
Silva Pontes v Portugal, (App no. 14940/89) (23 March 1994) Series A no. 286-A
Silver and Others v the United Kingdom, (App nos 5947/72, 6205/73 and 7052/75) (25 March 1983) Series A no. 61
Simaldone v Italy, (App no. 22644/03) (31 March 2009)
Simončič v Slovenia, (App no. 7351/04) (18 January 2011)
Sizov v Russia (no. 2), (App no. 58104/08) (24 July 2012)
Slaviček v Croatia, (App no. 20862/02) (4 July 2002) ECHR 2002-VII
Šleževičius v Lithuania, (App no. 55479/00) (13 November 2001)
Smirnova v Russia, (App nos 46133/99 and 48183/99) (24 July 2003) ECHR 2003-IX (extracts)
Sociedade de Construções Martins and Vieira, Lda. and Others v Portugal, (App nos 56637/10, 59856/10, 72525/10, 7646/11 and 12592/11) (30 October 2014)
Solomakhin v Ukraine, (App no. 24429/03) (5 March 2012)
Solovyevy v Russia, (App no. 918/02) (24 April 2012)
Šorgić v Serbia, (App no. 34973/06) (3 November 2011)
Sorokins and Sorokina v Latvia, (App no. 45476/04) (28 May 2013)
Sprotte v Germany (dec.), (App no. 72438/01) (17 November 2005)
Stakić v Montenegro, (App no. 49320/07) (2 October 2012)
Starokadomskiy v Russia (no. 2), (App no. 27455/06) (13 March 2014)
Stebnitskiy and Komfort v Ukraine, (App no. 10687/02) (3 February 2011)
Steel and Morris v the United Kingdom, (App no. 68416/01) (15 February 2005) ECHR 2005-II
Stefanou v Greece, (App no. 2954/07) (22 April 2010)
Stögmüller v Austria, (App no. 1602/62) (10 November 1969) Series A no. 9
Stoianova and Nedelcu v Romania, (App no. 77517/01 and 77722/01) (4 August 2005) ECHR 2005-VIII
Stoilkovska v the former Yugoslav Republic of Macedonia, (App no. 29784/07) (18 July 2013)
Stojc v Slovenia, (App no. 20159/06) (18 October 2012)
Streltsov and other 'Novocherkassk military pensioners' cases v Russia, (App nos 8549/06, 17763/06, 18352/06, 18354/06, 18835/06, 18848/06, 18851/06, 18856/06, 18916/06, 18952/06, 19350/06, 19352/06, 19353/06, 20423/06, 20904/06, 20906/06, 20907/06, 21081/06, 21123/06, 21124/06, 21179/06,

21189/06, 24041/06, 24048/06, 24055/06, 24058/06, 24816/06, 25029/06, 25043/06, 25044/06, 25442/06, 25717/06, 25721/06, 25827/06, 25831/06, 25920/06, 25922/06, 25923/06, 26440/06, 26654/06, 26706/06, 26709/06, 26766/06, 26972/06, 26981/06, 26983/06, 27709/06, 27710/06, 27714/06, 27716/06, 27718/06, 27833/06, 27840/06, 28105/06, 28231/06, 28886/06, 28888/06, 30481/06, 30494/06, 31422/06, 31424/06, 31436/06, 31410/06, 31411/06, 31414/06, 31427/06, 31429/06, 31433/06, 31419/06, 31309/06, 31324/06, 31439/06, 32419/06, 32421/06, 34443/06, 40256/06, 41560/06, 42694/06, 42695/06, 42696/06, 42697/06, 42701/06, 5648/07, 6167/07, 6902/07, 7869/07 and 39423/07) (29 July 2010)
Struc v the Republic of Moldova, (App no. 40131/09) (4 December 2012)
Styranowski v Poland, (App no. 28616/95) (30 October 1998) 1998-VIII
Sukobljević v Croatia, (App no. 5129/03) (2 November 2006)
Sürmeli v Germany [GC], (App no. 75529/01) (8 June 2006) ECHR 2006-VII
Süssmann v Germany, (App no. 20024/92) (16 September 1996) 1996-IV
Sutyagin v Russia, (App no. 30024/02) (3 May 2011)
Svetlana Orlova v Russia, (App no. 4487/04) (30 July 2009)
Svinarenko and Slyadnev v Russia [GC], (App nos 32541/08 and 43441/08, ECHR 2014)
Svinarenko and Slyadnev v Russia, (App nos 32541/08 and 43441/08) (11 December 2012)
Sylvester v Austria (no. 2), (App no. 54640/00) (3 February 2005)
Syngayevskiy v Russia, (App no. 17628/03) (27 March 2012)
Szabo and Others v Romania, (App no. 8193/06) (18 March 2014)
Taiuti v Italy, (App no. 12238/86) (27 February 1992) Series A no. 229-I
Taran v Ukraine, (App no. 31898/06) (17 October 2013)
Tarkan Yavaş v Turkey, (App no. 58210/08) (18 September 2012)
Tatjana Marinović v Croatia, (App no. 9627/03) (6 October 2005)
Todorov v Ukraine, (App no. 16717/05) (12 January 2012)
Tomé Mota v Portugal, (App no. 32082/96) (2 December 1999) ECHR 1999-IX
Triggiani v Italy, (App no. 13509/88) (19 February 1991) Series A no. 197-B
Trunk v Slovenia, (App no. 41391/06) (18 April 2013)
Tsareva v Russia, (App no. 43327/02) (1 April 2010)
Tsikakis v Germany, (App no. 1521/06) (10 February 2011)
Tumminelli v Italy, (App no. 13362/87) (27 February 1992) Series A no. 231-H
Tyrer v the United Kingdom, (App no. 5856/72) (25 April 1978) Series A no. 26
Uçan and Others v Turkey, (App no. 37377/05) (2 July 2013)
Unión Alimentaria Sanders S.A. v Spain, (App no. 11681/85) (7 July 1989) Series A no. 157
Ustyantsev v Ukraine, (App no. 3299/05) (12 January 2012)
V.K. v Croatia, (App no. 38380/08) (27 November 2012)
Vaney v France, (App no. 53946/00) (30 November 2004)
Varipati v Greece, (App no. 38459/97) (26 October 1999)
Vasilchenko v Russia, (App no. 34784/02) (23 September 2010)
Vassilios Athanasiou and Others v Greece, (App no. 50973/08) (21 December 2010)

Vayiç v Turkey, (App no. 18078/02) (20 June 2006) ECHR 2006-VIII (extracts)
Veiss v Latvia, (App no. 15152/12) (28 January 2014)
Velichko v Russia, (App no. 19664/07) (15 January 2013)
Velimirović v Montenegro, (App no. 20979/07) (2 October 2012)
Velinov v the former Yugoslav Republic of Macedonia, (App no. 16880/08) (19 September 2013)
Veliyev v Russia, (App no. 24202/05) (24 June 2010)
Veljkov v Serbia, (App no. 23087/07) (19 April 2011)
Ventouris and Others v Greece, (App no. 33252/08) (31 January 2012)
Veriter v France, (App no. 31508/07) (14 October 2010)
Vernillo v France, (App no. 11889/85) (20 February 1991) Series A no. 198
Vidas v Croatia, (App no. 40383/04) (3 July 2008)
Vilho Eskelinen and Others v Finland [GC], (App no. 63235/00) (19 April 2007) ECHR 2007-IV
Vlad and Others v Romania, (App nos 40756/06, 41508/07 and 50806/07) (26 November 2013)
Vladimir Melnikov v Russia, (App no. 38202/07) (17 January 2012)
Vladimir Romanov v Russia, (App no. 41461/02) (24 July 2008)
Vocaturo v Italy, (App no. 11891/85) (24 May 1991) Series A no. 206-C
Vorrasi v Italy, (App no. 12706/87) (27 February 1992) Series A no. 230-E
Vučković and Others v Serbia [GC], (App no. 17153/11) (25 March 2014)
Vučković and Others v Serbia, (App no. 17153/11) (28 August 2012)
Vukadinovič v Slovenia, (App no. 44100/09) (18 April 2013)
Vukelić v Montenegro, (App no. 58258/09) (4 June 2013)
Wasserman v Russia (no. 2), (App no. 21071/05) (10 April 2008)
Wasserman v Russia, (App no. 15021/02) (18 November 2004)
Wemhoff v Germany, (App no. 2122/64) (27 June 1968) Series A no. 7
Wiesinger v Austria, (App no. 11796/85) (30 October 1991) Series A no. 213
Włoch v Poland, (App no. 27785/95) (19 October 2000) ECHR 2000-XI
Wurzer v Austria, (App no. 5335/07) (6 March 2012)
X v France, (App no. 18020/91) (31 March 1992) Series A no. 234-C
Yagtzilar and Others v Greece, (App no. 41727/98) (6 December 2001) ECHR 2001-XII
Yakışan v Turkey, (App no. 11339/03) (6 March 2007)
Yavuz and Yaylalı v Turkey, (App no. 12606/11) (17 December 2013)
Young, James and Webster v the United Kingdom, (App nos 7601/76 and 7806/77) (13 August 1981) Series A no. 44
Yuriy Nikolayevich Ivanov v Ukraine, (App no. 40450/04) (15 October 2009)
Yuryeva and Yuryev v Ukraine, (App no. 3431/03) (31 July 2012)
Z. v Slovenia, (App no. 43155/05) (30 November 2010)
Zabovnik v Slovenia, (App nos 17596/06 and 17608/06) (18 October 2012)
Zandbergs v Latvia, (App no. 71092/01) (20 December 2011)
Zarb v Malta, (App no. 16631/04) (4 July 2006)
Zimmermann and Steiner v Switzerland, (App no. 8737/79) (13 July 1983) Series A no. 66

Zubko and Others v Ukraine, (App nos 3955/04, 5622/04, 8538/04 and 11418/04) (26 April 2006) ECHR 2006-VI (extracts)
Zulfali Huseynov v Azerbaijan, (App no. 56547/10) (26 June 2012)
Zunic v Italy, (App no. 14405/05) (21 December 2006)

Judgments Delivered in the Republic of Malta[2]

Constitutional Court

Al Sakalli v Prim Ministru, (7 April 2000) (Constitutional Court) as cited in Paul Fenech v Kummissarju Ta' L-Artijiet, (Constitutional Court) (App no. 31/2007/1) (20 February 2009)

Allied Newspapers Limited v Avukat Ġenerali Et, (Constitutional Court) (App no. 723/1999/1) (2 December 2003)

Attard v Ono. Prim Imhallef Et, (Constitutional Court) (29 October 1992) cited in Manduca v Avukat Ġenerali, (Constitutional Court) (Ref no. Volume 79 (1995) Part no. 1 Page 1) (23 January 1995)

Azzopardi v Reġistratur Tal-Qorti Et, (Constitutional Court) (Ref no. Volume 80 (1996) Part no. 1 Section − Page 4) (17 January 1996)

Bartolo v Avukat Ġenerali, (Constitutional Court) (Ref no. 2 App no. 571/96 GV) (28 December 2001)

Brincat v Avukat Ġenerali, (Constitutional Court) (Ref no. Volume 80 (1996) Part no. 1 Section Page 17) (21 February 1996)

Bugeja v L-Avukat Ġenerali u Il-Kummissarju Tal-Pulizija, (Constitutional Court) (App no. 29/2002/1) (11 August 2003)

Cachia Pawlu v Avukat Ġenerali Et, (Constitutional Court) (App no. 586/1997/1) (28 December 2001)

Cassar v L-Avukat Ġenerali, (Constitutional Court) (App no. 64/2006/1) (29 February 2009)

Central Mediterranean Development Corporation Limited v Avukat Ġenerali, (Constitutional Court) (App no. 21/2002/1) (8 May 2003)

Clayton Communications Company Limited v L-Onorevoli Prim'ministru Et, (Constitutional Court) (App no. 55/2008/1) (29 January 2010)

Consiglio v Air Supplies And Catering Company Limited, (Constitutional Court) (App no. 526/95) (11 August 2000)

Curmi Noe v Il-Kummissarju Tal-Artijiet Et, (Constitutional Court) (App no. 25/2005/1) (23 May 2005)

Debono Et v Reġistratur Principali Tal-Qrati Tal-Gustizzja U Onor. Ministru Tal-Gustizzja U Gvern Lokali, (Constitutional Court) (App no. 28/2002/1) (30 June 2003)

Ellul Sullivan Et v L-Avukat Ġenerali Tar-Republika U L-Kummissarju Tal-Pulizija, (Constitutional Court) (App no. 651/1998/1) (18 June 2008)

Farrugia, Maria v Kummissarju Ta' L-Artijiet, (Constitutional Court) (App no. 59/2005/1) (25 April 2008)

Fenech Et v Kummissarju Ta' L-Artijiet, (Constitutional Court) (App no. 31/2007/1) (20 February 2009)

Fino Bħala Direttur Għan-Nom U In Rappresentanza Ta' Strand Construction Limited v Awtorita' Ta' L-Ippjanar, Direttur Tad-Dipartiment Ta' L-Avjazzjoni Ċivili, U L-Avukat Ġenerali, (Constitutional Court) (App no. 604/1997/1) (16 April 2004)
Frendo Randon v Kummissarju Ta' L-Art Et, (20 July 2009) (Constitutional Court) (App no. 17/2002/1) (16 April 2004)
Gaffarena v Kummissarju Tal-Pulizija, (29 October 1993) cited in Paul Fenech v Kummissarju Ta' L-Artijiet (Constitutional Court) (App no. 31/2007/1) (20 February 2009)
Gasan Enterprises Limited v Awtorita' ta' Malta Dwar L-Ambjent U L-Ippjanar, (Constitutional Court) (App no. 29/2001/1) (3 February 2009)
Hall v Director for the Department of Social Accommodation Et, (Constitutional Court) (App no. 1/2003/1) (18 September 2009)
Manduca v L-Onorevoli Prim Ministru, (Constitutional Court) (App no. Volume 79 (1995) Part no. 1 Section 1 Page 1) (23 January 1995)
Mckay v Kummissarju Tal-Pulizija, (27 July 1995) cited in Paul Fenech v Kummissarju Ta' L-Artijiet (Constitutional Court) (App no. 31/2007/1) (20 February 2009)
Mifsud v Supretendent Bonello Et, (Constitutional Court) (App no. 176/1987/2) (18 September 2009)
Mintoff Et v Prim Ministru Onor. Et, (Constitutional Court) (App no. 470/1994/2) (28 July 2006)
Pace v Avukat Ġenerali Et, (Constitutional Court) (App no. 753/2000/2) (20 October 2004)
Ramesh Chetenram Sharma v Avukat Ġenerali Et, (Constitutional Court) (Ref no. Volume 73 (1989) Part no. 3 Section Page 808) (6 June 1989)
Said Et v L-Avukat Ġenerali, (Constitutional Court) (App no. 10/2007/1) (3 February 2009)
Said v L-Avukat Ġenerali, (Constitutional Court) (App no. 30/2007/1) (12 February 2010)
Scicluna v Avukat Ġenerali Et, (Constitutional Court) (App no. 463/1994/1) (15 October 2003)
Spiteri, Melchior v Avukat Ġenerali, (Constitutional Court) (App no. 5/2002/1) (31 October 2001)
Spiteri, Vincenti v Onor. Prim Ministru Et, (Constitutional Court) (31 August 1977) referred to in Scicluna v Avukat Ġenerali Et, (Constitutional Court) (App no. 463/1994/1) (15 October 2003)
Vella v L-Onorevoli Prim Ministru Et, (Constitutional Court) (Ref no. Volume 74 (1990) Part no. 1 Section Page 159) (18 July 1990)
Visual and Sound Communications Limited v Il-Kummisarju Tal-Pulizija Et, (Constitutional Court) (App no. 34/2001/1) (2 December 2002)
Xuereb v Reġistratur Tal-Qrati Et, (Constitutional Court) (App no. 742/2000/1) (8 November 2004)
Zarb v Avukat Ġenerali, (Constitutional Court) (App no. 6/2002/1) (31 October 2003)

Constitutional References, Constitutional Court

Constitutional Reference from the Court of Magistrates as a Court of Criminal Inquiry in Il-Pulizija v Ellul Sullivan Et decided by the Constitutional Court on the 24th January 1991: Il-Pulizija v Ellul Sullivan Et, (Ref no. Volume 75 (1991) Part no. 1 Section 1 Page 46)

First Hall Civil Court (Constitutional Jurisdiction)

Attard, Joseph v Avukat Ġenerali, (FHCC(CJ)) (App no. 624/97) (8 June 2000)
Azzopardi v Avukat Ġenerali Et, (FHCC(CJ)) (App no. 669/1998/1) (23 March 2007)
Blaschem (Malta) Ltd v Avukat Ġenerali Et, (FHCC(CJ)) (App no. 22/2003/1) (23 March 2007)
Bonnici v L-Avukat Ġenerali, (FHCC(CJ)) (App no. 3/2007) (5 July 2007)
Debono v Avukat Ġenerali, (FHCC(CJ)) (App no. 40/2006) (6 February 2007)
Farrugia, Luqa v Avukat Ġenerali, (FHCC(CJ)) (App no. 16/2005) (30 November 2006)
Farrugia, Nicholas v Kummissarju Tal-Pulizija Et, (FHCC(CJ)) (App no. 30/2002/1) (27 March 2003)
Lay Lay Co. Ltd. v L-Awtorita' Ta' Malta Dwar L-Ambjent U L-Ippjanar Et, (FHCC(CJ)) (App no. 30/2004/1) (29 September 2009)
Licari Bħala Likwidatur Għan-Nom U In Rappresentanza Ta'Farr Ltd. (C 1402) v Kummissarju Ta' L-Artijiet Et, (FHCC(CJ)) (App no. 19/2005) (20 October 2005)
Pulis Francesca v Kummissarju Tal-Artijiet Et, (FHCC (CJ)) (App no. 34/2005) (28 June 2006)
Xuereb v Avukat Ġenerali, (FHCC(CJ)) (App no. 14/2003/1) (28 January 2005)

Constitutional References, First Hall Civil Court

Constitutional Reference of the 29th November 2002 from the Lands Arbitration Board – Kummissarju Tal-Artijiet v Violet Briffa Et, (FHCC(CJ)) (App no. 14/2001)
Il-Pulizija (Spettur Carmelo Magri) v Attard, Constitutional Reference of the 14th November 2004 from the Court of Magistrates acting as a Court of Criminal Inquiry to the FHCC(CJ), (App no. 33/2003/1) (1 July 2004)

First Hall Civil Court (General Jurisdiction)

Mifsud Bonnici v Tabone, (FHCC(GJ)) (App no. 296/2002/2) (24 September 2002) cited in Paul Fenech v Kummissarju Ta' L-Artijiet, (Constitutional Court) (App no. 31/2007/1) (20 February 2009)
Zammit v Borg Barthet Noe, (FHCC(GJ)) (App no. 1768/1993/1) (16 January 2003)

Court of Appeal (Civil, Superior)

Attard v Attard, (Court of Appeal (Civil, Superior)) (App no. 214/2000) (30 May 2008)

Baldacchino v Kummissarju Tal-Artijiet, (Court of Appeal (Civil, Superior)) (App no. 273/1993/2) (23 Septtember 2009)

Busuttil v Xuereb u AX Construction Limited, (Court of Appeal (Civil, Superior)) (App no. 1728/1995/1) (27 February 2009)

Consiglio v Air Supplies and Catering Limited, (Court of Appeal (Civil, Superior)) (App no. 881/2002/1) (1 February 2008)

Fiorino D'Oro v Direttur Tat-Toroq, (Court of Appeal) (App no. 1781/2001/1) (17 February 2006)

Pending Cases

Gatt v Avukat Generali, (FHCC(CJ): Giannino Caruana Demajo) (App no. 52/2007) (Registered 17 October 2007 and adjourned to 25 May 2010)

Mifsud v Avukat Generali, (FHCC(CJ): Joseph Zammit McKeon) (App no. 2/2010) (Registered 3 January 2010 and adjourned to 21 June 2010)

Notes

1 Referencing in accordance with OSCOLA 2006, details obtained from HUDOC website 'Alphabetical citation list of all judgments and published decisions' and 'Case-law references of judgments, advisory opinions and published decisions' which is 'a master list of all judgments delivered by a Grand Chamber or Chamber, all advisory opinions issued by the Court under Article 47 of the Convention and all decisions that have been published or selected for publication in the Court's official series. It replaces the former alphabetical and chronological lists, which have been discontinued.' <http://www.echr.coe.int> accessed April 2015. Referenced judgments span the case law of the European Court of Human Rights from inception up to February 2015.

2 Referenced local judgments span the period between August 1987 and May 2010, for the purpose of the study outlined in the *Chapter Introduction* to Chapter 3. For purposes of clarification, the official title of the respondent has in some cases been translated into English, but left in the original language in *Judgments* so as to enable searches in public registers. The case reference number is always given for accuracy of identification.

Abbreviations

Preliminary Note

Where a legal provision is referred to in capitalised form (for example Article 6, Article 41, and so forth), this refers to articles of the European Convention on Human Rights. Other legal provisions are referred to *via* an uncapitalised reference to the relevant statute. The full text of the relevant legal provision can be found in *Statutes*.

'*Article 6*' and '*Article 39*'	Articles 6 and 39 of the European Convention on Human Rights, and, where the context so implies, the same articles as implemented into the relevant national legal system.
'*European Court*' or '*Strasbourg Court*'	European Court of Human Rights, Council of Europe, Strasbourg
'*(European) Convention*' or '*ECHR*'	Convention for the Protection of Human Rights and Fundamental Freedoms (European Convention on Human Rights); full instrument available at: <http://www.echr.coe.int/Documents/Convention_ENG.pdf>
'*FHCC(CJ)*'	First Hall Civil Court of Malta, Constitutional Jurisdiction
'*FHCC(GJ)*'	First Hall Civil Court of Malta, General Jurisdiction
'*Scordino-Type Cases*'	A set of judgments delivered by the Strasbourg Court and described in Chapter 2, Section 3.
'*Strasbourg Court*' or '*European Court*'	See '*European Court*'.
'*Strasbourg Jurisprudence*'	The body of case law emanating from the European Court of Human Rights, Council of Europe, Strasbourg.

Foreword

There is an inbuilt tension in our current conception of human rights, stemming from the attempt to marry an abstract understanding of the universal entitlements and freedoms of human beings to systems of enforcement that largely rest upon the laws and institutions of nation states. Within Europe, potential mismatches between universal rights and national remedies have been addressed through the mechanism of the European Convention of Human Rights. Residents of European states which have ratified the Convention and granted the right of individual petition enjoy the possibility of direct access to the European Court of Human Rights, which means that national remedies for human rights violations may be tested against the minimum standards set at a European level and, to the extent that they are found wanting, replaced by the latter.

While granting individuals access to the Strasbourg court greatly reduces the abovementioned tension to the victim's benefit, it would be simplistic to assume that it is thereby eliminated. Specific national understandings, both of the rights themselves and of the appropriate remedies for their violation, remain critical to the process of invoking and applying the Convention. Indeed the very possibility of access to the European remedy requires the applicant to first persuade the Strasbourg Court that an effective ordinary remedy is not available or was ineffective in the particular case. Such decisions can only be made after a thorough review of the national legal system involved, which must necessarily encompass all the areas of substantive and procedural law which might have a bearing on the case.

It is precisely such an exercise of reviewing, comparing and assessing national and European remedies that has been ably carried out by Caroline Savvidis in this professional monograph. It has been driven by a passionate belief that human rights can mean nothing unless they are a tool by which victims can obtain an effective remedy which is, as far as possible, commensurate to the harm they have suffered. It is, she points out, from the perspective of the parent who has been wrongly deprived of custody over his child pending separation proceedings, the innocent victim unjustly accused of committing a criminal offense and the entrepreneur whose envious rivals have managed to embroil in costly and protracted litigation, that the availability and effectiveness of remedies for excessive trial delays should be assessed.

This victim-centred perspective on national and European *remedies* is particularly appropriate when bearing in mind this book's focus on court delays. Article 6 of the Convention, which is here focused upon, is a human right which is itself inherently concerned with fairness in the way 'civil rights and obligations' are procedurally determined. As access to a European remedy for violations of the right to have a hearing determined in a reasonable time is only possible if the victim first manages to prove that an effective remedy was not made available by the *same national court system* which had allegedly violated his or her Article 6 rights in the first place, formidable obstacles stand in the path of such a victim.

This monograph should be welcomed primarily for the help it provides such individuals; empowering them to access the Strasbourg Court by indicating precisely which criteria this court employs to establish that a trial has exceeded the 'reasonable time' requirement and what kind of national remedy it considers sufficient to ensure that the case can be safely left to the national authorities. The former exercise is undertaken in the first two chapters of the book. The other chapters revolve around a case study of the Maltese jurisdiction, illustrating how the remedies available within a given legal system can be analysed against the standards set by the Convention.

As a mixed system[1] and one of the EU member states having the longest disposal times for court litigation,[2] the Maltese jurisdiction is an appropriate laboratory for observing the effects of breaching Article 6 'reasonable time' requirements. Conversely Dr Savvidis shows how the case law of the Strasbourg Court also provides a clear and logical vantage point from which a legal system can be viewed and assessed as a whole. Her analysis leads her to the observation of a structural schism within the studied legal system, as a result of which she observes that: '*The actual situation, therefore, is one where there are multiple remedies which are theoretically capable of providing effective redress, but not a single one which effectively does so in practice.*'

This conclusion is reached through a study which shows how ordinary private law remedies do not adequately compensate the victim for the moral damage sustained, while the public law remedies for human rights breaches give more importance to symbolically compensating damage than to fully compensating the victim for all the harm sustained. Since Maltese law does not permit the victim to access both private and public law remedies simultaneously, Dr Savvidis persuasively argues that Maltese law *as a whole* is unable to guarantee access to a proper remedy to most of the victims of such a breach of the European Convention, leading to the logical conclusion that such cases would have to be tried by the Strasbourg Court for a remedy attaining the Convention's minimum standards to be provided. Her suggestions aim to remove the need to resort to this supranational forum by pushing for the provision of effective domestic remedies so as to achieve the desideratum of a subsidiary implementation of the rights protected by the European Convention.

The author's argument is both subtle and prescient; showing how the interplay of constitutional and ordinary remedies can result in a situation where the theoretical availability of multiple remedies conceals the practical inexistence of any effective remedy. From a comparativist's perspective, it exemplifies the practical (mal-)functioning of a mixed jurisdiction; combining private law of continental derivation with public law influenced profoundly by common law. This legal mixing tends to generate systemic fissures, as can be exemplified by an internal tendency to treat human rights principles and civil law rules as occupying distinct and parallel universes. It also produces various unlikely conjunctions within the legal system in question. Maltese administrative law, for instance, follows common law by holding the government liable according to the same law applied to private citizens and before the same courts, with the paradoxical consequence that the substantive rules of governmental liability are civilian in character; Maltese tort law, while rooted in a code of clear civilian inspiration, is usually interpreted from a common law standpoint which prioritizes remedies over rights and assumes that heads of damages which are not expressly listed in coded provisions are not compensable. Even the Maltese Constitution, albeit drafted in the detailed and somewhat opaque common law style, diverges from its British progenitor, since it is a written text containing an enforceable bill of rights.

As Dr Savvidis shows, these various levels of hybridity can foster an inflexible and compartmentalized mindset which refuses to acknowledge the problems posed by areas falling outside pre-defined categories, or to think holistically and harmonize the remedies available under private and public law. Moreover, by highlighting the potential of human rights as declared in the Convention to unify these systems of remedies, she is accurately charting out the course which should be followed by the Maltese courts in order to respond appropriately to recent Strasbourg judgments. In particular I would refer to BRINCAT AND OTHERS, delivered in 2014,[3] in which judgment it was held that the Maltese courts could no longer consider their traditional interpretive stance that moral damages are not compensable in ordinary tort cases, as compatible with the understanding that Maltese tort law is an effective ordinary remedy for certain kinds of human rights violations. Ultimately, the point being made by the Strasbourg Court can be summed up in the words of Judge Giovanni Bonello in the earlier Strasbourg case of AQUILINA: *'I consider it wholly inadequate and unacceptable that a court of justice should "satisfy" the victim of a breach of fundamental rights with a mere handout of legal idiom.'*[4]

What particularly distinguishes this monograph, and the reason why I recommend it so strongly to the reader, is the careful, competent and stimulating manner by which Dr Savvidis pursues these questions of precisely *what* is acceptable, satisfactory and adequate and – most importantly – *how* such a remedy can be provided to victims stuck in endless Kafkaesque trials. In so doing, she challenges all professionals involved in the administration of justice to 'get real' about using domestic law to protect human rights. It is fervently hoped that they will get the message.

Dr David E. Zammit LL.D. Ph.D. (Dunelm)
Head of Department of Civil Law
Faculty of Laws
University of Malta

1 *Foreword*

Notes

1 See Vernon Valentine Palmer, Mixed Jurisdictions Worldwide: The Third Legal Family (2nd edition, Cambridge) pp. 528–76.
2 Thus the EU justice Scoreboard for 2014 shows that in Malta the average time at first instance needed to resolve litigious civil and commercial cases was close to 700 days. By comparison, Italy needed close to 600 days. See <http://ec.europa.eu/justice/effective-justice/files/justice_scoreboard_communication_en.pdf> accessed May 2015.
3 See case of BRINCAT AND OTHERS (App nos 60908/11, 62110/11, 62129/11, 62312/11 and 62338/11); judgment delivered by the European Court of Human Rights on the 24th July 2014.
4 See partly dissenting opinion of G. Bonello annexed to the case of AQUILINA (App no. 25642/94); judgment delivered by the European Court of Human Rights on the 29th April 1999.

Preface

The author aims to give legal and academic perspective to the theory and practice surrounding the right to a fair hearing within a reasonable time. This field of rights has been somewhat neglected academically, a fact which jars with the sheer volume of case law budding from this single, simple fundamental right and which bears testimony to widespread concern with delay in judicial proceedings which transcends the boundaries of states or legal systems.

The book provides a blueprint for analysing the effectiveness of legal remedies across entire legal systems, as well as in any given individual case. The first part focuses on deriving legal principles from the body of jurisprudence of the European Court of Human Rights in Strasbourg, while the latter parts contain illustrations of the practical application of such principles.

While it is academically interesting to observe the interplay between ordinary civil and extraordinary human rights or constitutional remedies, this endeavour also seeks to demonstrate the dangers which may result from an uneasy confluence of legal principles, resulting in legal systems which ostensibly offer multiple remedies but in practice are afflicted by a dearth of effective avenues for the redress of certain losses.

Caroline Savvidis

Acknowledgements

The light for this journey, which has matured into the publication of *Court Delay and Human Rights Remedies: Enforcing the Right to a 'Fair Hearing within a Reasonable Time'*, was provided by the constant encouragement and support of the remarkable people that surround me. My first, and most fundamental, debt of gratitude is owed to the members of my family, who gave me the required elan and support to digest and assimilate the mountains of case law and information prerequisite to embarking on this project. Barasco Savvidis, I am deeply moved by the love and pride in your eyes; having the enthusiasm and support of my husband, my soulmate, creates the harmony which gives fulfilment to my endeavours: thank you, my darling. Mama, your palpable pride and warm presence throughout our lives have instilled the confidence we need to be able to climb mountains when we believe our cause is just; there is infinite beauty in the strength of your dedication, love and support. Papa, I am deeply grateful for the courage you have instilled in me through your consistent belief in my abilities; you have always encouraged me to follow my heart in life and work alike, solid in your conviction that this is the road to achieving true fulfilment. Suzanne Busuttil Naudi, how many a time did I plonk myself onto your duvet, coffee mug and all, and receive the required boost from your warm words of encouragement to persevere in my endeavours? Thank you for priceless memories, cheerfully engraved over the years by tears of joy, exasperation, exhaustion and comraderie.

I owe a great debt to my learned mentors and colleagues Prof. Vernon Valentine Palmer, Dr David E. Zammit and Avv. Dr Tonio Azzopardi, without whose ongoing encouragement, patience, and enthusiasm for my work this would have been a lonely endeavour which would in all probability never have seen the light of day. David Zammit, for the endless dedication and support for the research at the basis of this study, and the ideas and feedback so patiently contributed, I shall be forever grateful. Vernon Valentine Palmer, I am deeply grateful for your unwavering support and encouragement to pursue the road of contribution to this area of study which, I think it is not amiss to say, is by far the one less travelled by. I have received precious encouragement and quality feedback from the members of Juris Diversitas and of the Mediterranean Hybridity Project, from my esteemed colleagues at the University of

Malta, Tulane University in New Orleans, Zhejiang University in Hangzhou and from the University of Limerick, and would like to thank everyone for their continued interest. I would like to acknowledge the contribution of each author, judge and academic whose work was material to enabling the modest contribution of this study. To the work's publishers, and all those who have been there to listen and exchange ideas, thank you for your valuable feedback and dedication.

I hope that, in its own way, this endeavour will itself provide a building block to encourage further development in the literature and focus on this area of human rights.

Grazie dal profondo del cuore.

Caroline Savvidis
April 2016

Introduction

Aims and Parameters of Research

In full knowledge of how multi-faceted this subject is, and of how many different approaches could have been taken to tackle the subject of delay in the determination of legal disputes, I will attempt to adumbrate the parameters of this study. This endeavour is not meant to consist of a series of animadversions on specific legal systems, and especially not on any particular individual or group of individuals. Neither is it intended as an anodyne commentary, for even the most cogent arguments in favour of the efficient and timely resolution of disputes will only be reiterating and reformulating that which, in essence, one can hear every day in the halls of law courts. Rather, the aim and motivations behind this study are as follows.

- To ground the subject in a human rights context

In order to give legal perspective and a human rights grounding to what may otherwise be perceived as the simple and general desideratum of efficiency in the law courts as in any other system offering a service, one must appreciate that persons have not just the wish for but *a fundamental human right to* the determination of their civil rights and obligations or of any criminal charge against them within a reasonable time.

The foundation of this study is an analysis of the principles emanating from the jurisprudence of the European Court of Human Rights, as it is this court that has given flesh to the bones of the Convention by interpreting its provisions. Clearly, a compleat understanding of this area implies that the starting point of our inquiry should be the Convention which enshrines the right in the first place. Were it not for this fundamental human right, which must be understood not only in a strictly positive sense, but in the light of the Strasbourg Court's interpretation, we would not speak of legal delay within the same parameters as we do today. It would not be a question of the violation of a fundamental right but rather simply a desideratum of efficiency in the justice system as in any other system. Otherwise stated, there wouldn't be the same impelling need for the state to ensure such efficiency above and beyond the efficiency of other governmental services, both at an international, national and even individual level.

Unlike the composite right to a fair trial, the reasonable time requirement emerging from Article 6 targets only one aspect of judicial proceedings. Through a study of length-of-proceedings Strasbourg Jurisprudence we can extrapolate a set of minimum standards against which to measure whether any given legal system is in compliance with the Convention as it is currently interpreted.[1] If such minimum standards are met, or even surpassed, surely there will always remain room for improvement; if they are not so met, however, and in particular if they are systematically not met in a large percentage of cases, then a state would be responsible for a practice which is incompatible with the same Convention which it has bound itself to uphold.

- To study Strasbourg Jurisprudence and derive a working knowledge of the relevant concepts by applying the principles identified to selected legal systems, cases and legal queries

The principles derived from our study of Strasbourg Jurisprudence in the first part of this work are applied, in the latter parts, to critically review selected case studies and answer a number of queries pertinent to the subject. These include the study of a set of similar cases brought against the Italian Republic to challenge the practical and continued effectiveness of a remedy introduced into the national law of Italy and which had been adjudged to constitute an efficient remedy, the analysis of whether it is possible to determine concrete rules for compensation on the basis of the guidance issued by the European Court of Human Rights, as well as a thorough examination of the legal system of the Republic of Malta, encompassing both its case law and legal remedies, in order to demonstrate how an entire legal system can be vetted for compliance with the Convention, utilising the guidance issued by the Strasbourg Court through its voluminous case law regarding the length of proceedings.

In terms of legal tradition, the Italian legal system is generally classified as civilian, while the Maltese legal system is considered to be hybrid, namely, a confluence of both common and civil law elements.[2] The reader should bear in mind, however, that when analysing any individual legal system or set of facts against the standards set by the European Convention on Human Rights, and while national courts and legislators have a margin of discretion in the implementation of their obligations under the European Convention, the principles and standards set down by the Strasbourg Court are universally applicable, irrespective of national differences or differences in legal tradition. Selected judgments handed down by national courts, as well as legal avenues for redress, are therefore analysed in order to assess whether divergences in the method of determining human rights cases regarding the length of proceedings falls within the margin of appreciation which a state enjoys in the implementation of Convention obligations, or whether the stance taken by the courts on certain legal issues is simply out of line with the minimum standards set by the Convention and the Strasbourg Court in its interpretation of it.

The analysis thus seeks to demonstrate what principles come into play in the determination of whether a given domestic ruling or legal procedure is compliant with the Convention; it sets out to equip the reader with sufficient knowledge of the principles at play to be able to assess issues such as whether, in the event of a challenge before the European Court of Human Rights, the Court would or would not proceed to hear the merits of the case, and whether, on the merits, a violation of Article 6 or, possibly, Article 13 of the Convention would be found. The study also aims to enable the reader to assess whether a given legal system, as a whole, offers redress for violations of the 'reasonable time' requirement of Article 6 which is 'effective' in terms of the jurisprudence of the Strasbourg Court and, if not, where it falls short, and how this could be remedied. In view of the fact that Article 6 expressly applies to both the determination of civil rights and obligations and of any criminal charge, the author aims to equip the reader with the tools to perform the abovementioned analysis in respect of both types of proceedings. The relevance of the nature of the main proceedings is thus not to the applicability of Article 6 *per se*,[3] but, as investigated throughout Chapter 2, to the Court's assessment of the merits of the case, such as in determining the start and end of the 'period to be considered',[4] or in determining the reasonableness of its duration, when assessing the gravity of the stakes of the case.[5] Furthermore, in view of the fact that the principles laid down by the Strasbourg Court apply across all kinds of legal systems, an analysis may be performed also irrespective of whether the legal system being studied is inquisitorial or adversarial, common or civil law, or other national differences, for the Convention seeks to establish minimum standards which apply irrespective of such factors.

- To underline the importance of forestalling human rights violations[6] – trite but true, prevention is better than cure

This is especially true in an area where *restitutio in integrum* is simply not possible. We shall be examining the various means which a state may adopt in order to compensate victims of a breach of the right in question, but this does not in any way detract from the fact that prevention of delay in legal proceedings is an obligation incumbent upon any state which is aware that the *status quo* will predictably occasion further breaches of the Convention in ongoing and future cases.

- To underline the fact that contracting states have *already* bound themselves to protect this fundamental human right yet treat it, somehow, as a right of inferior status

The author feels that this Convention right has been, in a manner of speaking, given a lesser status than other fundamental rights by the Convention's

4 *Introduction*

contracting states.[7] It is however, as the sheer volume of applications thronging in through the floodgates of the Strasbourg institutions following the ratification of the right of individual petition attests, at the forefront of citizens' concerns.[8] While every state recognises how laudable the cause of improving efficiency in the courts, tribunals and other public adjudicating bodies is, as well as the preeminent importance of the timely delivery of justice, most states have preferred to provide compensation *ex post facto* to citizens who have suffered due to excessive delay in legal proceedings rather than to effectively address, tackle and solve the causes of delay, thereby forestalling other violations. As we shall be seeing however, the compensatory remedies afforded may themselves be afflicted by shortcomings which may render them ineffective for the purpose sought to be achieved.

The Creation of a Blueprint for the Analysis of Cases and Remedies within Legal Systems: Outline of Approach

This study seeks to provide a blueprint for analysing the effectiveness of legal remedies for delay across entire legal systems, as well as in any given individual case. The first chapters are focused on deriving legal principles from the body of jurisprudence of the European Court of Human Rights in Strasbourg, while the latter chapters contain illustrations of the practical application of such principles to both selected case law and legal avenues for redress, in order to assess their effectiveness in Convention terms, and to allow the readers to further familiarise themselves with the principles derived from the initial chapters. Finally, a number of areas of concern are identified through the progressive build-up and application of principles deriving from the European Convention on Human Rights, followed by the author's proposed solutions and conclusions.

The cases examined under the various headings will be examined not in chronological order, but according to relevance, with particular emphasis placed on the authority of the ruling.[9] The abbreviations and referencing method broadly follows the OSCOLA 2006 guidelines.[10] Strasbourg Jurisprudence will be referred to, throughout the text and footnotes, by a capitalised reference to the applicant, while national jurisprudence will be referred to by a capitalised reference to the applicant and respondent.[11] Where this approach may, in the author's view, cause confusion or be insufficient, additional details, such as the application number or date may also be provided. Full case details can be found in *Judgments*, wherein the cases are enlisted in alphabetical order. Citations from judgments delivered in foreign languages have been translated into English by the author in the manner which, to the best of her abilities, most accurately reflects the meaning and purport of the relevant passage. Awards in foreign currencies have been converted to the euro equivalent as at end January 2015. Except as otherwise specified,[12] this study, and the opinions expressed in it, have been compiled on the basis of selected literature, publicly available information, legislative instruments and judgments delivered up to the beginning of February 2015.[13]

The Strasbourg Pot Calling the National Kettles Black? A Vicious Circle

Under Article 6 of the Convention, states have a 'duty to organise their judicial systems in such a way that their courts can meet each of its requirements, including the obligation to hear cases within a reasonable time.'[14] Widespread dissatisfaction with the length of judicial proceedings in the member states of the Council of Europe has placed enormous stress on the workings of the Strasbourg Court itself. There is some irony in the fact that the ultimate court which upholds Convention rights, due to an inundation of length-of-proceedings cases,[15] finds itself unable to guarantee the hearing of its own cases within a reasonable time. It is in this vein that the Strasbourg Court has been referred to as a victim of its own success.[16]

> The Court has to deal with a large number of repetitive cases, admittedly well-founded, but which should be disposed of at national level once the relevant principles have become well-established in Strasbourg case-law. The States must bear responsibility for this second problem if they have failed to implement the necessary internal reforms or if reforms have been delayed. Two examples of problems that should be dealt with nationally are the excessive length-of-proceedings and the failure to enforce domestic judgments. Some commentators have argued that the Convention case-law should be binding *erga omnes*, and that this would improve matters because all States would have to amend their legislation, and domestic courts would have to develop their own case-law, in line with a judgment of the Court against another State. Increasingly – and fortunately – domestic authorities and courts have been learning from case-law that does not concern them directly, thus creating an *erga omnes* effect *de facto* ...[17]

It is therefore against this backdrop that one finds a consistent reiteration of the importance of the principle of subsidiarity in the annual speech of the President of the European Court of Human Rights.

Subsidiarity – The Need for Effective Remedies at a National Level to Uphold Convention Rights

The concept of the need for effective protection of the individual's fundamental human rights at a domestic level, referred to as 'subsidiarity' in the implementation of Convention rights, lies at the very heart of an effective implementation of the rights enshrined in the Convention; this investigation drives at understanding the extent to which Convention principles have been drawn on in this field of rights, and to equipping the reader with the necessary tools to understand and analyse the implementation of the Convention's principles at a domestic level.

6 Introduction

The practical need for national courts to apply the standards set down by the Strasbourg Court is seen as a desideratum which would in turn reduce the Court's caseload. A dramatic instantiation of this, which illustrates the 'potential impact of effective domestic remedies on the workload of the Court and underlines their importance as a factor in keeping the volume of applications within manageable limits'[18] was the sudden drop in the number of length-of-proceedings applications lodged with the Strasbourg Court in 2003 pursuant to the provision of an effective domestic remedy for length-of-proceedings complaints in the Italian Republic.[19]

The subsidiary nature of the Convention mechanism is key to several of the concepts we shall be drawing on in following chapters.[20] An analysis of the implications which a radical implementation of this concept would have on an entire legal system can be found in a recent paper by Chief Justice Emeritus Said Pullicino's insistence that:

> A human rights culture implies an awareness of the need to ensure their observance at all levels of public administration. It means that every action or inaction of public administration has to be taken in the knowledge that fundamental rights and freedoms are not violated or threatened.[21]

Subsidiarity, he stresses, thus requires *proactive promotion* of Convention rights by 'all those who are in any way involved in public administration', so that responsibility for the upholding of rights is 'decentralised'. Said Pullicino refers to a multi-tiered, hierarchical structure with the European Court of Human Rights at the apex ensuring uniformity, followed by the national judicial organs as supervisors or 'natural guarantors' of human rights at a national level and, finally, all those levels of public administration including judicial and quasi-judicial bodies, up to the 'grassroots' of the administration. A 'human rights culture', as the most extensive and effective form of protection of human rights, can best be achieved where awareness of the importance to proactively promote such rights 'permeate[s] all administrative actions'.

Notes

1 The Convention has been referred to as 'a living instrument which must be interpreted in light of present-day conditions' (TYRER); see Chapter 2, Section 1, *The Strasbourg Court's Method of Examination*, Sub-Section 1, *The framework for an examination of the merits of an alleged violation of Article 6*, regarding gradual evolution of the interpretation of what is 'reasonable'.

2 See Vernon Valentine Palmer, *Mixed Jurisdictions Worldwide: The Third Legal Family* (2nd edition, Cambridge), pp. 528–76 and John Henry Merryman, *The Civil Law Tradition* (2nd edition, Stanford University Press, Stanford 1985).

3 Regarding the applicability of Article 6 to constitutional proceedings, see Chapter 2, Section 1, Sub-Section 3, *Guidance on the length of proceedings for constitutional remedies*.

4 See Chapter 2, Section 1, *The Strasbourg Court's Method of Examination*, Sub-Section 1, *The framework for an examination of the merits of an alleged violation of Article 6*.

5 Ibid. See Chapter 2, Section 1, *The Strasbourg Court's Method of Examination*, Sub-Section 1, *The framework for an examination of the merits of an alleged violation of Article 6* under the heading, *iv What was at stake for the applicant*.
6 'All the contact I have been able to have with national authorities has shown me that there is a growing awareness among executive, legislative and judicial authorities of the need for states to forestall human rights violations and to remedy those it has not been possible to avoid.' Jean Paul Costa, 'Annual Report 2008 of the European Court of Human Rights, Council of Europe' <http://www.echr.coe.int> accessed January 2015, p. 38.
7 See Ugo Mifsud Bonnici, 'Human Rights in Maltese Legislation' in David E. Zammit (ed.), *Maltese Perspectives on Human Rights* (University of Malta, Malta 2008) p. 111.
8 See Appendix B.
9 Gauged according to how extensively such judgment is quoted in subsequent rulings, and from the impact it has had on the consideration of future cases, even if the case is not directly cited.
10 <http://denning.law.ox.ac.uk/published/oscola_2006.pdf.>
11 Or plaintiff and defendant, as applicable. Where judgments of the Strasbourg Court are only referenced by the applicant's initials, the respondent state is also cited in the capitalised reference.
12 See Chapter 3, *Chapter Introduction* regarding the start and end dates for the case study undertaken in that chapter.
13 Supplementary editions or supplements may be published. See <http://www.routledge.com.>
14 SÜSSMANN, BOTTAZZI, SCORDINO, COCCHIARELLA.
15 See Appendix A.
16 Louise Arbour, 'Annual Report 2008 of the European Court of Human Rights, Council of Europe' <http://www.echr.coe.int> accessed January 2015, p. 43.
17 Jean-Paul Costa, 'Annual Report 2008 of the European Court of Human Rights, Council of Europe' <http://www.echr.coe.int> accessed January 2015, p. 5.
18 'Annual Report 2003 of the European Court of Human Rights, Council of Europe' <http://www.echr.coe.int> accessed January 2015, p. 1.
19 See Appendix A.
20 See KUDŁA [152].
21 Joseph Said Pullicino, 'The Ombudsman: His Role in Human Rights Promotion and Protection' in David E. Zammit (ed.), *Maltese Perspectives on Human Rights* (University of Malta, Malta 2008) pp. 126–30.

1 Preliminary Pleas and Fundamental Concepts Relevant to Length-of-Proceedings Cases Brought Before the European Court of Human Rights

Chapter Introduction

The scope of this section is to analyse some of the preliminary pleas which are most commonly raised by respondent states, specifically in regard to applications based on the length of proceedings. In order to eventually analyse whether the remedies available in a given domestic system are 'effective' in terms of the Convention, as well as whether the redress afforded by national courts is sufficient by Convention standards, an understanding of the principles governing the Strasbourg Court's assessment of the following two preliminary pleas is crucial.

i   ECHR Article 35(1): Exhaustion of domestic remedies[1]

> The Court may only deal with the matter after all domestic remedies have been exhausted, according to the generally recognised rules of international law, and within a period of six months[2] from the date on which the final decision was taken.
>
> – ECHR Article 35 (admissibility criteria) sub-section 1

ii ECHR Article 35(3)[3]: Inadmissibility *ratione personae* and loss of victim status as per ECHR Article 34[4]

> The Court may receive applications from any person, non-governmental organisation or group of individuals claiming to be the victim of a violation by one of the High Contracting Parties of the rights set forth in the Convention or the protocols thereto. The High Contracting Parties undertake not to hinder in any way the effective exercise of this right.
>
> – ECHR Article 34 (individual applications)

> The Court shall declare inadmissible any individual application submitted under Article 34 if it considers that:
>
> (a) the application is incompatible with the provisions of the Convention or the Protocols thereto, manifestly illfounded, or an abuse of the right of individual application; or

(b) the applicant has not suffered a significant disadvantage, unless respect for human rights as defined in the Convention and the Protocols thereto requires an examination of the application on the merits and provided that no case may be rejected on this ground which has not been duly considered by a domestic tribunal.
– ECHR Article 35 (admissibility criteria) sub-section 3

The attention of the reader is drawn to the fact that the preliminary pleas examined in this Chapter are the ones most relevant to and most frequently raised in length-of-proceedings cases, but they are not the only preliminary pleas or considerations which need to be considered when filing or considering an application alleging a violation of Convention rights due to delay in judicial proceedings. A general understanding of all the preliminary concepts which any application claiming a violation of a Convention right should draw on would be beyond the focused scope of this study, where the author feels it is preferable to delve into those pleas in respect of which the case law of the Strasbourg Court in length-of-proceedings cases has reached a particular level of maturity in connection with the subject matter.

It is also worth noting that, aside from the two preliminary pleas enlisted above, since the introduction of Protocol 14 to the European Convention on Human Rights, another provision which seems to be playing a role of increasing relevance in a length-of-proceedings context is the newly amended limb of Article 35(3) which allows the Court to reject an examination where the applicant 'has not suffered a significant disadvantage'. One such case was that of GAGLIANO GIORGI, where the respondent government successfully argued that the applicant had not suffered any significant disadvantage as envisaged in Article 35(3), on the basis that the delay in the relevant proceedings had actually allowed the applicant to benefit from a reduction in the penalty due to the time barring of the action for corruption. While noting that the introduction of this qualifying caveat stems from the desirability of implementing the principle of *de minimis non curat praetor*, so as to allow the Court to focus on alleged violations of a minimum threshold of severity, the Court has underlined that this threshold is relative, and depends on the circumstances of the case. It further noted in GAGLIANO GIORGI that the criteria it will consider when assessing whether an application for an alleged violation has reached this minimum level of severity include the nature of the right allegedly infringed, the impact of the alleged violation on the exercise of the right and/or the consequences of the violation on the personal situation of the applicant.[5]

Chapter 1 – Section 1 – Article 35(1) Exhaustion of (Effective) Domestic Remedies

Mifsud Bonnici observes that the sheer volume of length-of-proceedings cases has obliged the Strasbourg Court to stringently enforce the requirement of the exhaustion of national remedies.[6]

The purpose of Article 35 § 1, which sets out the rule on exhaustion of domestic remedies, is to afford the Contracting States the opportunity of preventing or putting right the violations alleged against them before those allegations are submitted to the Court ... The rule in Article 35 § 1 is based on the assumption, reflected in Article 13 (with which it has a close affinity), that there is an effective domestic remedy available in respect of the alleged breach of an individual's Convention rights.[7]

1.1.1 *The general rules*

The general rules regarding the exhaustion of domestic remedies are, in essence, the following. The applicant must first have recourse to those remedies at a domestic level which relate to his complaint. Only those remedies which are normally available and sufficient need be resorted to, and not every possible avenue of redress available. The applicant need not resort to remedies which are not **certain,** both *in theory* and *in practice,* or inadequate to redress his grievances. If the availability of the remedy is unclear then it will lack the requisite **accessibility** and **effectiveness** required.[8] A remedy which requires exhaustion must be capable of directly remedying the state of affairs causing the violation, and must offer reasonable prospects of success. The existence of mere doubts as to the prospects of success of a particular remedy which is not obviously futile, however, is not a valid reason for failing to exhaust that avenue of redress.[9]

These requirements are interlinked. In PARIZOV the plea of non-exhaustion of domestic remedies was dismissed since although there was a compensatory remedy available, the law was unclear as to which court had jurisdiction to take cognizance of the claim where the case was still ongoing, and, being a recently introduced remedy, there was no case law to clarify this point. In HORVAT[10] the government's preliminary plea regarding non-exhaustion of domestic remedies was also dismissed. The availability of the remedy in question was predicated upon the constitutional court's decision to examine the complaint, and in order to achieve such a ruling the application had to satisfy two conditions: it had to be proved that a gross violation of constitutional rights had been incurred by reason of the absence of a decision within a reasonable time, and that there existed the risk of serious and irreparable consequences ensuing as a result of the delay. Only one case had ever been decided by the constitutional court, a fact which reaffirmed the uncertainty of the applicant's legal position.

In essence, what is required of applicants is that they afford the state an opportunity to redress the violation by presenting the complaints intended to be made subsequently in Strasbourg to the appropriate domestic body, 'at least in substance and in compliance with the formal requirements and time-limits laid down in domestic law and, further, that any procedural means that might prevent a breach of the Convention should have been used'.[11] The Court has demonstrated itself ready to apply this Convention requirement 'with some degree of flexibility and without excessive formalism', noting that it is essential to have regard to the particular circumstances of the case:

> This means, in particular, that the Court must take realistic account not only of the existence of formal remedies in the legal system of the Contracting State concerned but also of the general context in which they operate, as well as the personal circumstances of the applicant.[12]

It is only remedies which qualify in accordance with the above enlisted criteria that require exhaustion in terms of Article 35(1). In the Grand Chamber ruling of VUČKOVIĆ AND OTHERS the Court further noted that:

> In addition, according to the "generally recognised rules of international law" there may be special circumstances which absolve the applicant from the obligation to exhaust the domestic remedies at his or her disposal. The rule is also inapplicable where an administrative practice consisting of a repetition of acts incompatible with the Convention and official tolerance by the State authorities has been shown to exist, and is of such a nature as to make proceedings futile or ineffective.

1.1.2 The burden of proof lies with the respondent state

The state must demonstrate how the remedy it alleges should have been exhausted was 'an effective one available in theory and in practice at the relevant time, that is to say, that it was accessible, capable of providing redress in respect of the applicant's complaints and offered reasonable prospects of success'.[13] Only remedies which the state proves to be effective for the purposes of Article 13 need be exhausted for the purposes of Article 35. Such effectiveness is generally assessed by reference to other domestic decisions.[14] As exemplified by the case of MERIT, emphasis is placed by the Court on the need for the government to demonstrate how the local remedies, which it pleads the applicant could have resorted to, are effective in practice.

The state must prove that the remedy offered the applicant reasonable prospects of success.[15] This has been held to mean a genuine possibility of obtaining redress at domestic level in respect of their complaint. It is an objective test and can be assessed by reference to previous decisions of the court and the chances of success of the particular case.[16] The need for proof of judicial precedent is not set in stone. In SLAVIČEK the Court declared the application inadmissible on the basis of non-exhaustion of domestic remedies after examining the wording of a new remedy introduced into national law a few days after the application to the Strasbourg Court had been lodged. The wording of the new remedy was sufficiently clear to render it effective, even though there had been no decision on those lines as yet.[17] If the state successfully discharges this burden of proof, then the burden is shifted onto the applicant to show that these remedies were actually exhausted or were 'for some reason inadequate and ineffective in the particular circumstances of the case or that there existed special circumstances absolving him or her from the requirement.'[18]

1.1.3 A domestic remedy can acquire and lose the status of being sufficiently certain to be in need of exhaustion[19]

Once the Strasbourg Court has found a remedy to be effective at law and in practice, it will declare that applicants must, on pain of having their application declared inadmissible on the basis of non-exhaustion of domestic remedies, henceforth make use of that domestic remedy first. There are situations however, where this effectiveness may once again be called into question. The Court has consistently reiterated[20] that the remedy must *remain* effective, so that if a new application is brought before it alleging the ineffectiveness of such a remedy,[21] the Court will always ascertain that the remedy has remained effective *in practice* and in that particular case.

Once a remedy has been declared by the Court to have achieved this status, the prospects for future applications are the following. Firstly, an applicant might attempt to bypass the domestic remedy *in toto* without alleging any shortcomings of such remedy. In such a case the Court would accept the plea of non-exhaustion of domestic remedies. Secondly, an applicant could bypass the domestic remedy *in toto* and claim that the remedy is no longer effective generally, or not effective in regard to the particular circumstances of the case. In this latter case the Court would examine whether the claims are founded, and adjudge accordingly. Finally, an applicant might resort to domestic proceedings but either during those proceedings or subsequently file an application to the Strasbourg Court. If such application is filed during the pendency of domestic proceedings for redress, the Court will examine whether the remedy which is being afforded is *itself* taking too long. If the domestic proceedings are being heard with due diligence, it will accept the plea of non-exhaustion of domestic remedies. If not, then it will deny the preliminary plea and go on to examine the merits. If the application is filed subsequently to the domestic proceedings, the claim at the basis of the application would be that the compensation afforded was inadequate or that the domestic award is taking or took excessively long to be enforced. In such a case the plea raised by the respondent state would relate to the applicant's loss of victim status. As we shall be examining further, the Court may find that the applicant has *not* lost his victim status as the remedy in question, albeit being generally considered effective, did not amount to sufficient acknowledgement of the breach in that particular case. The general efficiency of the remedy will not be called into question unless that application belongs to a larger class of cases which call the general effectiveness of the remedy into question once again, raising issues under Article 13. The Scordino-Type Cases examined in Chapter 2, Section 3, fall under this category.

1.1.4 What forms of remedies has the Court considered to be effective and in need of exhaustion for the purposes of Article 35?

Those remedies which would satisfy the Court if it came to assess whether the applicant had an effective remedy under Article 13 need to be exhausted for the purposes of Article 35. In KUDŁA the Court explained that a remedy is 'effective' for the purposes of Article 13 'in the sense either of preventing the alleged violation or its continuation, or of providing adequate redress for any violation that had already occurred'.[22] A remedy which is in need of exhaustion, therefore, would equally fall within either of these categories.

An aggregate of remedies may together be considered effective[23]

These characteristics may be satisfied not only by a single remedy, but also by a set of options available to the individual *at different* stages of the proceedings[24] (although in a length-of-proceedings context, not at the *same* stage of proceedings, for requiring the applicant to resort to multiple remedies at any one stage is considered unreasonable[25]). It was in this vein that the Court in KAIĆ AND OTHERS[26] made note of the danger in requiring an applicant to have recourse to several domestic remedies where the result would be a 'vicious circle where the failure of one remedy would have constantly given rise to an obligation to make use of another one.'

If the domestic proceedings for compensation themselves took too long, it is unreasonable to expect the applicant to bring a second set of domestic proceedings complaining of the length of the compensation proceedings

One such case was SUKOBLJEVIC where against a backdrop of ongoing civil and bankruptcy proceedings which had lasted nine years, proceedings for compensation before the constitutional court took five years to be determined. The Court noted that it would have been unreasonable to require the applicant to file a second constitutional complaint to exhaust domestic remedies, and dismissed the government's preliminary objection.

The requirement to bring enforcement proceedings is more than can be reasonably expected of an applicant pursuant to Article 35: enforcement proceedings are not part of the remedies normally available and sufficient, and therefore need not be exhausted

The Court has repeatedly held that a person who has obtained a final and enforceable judgment *via* the appropriate state organs is not expected to bring separate enforcement proceedings. Consequently, any respondent state's plea to the effect that the applicant could, before lodging his application, have brought such proceedings, has been consistently rejected.[27]

1.1.5 The nexus between the plea of non-exhaustion of domestic remedies and the right to an effective remedy under Article 13 lies in the subsidiarity of the Convention's mechanism

We have already seen how the Court in KUDŁA underlined the mechanism which renders Articles 35 and 13[28] complementary and interdependent. In LUKENDA the Court recalled that:

> The primary responsibility for implementing and enforcing the guaranteed rights and freedoms is laid on the national authorities. The machinery of complaint to the Court is thus subsidiary to national systems safeguarding human rights. This subsidiary character is reflected in Articles 13 and 35(1) of the Convention.[29]

The affinity between these two provisions was clearly demonstrated in LUKENDA, where in its examination of the merits of the application in regard to Article 13 the Court simply referred to the reasoning whereby it had motivated the denial of the government's preliminary objections in regard to the non-exhaustion of domestic remedies.

1.1.6 Does a dismissal of the preliminary plea for non-exhaustion of domestic remedies mean the eventual finding of a violation of Article 13?

The answer is in the negative. For there to be a violation of Article 13 what is required is the absence of a legal avenue of effective redress to remedy the violation of a Convention right; it is a question of structure. If this avenue was attempted, yet failed to be effective in the particular case, then the preliminary plea on the basis of Article 35 will be dismissed, but there will be no violation found in regard to Article 13. One case which followed this pattern was ZARB, examined in Chapter 3.

Chapter 1 – Section 2 – Article 34 Loss of Victim Status – Incompatibility *Ratione Personae*

> It is the Court's settled case-law that where the national authorities have found a violation and their decision constitutes appropriate and sufficient redress, the party concerned can no longer claim to be a victim within the meaning of Article 34 of the Convention.[30]

1.2.1 Have the authorities acknowledged the violation, 'either expressly or in substance',[31] and was that acknowledgment adequate?

In determining this preliminary plea, the Court will first check whether there has been some form of acknowledgement that the applicant has sustained a violation, and will then assess whether this acknowledgement was appropriate, sufficient, adequate and proportionate, given the circumstances, to cause the applicant to lose victim status under the Convention and whether the remedy itself was an efficient, adequate and accessible remedy.[32] These elements are to be assessed by reference to the characteristics of the particular redress afforded. Where the redress consists in compensation proceedings for instance, the Court will base its assessment on the following points:

i *Comparison of the level and nature of compensation awarded to what the Court would itself have awarded*:[33] 'an applicant's victim status may depend on the level of compensation awarded at domestic level on the basis of the facts about which he or she complains before the Court.'[34] The Court will allow the domestic authorities a margin of discretion, as we shall be examining in further detail. Ultimately however, the quantum of compensation in respect of a breach must not be 'manifestly unreasonable' in the light of the Court's own case law.

In SIMALDONE, for instance, the Court noted that the Pinto laws of the Italian Republic allowed compensation to be awarded only for that part of the proceedings which surpassed the 'reasonable time' requirement, and that while this diverged from the Court's own practices, this fell within the state's margin of appreciation in implementing Convention rights; nevertheless, the Court went on to note that the sum of compensation ultimately awarded, irrespective of the method of calculation, must not be manifestly unreasonable by comparison to what it itself would have awarded. Similarly, in BAKO the Court was faced with a plea of loss of victim status in regard to civil proceedings lasting over nine years, where the domestic court had awarded € 3,000 by way of non-pecuniary compensation. In accepting the government's plea, the Court noted that the constitutional court's method of analysing whether there had been undue delay, even though different from its own approach where the overall length of proceedings is taken into consideration, rather than breaking the proceedings down into the periods before the different courts, still amounted to sufficient acknowledgement of the violation.

The Court has held that when there are several remedies[35] – one to speed proceedings up and another for compensation – the amounts awarded may be lower than those which the Court would have awarded, as long as these are not 'manifestly unreasonable', are in line with the legal tradition and standard of living of the country concerned and are speedy, reasoned and rapidly executed.

The Court has also consistently held[36] that an effective compensatory remedy must be capable, both in theory and in practice, of affording *both* pecuniary and non-pecuniary compensation where such damages are occasioned by delay, and that the remedy should provide for a presumption, in no need of further proof, that non-pecuniary compensation should be awarded for the moral damage suffered.

ii *The length of the remedial proceedings themselves*: 'It cannot be ruled out that excessive delays in an action for compensation will render the remedy inadequate'.[37] The Court has allowed the possibility for the domestic courts to acknowledge their own delay (in proceedings for compensation) and in the light of such further breach to award a particularly high amount in order to provide the applicant with redress.

iii *The effectiveness of the enforcement proceedings*: The Court has held that a six month time limit is reasonable for the enforcement of compensation awarded in length-of-proceedings cases.[38] A state should make budgetary provision for any remedy which is to be considered 'effective', but enjoys a margin of discretion as to the procedure to be followed in remedial actions in order to best achieve efficiency. Rules regarding legal costs should not however impose an excessive burden on a party seeking a remedy for the length of proceedings, as this could constitute a bar to the right of access to court. In SIMALDONE the interest paid in respect of a one year delay in the enforcement of a judgment awarding compensation was not held to be sufficient to compensate for the frustration in awaiting the enforcement of a final and binding judgment.

In this way, the Court's approach has been described as an *a posteriori* examination of the compensation proceedings.[39] If these characteristics are not met, the applicant will not be considered to have lost his victim status under Article 34. This will be considered an aggravation of any breach eventually proved on the merits.

Remedies which could cause the loss of victim status are not, however, limited to financial compensation.[40]

> Another measure that can, in certain situations, make good past delays is the possibility to obtain a reduction in the penalty imposed on a convicted defendant ... However, to be able to redress the breach of the defendant's right to a hearing within a reasonable time, such a measure must meet three conditions. First, the courts must acknowledge the failure to observe the reasonable time requirement of Article 6 § 1 in a sufficiently clear way. Secondly, they must afford redress by reducing the sentence in an express and measurable manner. Lastly, the opportunity to request such a reduction, whether based on express statutory language or clearly established case law, must be available to the convicted defendant as of right. Naturally, that does not mean that the courts must as a rule accede to such requests; in situations where a reduction of sentence would not be an appropriate measure, they may refuse to do so, and it will then be for the defendant to seek other forms of redress, such as pecuniary compensation. ... Conversely, in cases of extreme delay or delay which has been exceptionally prejudicial to the accused, consideration may even be given to discontinuing the proceedings altogether ... provided that the public interest is not adversely affected by such a discontinuance.

A comparison of the following cases clearly brings out the analytical exercise conducted by the Court in the face of such a plea. The government's preliminary pleas were dismissed in the first two cases, and upheld in the third and fourth. In BURDOV the government pleaded that in view of the fact that the amount due to the applicant would be adjusted to cater for inflation in accordance with an official price index, he had been adequately compensated for any delay in the payment of the award. The Court noted that this method of compensation made good only for inflation-related losses but took no account of pecuniary or non-pecuniary damage sustained by the applicant.[41] In JENSEN the domestic court reduced the length of the applicant's sentence by six months on appeal, citing the length of proceedings and the applicant's cooperation as its motivation, expressly rejecting however that there had been any breach of the applicant's right to have his case determined within a reasonable time. The government pleaded loss of the applicant's victim status. The Court noted that the sentence was nebulous in regard to what part of the six months was reduced as a result of the length of proceedings, noting also that the appellate court had rendered the sentence enforceable, albeit reduced, unlike the sentence of the court of first instance which had been suspended.

These cases stand in contrast to those of FOLDES AND FOLDESNE HAJLIK, in which lenient sentences were imposed as a result of the acknowledgement of the length of criminal proceedings against the applicants, which had lasted twelve and a half years at three instances. The Court noted that the offences of which the applicants had been convicted carried a two- to five-year imprisonment term, and that upon conviction, moderate fines, but no jail term, had been imposed. It consequently ruled that this amounted to adequate and sufficient acknowledgement for the violation of the applicants' rights under Article 6. In SPROTTE the applicant was held to have lost his victim status as a result of the discontinuance of criminal proceedings which had taken eleven years at four instances. The domestic court had also ordered that the court fees, and half of the applicant's expenses, were to be borne by the treasury.

It is clear therefore, that not just any measure taken by the state, being favourable to the applicant, will suffice to redress his position if it is not proportionate to the violation incurred.[42] Otherwise stated, unless the 'decision or measure' in question amounts to appropriate or sufficient acknowledgement, whether express or in substance, of the breach, the Court will dismiss the government's preliminary plea.[43]

1.2.2 State failure to cause loss of victim status notwithstanding the affording of domestic redress

If a breach of the reasonable time requirement has occurred, then the applicant will hold victim status in terms of Article 34. The Strasbourg Court will not find that an applicant has lost such status if there is no effective remedy through which the applicant can obtain redress at a domestic level, or if having had recourse to an available remedy, this was not effective in that particular case. We have seen some examples in cases cited above in this Section, but generally speaking, this latter possibility could ensue either where:

- The authorities did not recognise that a breach occurred[44]

On the merits this would lead to a breach of Article 6, but not of Article 13, as the reason for the remedy not being effective would be independent of the structural availability of such remedy. If there is an action for compensation at a domestic level therefore, and this *is* resorted to, but the action fails on the merits, the applicant would not have lost his victim status. In KOZLICA and SUKOBLJEVIC the Court noted that the remedy the applicant had availed himself of had already been adjudged to be an effective remedy in SLAVIČEK, but went on to note that nevertheless it would continue to verify whether the way in which the domestic court 'interpreted and applied the relevant provisions of the domestic law' was consonant with Convention principles.

- Through delay in the remedial proceedings themselves

On the merits this would lead to a breach of Article 6, but not of Article 13, unless the delay is systematic.[45] In the 2010 judgment of BELPERIO ET CIARMOLI, having examined several applications complaining about the length of Pinto-law based compensation proceedings for delays in judicial proceedings in Italy, the Court fixed at one year and six months for hearings at a single instance, and two years and six months for a hearing at two instances, the maximum thresholds within which Pinto law-based proceedings should be heard, failing which a violation of Article 6 would be found.[46]

- By awarding compensation that is 'manifestly unreasonable' to remedy the violation

This would lead to a Scordino-Type Case[47] and entail a breach of Article 6, but not Article 13, unless this is part of a wider practice. In DELLE CAVE AND CORRADO, a Scordino-Type Case, the Court noted that although domestic proceedings for compensation had been expeditious, lasting for only five months, the amount of non-pecuniary damage awarded by the Court in the Pinto law-based proceedings was a mere 10 per cent of that generally awarded by the Court in similar cases. The applicants could therefore still claim victim status. These cases can be contrasted with ESPOSITO, wherein the award the applicant received at a domestic level amounted to 70 per cent of that which would have been awarded by the Court, and was thus held to constitute appropriate and sufficient acknowledgement of the violation.

In addition to a direct comparison between the sum awarded and what the Court itself would have awarded, the Court's rulings have been also been guided by other factors which affect the materiality of the award. At the basis of the inadmissibility of the application in KALAJZIC, for instance, lay the consideration that although the sum of € 1,130 awarded by the domestic court in respect of civil proceedings which had taken fourteen years was lower than what it would itself have awarded, this did not automatically render it manifestly inadequate and that:

> Whether the amount awarded could be regarded as reasonable fell to be assessed in the light of all the circumstances of the case. These included not merely the duration of the proceedings in the specific case but the value of the award judged in the light of the standard of living in the State concerned, and the fact that under the national system compensation would in general be awarded and paid more promptly than would be the case if the matter fell to be decided by the Court.

- By awarding compensation which is not promptly paid (delay in enforcement)

Delay in the enforcement of the award will lead to a breach of Article 6, and possibly Article 13 if there is a widespread practice of non-enforcement or delay in enforcement. In some cases a breach of the right to the protection of property under Article 1 of the Convention's First Protocol has also been found.[48] As we shall be examining in Chapter 2.1.2, proceedings for enforcement are considered part and parcel of the 'period to be considered'.

In Chapter 2 we delve into further depth in regard to the measures which domestic authorities must take in order to afford sufficient redress to the victim of a breach of the reasonable time requirement emanating from Article 6. It is important to note that the above enlisted heads are cumulative conditions, and a state does not have the option of satisfying them in the alternative. In the case of SARTORY for instance, the Court concluded that the remedy itself had taken too long[49] and that therefore, the applicant was still to be considered a victim, noting that if the compensation procedures had not been afflicted by delay, € 3,000 would have sufficed to cause the loss of the applicant's victim status.[50] It further noted that where domestic proceedings do not succeed in providing sufficient redress for the violation suffered, this amounts to an aggravating factor in the calculation of the compensation due, saving the possibility for a domestic court to acknowledge its own delay and award a particularly high amount to offer redress for this further delay.[51] There have been cases where the Court reserves the issue as to the victim status of the applicant, as it is too intimately imbricated with the merits of the case.[52]

Notes

1 See *Statutes* for entire provision.
2 Regarding the timing for the lodging of applications, see RIBIČ and the dissenting opinion of judges Myjer and López Guerra: '... an applicant who brings an unnecessary or inappropriate appeal and then waits until the final decision before lodging an application

with the Court faces the danger that his application will be declared inadmissible as out of time.' ... '... if, and only if, an applicant wishes to pursue further domestic remedies but has genuine reason to doubt their effectiveness. In such a case it is not unacceptable for the applicant – in order not to run the risk that his application will be rejected under the six-month rule or under the rule on non-exhaustion of domestic remedies – to lodge an application before embarking on the further national remedy, as long as he informs our Court accordingly.' Reference should also be made to the status of ECHR Protocol 15, and other legislative updates which may come into force from time to time, when considering an application.

3 See *Statutes* for entire provision.
4 See *Statutes* for entire provision.
5 [56] and GIUSTI [34].
6 David E. Zammit, 'Introduction' in *Maltese Perspectives on Human Rights* (University of Malta, Malta 2008) *op. cit.* p. 10.
7 KUDŁA [152], SCORDINO [141], SELMOUNI [74], BEZZINA WETTINGER AND OTHERS [58].
8 SCORDINO, VERNILLO, DALIA, CALLEJA, VLADIMIR ROMANOV.
9 VUČKOVIĆ AND OTHERS [74]. See also DELLE CAVE AND CORRADO, AKDIVAR AND OTHERS, VASSILIOS ATHANASIOU ET AUTRES [55]. Note also VUČKOVIĆ AND OTHERS at [75] relating to the requirement to exhaust those remedies geared to redress Convention violations, and not others unrelated to such breach, and how this is linked to the subsidiary mechanism of the Convention: 'It is not sufficient that the applicant may have unsuccessfully exercised another remedy which could have overturned the impugned measure on other grounds not connected with the complaint of a violation of a Convention right. It is the Convention complaint which must have been aired at national level for there to have been exhaustion of "effective remedies". It would be contrary to the subsidiary character of the Convention machinery if an applicant, ignoring a possible Convention argument, could rely on some other ground before the national authorities for challenging an impugned measure, but then lodge an application before the Court on the basis of the Convention argument.'
10 Also CERIN.
11 AKDIVAR [66], VLADIMIR ROMANOV [46], VUČKOVIĆ AND OTHERS [72].
12 KHASHIYEV AND AKAYEVA [117], AKSOY [53], AKDIVAR [69].
13 LUKENDA [44].
14 COCCHIARELLA, MUSCI, RICCARDI PIZZATI, MOSTACCIUOLO (NO 1), MOSTACCIUOLO (NO 2), APICELLA, ERNESTINA ZULLO, GIUSEPPINA AND ORESTINA PROCACCINI, ANDRÁŠIK, SIERMIŃSKI.
15 DI COLA.
16 CALDAS RAMIREZ DE ARRELLANO.
17 Cf. HORVAT.
18 LUKENDA [44], HORVAT [39].
19 MIFSUD, GIUMMARRA AND OTHERS, KRASUSKI, DI SANTE.
20 PAULINO TOMAS, GOUVEIA DA SILVA TORRADO, SCORDINO.
21 *Viz.* one declared previously to have acquired sufficient certainty to constitute an effective remedy which requires exhaustion for the purposes of Article 35(1).
22 [158]. See also LUKENDA [67]. KUDŁA was a landmark judgment in the context of the length-of-proceedings case law of the Court, and remains, to date, the basis for how the interplay between Articles 6 and 13 of the Convention is interpreted: see Chapter 2, *Chapter Introduction*. See also KUPPINGER [137], but note the comments of the Court in SCORDINO [185].

23 LUKENDA.
24 SILVER AND OTHERS, GRZINČIČ, CHAHAL. See also DEGUARA CARUANA GATTO AND OTHERS [67]: 'when a remedy has been pursued, use of another remedy which has essentially the same objective is not required'.
25 For instance LUKENDA [70].
26 [32] Also VANEY [52].
27 COCCHIARELLA, MUSCI, RICCARDI PIZZATI, MOSTACCIUOLO (NO. 1), MOSTACCIUOLO (NO. 2), APICELLA, ERNESTINA ZULLO, GIUSEPPINA AND ORESTINA PROCACCINI, YURIY NIKOLAYEVICH IVANOV, METAXAS, LIZANETS, DELLE CAVE AND CORRADO.
28 Text to n 7 (Chapter 1).
29 [41].
30 SCORDINO [181], HOLZINGER (NO. 1) [21].
31 BURDOV, KALAJZIC, CENTRAL MEDITERRANEAN DEVELOPMENT CORPORATION LIMITED, ECKLE, COCCHIARELLA, WASSERMAN.
32 SARTORY, COCCHIARELLA.
33 SCORDINO, COCCHIARELLA, MUSCI, RICCARDI PIZZATI, MOSTACCIUOLO (NO. 1), MOSTACCIUOLO (NO. 2), APICELLA, ERNESTINA ZULLO, GIUSEPPINA AND ORESTINA PROCACCINI, DELLE CAVE AND CORRADO.
34 SCORDINO [202].
35 SCORDINO [206].
36 Explicitly laid out in SÜRMELI [113], GRÄSSER [49], HARTMAN [68], LUKENDA [59] and can also be inferred from several other cases such as the Court's reasoning in SCORDINO [204] and COCCHIARELLA [95].
37 SCORDINO [195]; Also see PAULINO TOMÁS, BELINGER, ÖNERYILDIZ, VIDAS, SCORDINO, COCCHIARELLA, MARTINS CASTRO ET ALVES CORREIA DE CASTRO.
38 See Chapter 2, Section 1, *The Strasbourg Court's Method of Examination*, Sub-Section 2, *Guidance on the length of proceedings for the enforcement of judgments*.
39 SARTORY, COCCHIARELLA, DELLE CAVE ET CORRADO.
40 See DIMITROV AND HAMANOV [128–129].
41 Point decided earlier in MOROKO.
42 ZARB, CENTRAL MEDITERRANEAN DEVELOPMENT CORPORATION LIMITED.
43 BURDOV, SCORDINO, COCCHIARELLA.
44 CALLEJA, DEBONO.
45 See Chapter 2, Section 1, *The Strasbourg Court's Method of Examination*, Sub-Section 2, *Guidance on the length of proceedings for the enforcement of judgments*.
46 See GAGLIANO GIORGI [72].
47 See Chapter 2, Section 3, *Case Study Based on the Legal System of Italy: The Scordino-Type Cases*.
48 YURIY NIKOLAYEVICH IVANOV, SIMALDONE, BURDOV.
49 Having exceeded four years and five months.
50 The length of main proceedings exceeded six years and seven months at two instances.
51 See Chapter 1, Section 2, *Article 34 Loss of Victim Status – Incompatibility* Ratione Personae, Sub-Section 1, *Have the authorities acknowledged the violation, 'either expressly or in substance', and was that acknowledgment adequate?*
52 BECK.

2 Guidance Drawn from Judgments of the European Court of Human Rights; the Relevance and Utility of ECHR Articles 6 and 13 to Length-of-Proceedings Cases

Chapter Introduction

> In the determination of his civil rights and obligations or of any criminal charge against him, everyone is entitled to a fair and public hearing within a reasonable time by an independent and impartial tribunal established by law. ...
>
> – ECHR Article 6 (right to a fair trial) sub-section 1

> Everyone whose rights and freedoms as set forth in this Convention are violated shall have an effective remedy before a national authority notwithstanding that the violation has been committed by persons acting in an official capacity.
>
> – ECHR Article 13 (right to an effective remedy)

The right to the determination of civil rights or obligations, or of any criminal charge, 'within a reasonable time' has dichotomous ramifications under the European Convention on Human Rights which stem from the interplay between Articles 6 and 13. The Strasbourg Court has required of states, in addition to ensuring that each particular case is heard within a reasonable time, a further level of compliance in terms of the provision of effective legal remedies to provide redress for breaches of this right. In order to determine whether a state is in compliance with Convention standards therefore, regard must be had to the avenues of redress provided by the legal system in order to determine whether, both in theory and in practice, an effective remedy to prevent and compensate for unreasonable delay in judicial proceedings exists.

The relevance of this second chapter will be to illustrate the pattern or framework approach of the European Court of Human Rights to the examination of the merits of length-of-proceedings cases. An in-depth understanding of the elements vying for expression in the final pronouncement of the Court will be central to an understanding, undertaken in Chapter 3, of how and why certain national courts have reached differing conclusions to the Strasbourg

Court on the basis of the same facts, as well as to academically speculate as to whether a selection of cases which were not brought before the Strasbourg Court would have benefited from a different upshot if an application had been filed before such latter court. This chapter is crucial both to an understanding of how the Strasbourg Court approaches a length-of-proceedings complaint to assess whether there has been a Convention violation, as well as to understand what form of remedy the Court expects states to provide once a violation has been found.

The *locus classicus* for a complaint regarding the length of proceedings, whether these are of a civil, administrative, criminal or constitutional nature, is ECHR Article 6. Prior to KUDŁA, the Court would, in the face of proceedings which exceeded the reasonable time requirement, find a violation of Article 6 and stop its examination at that point, finding it unnecessary to examine also whether the applicant had an effective remedy in regard to his right to have the dispute determined within a reasonable time. In view of the mounting pressure on the Court and the increased need for the issue of delay in legal proceedings to be resolved at a domestic level however, the Court revised its approach and today consistently examines also whether, in the particular case (and if there are multiple pending applications against the same state, bearing the possibility of a pilot judgment in mind[1]), the applicant had an effective remedy. Otherwise put, the Court has accepted that there is *no overlap* between the two distinct rights to have one's case determined within a reasonable time, and the right to have an effective remedy provided to safeguard such right. Length-of-proceedings applications are consequently framed either on the basis of Article 6 alone, or on the basis of Article 6 in conjunction with Article 13, depending on the material facts.

> Kudła was important because the Court expressly reacted to the threat posed to the effectiveness of the Convention system by the accumulation of large numbers of same issue cases, the so-called repetitive or clone cases. It also pointed to what, in the long term, will be the only solution to this problem, namely the introduction of effective remedies at the national level.[2]

Chapter 2 – Section 1 – The Strasbourg Court's Method of Examination

2.1.1 The framework for an examination of the merits of an alleged violation of Article 6

When examining the merits of an application claiming a violation of the length of proceedings requirement prescribed by Article 6, the Strasbourg Court has traditionally adopted a structured approach in its analysis. The Court first proceeds to determining the 'period to be considered' by establishing the start and finish of a period, the reasonableness of which is to be then examined in the light of the 'particular circumstances of the case'. In establishing this period a plethora of considerations apply, including:

- the temporal application of the Convention,[3]
- whether the proceedings complained of were criminal[4] or civil[5] in nature, and the corresponding rules regarding the start[6] and the end[7] of the 'period to be considered',
- whether the applicant was a party to the proceedings complained of or the heir of such party and, if so, whether they are applying in their own right or in their quality as heir,[8]
- whether any periods should be subtracted from the total duration due to delay caused by the applicant (such as a period during which the applicant absconded pending criminal proceedings[9]) and
- whether there were any administrative proceedings preceding the filing of the judicial demand which were necessary precursors to such action and which would therefore have to be considered as part and parcel of the 'period to be considered'.[10]

Once this has been established, two possibilities will subsist *prima facie*:

i *The period is prima facie unreasonably long*[11] – This leads to a rebuttable presumption that there has been a violation of Article 6. Different authors have reached varying conclusions as to whether the jurisprudence of the Strasbourg Court provides any particular threshold or period which, once breached or elapsed, will generally result in the finding of a violation of the reasonable time requirement. Harris, O'Boyle and Warbrick have set this threshold at eight years.[12] Stavros feels that no conclusion can be drawn for certain as the Court has reached divergent conclusions on the basis of equivalent periods, particularly below the nine-year mark.[13] An interesting dissenting opinion was entered by Judge Borrego Borrego in the case of DEBONO in which, while disagreeing with the majority as to the finding of a violation on the facts of the case (being a period of around three years), he noted that what constitutes 'a reasonable time' is 'gradually becoming shorter', with the objective cut-off point standing currently at five years.[14]

ii *The period is prima facie reasonable in length* – In this event the Court will still examine the merits in order to assess whether the period in question was reasonable in the 'particular circumstances of the case'. The period may still be considered unreasonable, and thus in violation of the applicant's rights due either to the fact that:

- The nature of the case is so straightforward as to render any delay unjustified. One example clearly falling within this category would be enforcement proceedings of the final and executable judgment of a competent court; or

- The high stakes of the case required particular expedition and a higher level of diligence than that ordinarily required of the judicial authorities. We shall be examining which cases fall within this category below in this Section.[15]

The Court will generally next assess the reasonableness of the period in the light of the 'particular circumstances of the case' which are to be assessed by reference to four heads of examination.[16] The Court frequently not only enters a general reference to these criteria by way of a citation from a previous judgment, but actually analyses the facts of the case under the following four headings:

i Complexity of the factual or legal[17] issues raised by the case[18]

These may include:

- The nature,[19] gravity, novelty or technicality of the subject matter of the proceedings
- The number of parties to the case if civil, or co-defendants[20] if criminal,[21] including the participation of joinders or intervenors[22]
- The number of judicial demands if civil, the number and gravity of accusations if criminal[23] and the number of corresponding pleas; the same applies to the appeal application and pleas upon appeal, as well as the existence of any cross appeal
- The need for expert reports[24]
- Whether the facts are disputed
- The volume of written or oral evidence[25] or number of witnesses[26]
- The need to obtain foreign expert evidence[27] or material[28]
- Obstacles to the production of evidence such as, in criminal proceedings, the need to obtain evidence of a co-accused where the rights of such co-accused come into conflict with those of the relevant accused person
- Any international elements, whether issues of conflict of laws, jurisdictional issues or concurrent jurisdiction, the need for foreign witnesses or letters rogatory[29] (the state will not be held responsible for delays caused by foreign jurisdictions)[30]
- The number of instances
- The joinder of the case to other cases[31]
- Any other relevant factors[32]

ii The conduct of the applicant(s)[33]

The general rule is that while the state, *via* its judicial authorities, is obliged to conduct proceedings with due – and in certain cases special or extraordinary – diligence, Article 6 does not does not require accused persons actively to co-operate with the judicial authorities or civil parties to expedite proceedings.[34]

All this is not to say that efforts on behalf of applicants to expedite proceedings would not be favourably looked upon by the Court. In UNIÓN ALIMENTARIA SANDERS SA, the Court described the applicant's duty as being:

> Required only to show diligence in carrying out the procedural steps relating to him, to refrain from using delaying tactics and to avail himself of the scope afforded by domestic law for shortening the proceedings. He is under no duty to take action which is not apt for that purpose.[35]

Applicants cannot be held to be at fault where they make use of legitimate procedural rights to defend their claim, or where they make full use of the remedies provided by domestic legislation.[36] In the case of PISHCHALNIKOV for instance, the Court held that the applicant could in no way be blamed for taking time to study his case file for this was a measure afforded by domestic law for the protection of his interests. Periods of delay attributable to the applicants consist of deliberate dilatory tactics,[37] abuse of procedural rights, outright obstructionist tactics[38] and delay resulting from gross negligence.

While a party will not be faulted for exercising legitimate procedural activity, and neither for periods elapsed pending the examination of applications filed in the course of the legitimate exercise of the right of *audi alteram partem*, 'Nonetheless, such conduct constitutes an objective fact, not capable of being attributed to the respondent State.'[39] When unreasonable delay stems from the applicant's own actions, therefore, the respondent state would not be held accountable for such period, unless the delay resulted from the legitimate exercise of the applicant's procedural rights. Consequently, if national adversarial proceedings were unreasonably delayed due to tactics of the counterparty, or national criminal proceedings unreasonably delayed due to the inefficiency of the prosecution, where additional delay is caused by the applicant in the course of the legitimate exercise of the rights of defence, the respondent state would have to answer for the entire period of time (including the time the applicant took to respond), for no applicant can be expected to forego their rights of defence in order to obtain efficiency in the delivery of justice.

In ŁOBARZEWSKI[40] the Court observed that an applicant can make full use of the procedural rights allowed to him, such as the extension of his claim, however 'he must be aware that it may lead to delays the consequences of which he would have to bear'. In essence the Court was setting out the self-evident fact that the applicant must bear the reasonable consequences of his actions, and that if a modification of his claim results in a transfer of the case to another court, he cannot complain of reasonable delay occasioned by the transfer. In this case, however, the proceedings had already been pending for thirteen years before the applicant modified the claim, and the Court concluded that the authorities were responsible for this delay.

LIADIS concerned a civil case spanning over twenty years where no violation of Article 6 was found as the numerous adjournments which accounted for the delay in question were required on account of the applicant's repeated absence. Failure to appear and demands for adjournments were also at stake in PATRIANAKOS. In that case, the applicant allowed a period of one year and two months to elapse before the filing of his appeal application. The applicant's conduct was the decisive factor in the Court's finding that there had been no violation notwithstanding the significant length of the proceedings.[41] In HUMEN the delay caused by the failure of the applicant to inform the Court of his refusal to submit himself to certain medical tests to determine the extent of his injuries, as well as inaccurate testimony of the facts, which complicated the proceedings, were held to be the reasons for delay in proceedings which had lasted two years and eleven months; no violation was found.

A state will not be held responsible for delays occasioned by the parties' own representatives.[42] Delays attributable to the advocates of parties are to be borne by such parties. If the cause of the delay is the opposing party (or the representative of such party), on the other hand, the court has a duty, pursuant to its positive obligations under the Convention, to safeguard the right of the other parties to the proceedings to have their case determined within a reasonable time. In PISHCHALNIKOV, in the context of criminal proceedings and in relation to the state's argument that delay was caused by the applicant's co-defendants, the Court held that:

> It was incumbent on the court dealing with the case to discipline the parties in order to ensure that the proceedings were conducted at an acceptable pace ... It therefore considers that the delay occasioned by the Regional Court's failure to discipline the co-defendants and their lawyers is attributable to the State.[43]

iii The conduct of the competent authorities

Only delays attributable to the state may justify a finding of a failure to comply with the 'reasonable time' requirement.[44] Delays attributable to foreign authorities will not be considered.[45] Stavros sets out the following scenarios in which the state may be found responsible for unreasonable delay in proceedings:

> The competent authorities may be criticised in any of the following ways for failing in their duty to conduct the proceedings within a reasonable time: first, for allowing the proceedings to stagnate refraining to take any substantial procedural measures for a considerable amount of time; second, for taking unreasonable in the circumstances time for the completion of specific measures, although they kept the case under constant review; third for protracting the proceedings by taking unnecessary procedural measures; and fourth, for failing to positively expedite already delayed proceedings by not taking, for example, measures to neutralise the applicant's dilatory tactics. Finally the system itself could be the object of criticism for displaying inherent features which inhibit the speedy conclusion of a criminal case.[46]

Irrespective of the domestic structure of procedure, whether inquisitorial or adversarial, and also irrespective of whether domestic law provides that the management of the case lies mostly in the hands of the parties or with the court, 'a special duty rests upon the court concerned to see to it that all those who play a role in the proceedings do their utmost to avoid any unnecessary delay.'[47] The court is ultimately responsible for ensuring that the rights of the parties, including the right to have the case determined within a reasonable time, are observed.

> Even in legal systems applying the principle that the procedural initiative lies with the parties, the latter's attitude does not absolve the courts from the obligation to ensure the expeditious trial required by Article 6 § 1.[48]

Providing avenues through which parties may expedite proceedings does not detract in any manner from a court's obligation to ensure that the reasonable time requirement is complied with, 'as the duty to administer justice expeditiously is incumbent in the first place on the relevant authorities.'[49] The positive obligations incumbent upon the state may therefore require it to take active measures to uphold the parties' rights, irrespective of the source of delay. This is true also where delay could result from the appointment of experts. Indeed the Court has held that 'the primary responsibility for delays resulting from the provision of expert opinions rests ultimately with the State.'[50]

If there are several co-defendants, or co-accused, the Court will look to whether the proper administration of justice required the cases to be heard simultaneously, usually due to common evidentiary elements, in order to assess whether the benefits of so joining the cases justified protraction of the determination of the individual case.[51] Harris, O'Boyle and Warbrick opine that while it may be sensible to hear cases against two or more co-accused persons together, this cannot justify substantial delay in the bringing of a case against any one of them.[52]

The Court will run through the manner in which the case was handled by the domestic court, pointing out any periods of delay, inactivity[53] or inefficiency, including those attributable to state prosecution in criminal cases. It will run through any delays or lengthy periods between adjournments, the causes of adjournments and the delay, if any, in appointment of the case for hearing, whether at first instance or at an appellate stage. In criminal cases it will look at the length of the investigation period conducted by the state authorities. It will search for any systemic causes of delay including chronic overload, or an isolated case of backlog, which may have had an effect on the particular case.

While the Strasbourg Court has been ready to concede that the vicissitudes of life are such that a sudden influx of applications may slow down the most efficient of judicial systems, a violation of the Convention will result where systematic delay exists. While chronic backlog of cases will not be accepted as valid justification for delay,[54] a temporary delay due to particular circumstances, such as the substitution of a judge or a temporary backlog may be acceptable if the state adduces evidence that it took all possible remedial measures to minimise the resultant delay.[55]

> Methods which may fall to be considered, as a provisional expedient, admittedly include choosing to deal with cases in a particular order, based not just on the date when they were brought but on their degree of urgency and importance and, in particular, on what is at stake for the persons concerned. However, if a state of affairs of this kind is prolonged and becomes a matter of structural organisation, such methods are no longer sufficient and the State will not be able to postpone further the adoption of effective measures.[56]

In the case of ZIMMERMANN AND STEINER what was thought to be an isolated excess of work resulted to be a progressive increase in the volume of litigation which could no longer be considered an isolated event; this increase would have necessitated structural reforms. In LEDONNE (NO. 2) a violation was found in relation to a year's adjournment due to a lawyer's strike, as while such isolated events are not necessarily always imputable to the state, proof of the measures implemented to minimise the resultant delay was not adduced.

Failure to abide by a particular time limit set down by law will not in and of itself mean that the reasonable time requirement has been exceeded.[57] Indeed, whether or not the length of proceedings is unreasonable will undergo the ordinary examination conducted by the Court irrespective of the breach of domestic time frames, which at most could be considered corroborating proof of the attitude with which the authorities handled the case.[58]

iv What was at stake for the applicant

'One of the purposes of the right to trial within a reasonable period of time is to protect individuals from "remaining too long in a state of uncertainty about their fate" '.[59] The general duty incumbent on the authorities is that of due diligence in ensuring that proceedings are conducted expeditiously in all cases irrespective of the subject matter. In SÜRMELI for instance, the Court noted that the action for damages in question did not call for special expedition, but a violation of Article 6 was still found in the light of the sixteen and a half year period, still pending at the time of the Court's decision, considered in that case. In HADJIKOSTOVA the Court considered a period of five years and one month at three instances in regard to property rights claims. While the periods of delay[60] it identified would have amounted to a violation if the stakes had been high for the applicant, this was an ordinary case which was somewhat complex and had been examined at multiple levels of jurisdiction.

Where certain issues are at stake for the applicant however, special diligence may be required. In these cases, the Court will readily find a violation on the basis of shorter delays and periods which would otherwise not be considered unreasonable. Cases which the Court has recognised to require special diligence on the part of the authorities include:[61]

- Personal circumstances such as the applicant's health,[62] age[63] or reputation[64] – The Court has, on occasion, referred to instances where what was at stake for the applicants required 'exceptional diligence' on the part of the authorities. In X V FRANCE the applicant was awarded € 22,900 by way of non-pecuniary damages in respect of civil proceedings lasting twenty four months where what was at stake was a disability allowance. The life expectancy of the applicant, as an infected haemophiliac, was of 16.7 to 28.5 months.
- 'Industrial disputes',[65] 'labour disputes',[66] 'employment disputes',[67] pension disputes[68] or cases involving the right to practice a profession[69] due to the impact these have on the applicant and on personal and family life including one's career[70] as well as involving the applicant's means of subsistence.[71]
- High financial stakes – cases where the applicant's economic existence was at stake[72]
- Commercial and professional matters[73] – DE CLERCK concerned a criminal investigation which was still pending and which had lasted sixteen years and ten months by the time the case was brought before the Court. In assessing the importance of the stakes of the case, the Court made note of the fact that in regard to moral persons the stakes may be high due to financial uncertainty and professional prejudice, both in regard to the individuals involved, as well as in regard to the enterprise itself. In this case this was further compounded by the fact that there were also questions regarding the advanced age of witnesses, and the consequent problem of safeguarding the rights of the defence.
- Property disputes, title to land[74]
- Criminal cases[75] – in particular where the accused is in custody[76]
- Actions of retrial[77]
- Actions for compensation in regard to violations of the Convention – including actions on the basis of Article 2 (such as actions for compensation for deaths caused by negligence[78]), Article 5,[79] Article 6 (such as length-of-proceedings cases themselves[80] and non-enforcement cases), Article 8 (such as cases involving the custody of children,[81] public care of children,[82] civil status[83] and legal capacity[84] and cases which may have an impact on the right to enjoyment of and the right to respect for family life and Article 13 (this category includes cases where the applicant was a victim of a criminal offence committed by the authorities[85]). In H. V THE U.K. the Court noted that the matter at stake, relating to an adoption, was both irreversible and decisive of the applicant's future relations with her child. Delay had resulted in serious prejudice to the applicant's case due to a *de facto* resolution of the dispute. Regarding disputes where children are affected, the Court in HOHOLM forcefully noted that:

> ... it reiterates the critical importance attached to the passage of time in proceedings of this type, which is often – and in this case appears

actually to have been - instrumental in the ultimate determination of the merits ... the present proceedings appear to have created a downward spiral, since the delay with which the evidence was examined resulted in the need for the re-taking of the same evidence which, in view of all the circumstances, bordered on a denial of justice.[86]

- Enforcement proceedings[87]
- A combination of several factors such as the case in KUDŁA, where the fact that the applicant was retained in custody pending the trial (which, being a deprivation of liberty, in itself required a special level of diligence) took its toll on the mental health of the applicant.

Having performed the exercise of assessing the reasonableness of the 'period to be considered' in the light of the 'particular circumstances of the case', with reference to the four heads of examination, the Court will only find a violation where, due to delays attributable to the respondent state,[88] the overall length of proceedings can be considered unreasonable[89] or there were unreasonable and unjustified periods of delay within the proceedings which may be held to cause a violation in themselves. Delays are attributable to the respondent state both where an organ of the state itself caused unreasonable delay (as in the case of the inefficiency of the prosecution), as well as where the state is responsible for an omission to uphold the rights of the applicant, pursuant to its positive obligations under the Convention, in the face of unreasonable delays caused by the counterparty, experts appointed, witnesses summoned or any other third party or factor which impacts the efficiency of the conduct of proceedings, and in respect of which the state could have taken remedial action. Certain delays, such as delays proportionate to the complexity or novelty of a case, may be permissible if the overall length of the proceedings remains reasonable. The Court's assessment of the reasonableness of the length of the 'period to be considered' and the extent to which it is attributable to the state, is therefore concretised in the light of the 'particular circumstances of the case', assessed by reference to the four heads of examination.[90]

Having determined whether there is or is not a violation of Article 6 in the instant case, the Court may be called, or may proceed of its own motion,[91] to examine the issue separately under Article 13. If the situation calls for a pilot judgment, or the finding of a practice incompatible with the Convention, the Court will enter its observations under Article 46. The pilot judgment has been developed by the European Court to attempt to tackle repetitive cases, and reduce its own caseload, by giving broad instructions to the relevant state as to how to remedy systemic defects.[92] Notwithstanding the issuance of a pilot judgment however, a state may fail to implement an effective remedy within the given time frame, and, thus, the Court may be obliged to rule that an application directly to it remains the only effective remedy to seek compensation in respect of a violation.[93]

In view of the fact that the Court may 'freeze' concurrent applications based on the same root cause as the case in respect of which the pilot judgment is being delivered, thereby adjourning such other cases for a specified period during which time is afforded to the relevant state to remedy the systemic defect,[94] a pilot judgment accompanied by an order to adjourn similar cases in the context of the length of proceedings may come *at a supremely high price* to the individual applicant. The applicant whose application is adjourned may thus have sustained delay and a breach of his rights at a national level, have exhausted national remedies without obtaining satisfaction, have had his application frozen before the Strasbourg Court, be forced to reattempt to resort to a national remedy after waiting for this to be introduced and, where effective relief is not delivered, be expected to re-apply to the Strasbourg Court, possibly being asked to wait once again pending the period during which the relevant state develops new practices on the basis of which the Court may judge the efficiency of the new remedial system.

Finally, under the heading of 'just satisfaction', the Court will assess the redress due in respect of the violation, and determine the costs of the case. In Chapter 2, Section 4, we shall be examining the criteria applied by the Court in the calculation of 'just satisfaction' under ECHR Article 41.

The more recent case law of the European Court of Human Rights seems to have shifted towards a less meticulous analysis of the circumstances of the case under the four headings of examination, but has consistently done so in favour of the applicant.[95] This lack of detail is clearly symptomatic of the sheer volume of cases which have been brought before the Strasbourg Court, which is in turn finding it unnecessary to examine each application in depth, in view of the general knowledge it has garnered. A typical examination of a length-of-proceedings case may therefore resolve itself, as in the cases of KINCSES, where what was at stake was a period of seven years at two instances of hearing, into a statement by the Court that it has 'frequently found violations of Article 6 § 1 of the Convention in cases raising issues similar to the one in the present application (see Frydlender, cited above)' and that 'Having examined all the material submitted to it, the Court considers that the Government have not put forward any fact or convincing argument capable of persuading it to reach a different conclusion in the present circumstances.' This attitude was criticized by Judge Power-Forde in BARIŠIĆ who opined that:

> Latterly, there has been a growing tendency to take a 'broad brush' approach to 'length of proceedings' claims – to look at the overall period of proceedings and, with very little analysis of what, in fact, transpired at national level, to conclude that a given period was 'unreasonable'. ... to find that a State has breached an international treaty is a serious matter. Every case stands alone and a prior and detailed examination of all the relevant events that occurred during the course of the litigation is an essential element in any judgment that censures a State for violating an individual's fundamental human right. The case law reiterates that the reasonableness of the length of proceedings must be assessed "in the light of the circumstances of the case".

2.1.2 Guidance on the length of proceedings for the enforcement of judgments[96]

Enforcement proceedings are to be considered another stage of proceedings, within the 'period to be considered' in length-of-proceedings cases, for the execution of a judgment given by a court must be regarded as an integral part of the 'trial' for the purposes of Article 6. Convention rights must be effective in practice and the rights guaranteed by the Convention:

> Would be illusory if a Contracting State's domestic legal system allowed a final, binding judicial decision to remain inoperative to the detriment of one party. Execution of a judgment given by any court must therefore be regarded as an integral part of the 'trial' for the purposes of Article 6.[97]

In Chapter 1.1.4 we observed how the Court has held that an applicant is not, under the rule relating to the exhaustion of domestic remedies, required to resort to enforcement proceedings. In LISEYTSEVA AND MASLOV the Court noted that in assessing the reasonableness of the delay in the execution of a judgment, it will have regard to the complexity of the enforcement proceedings, the conduct of the applicants and the authorities respectively, and what the nature of the award was.[98] One must also bear in mind that, being part of the 'period to be considered' in relation to the trial as a whole, the application of such criteria to the enforcement proceedings *per se* is an analysis subsidiary to that which is carried out in respect of the entire period in question; much depends on the way the application is framed. Therefore, when applying to the Court to find a violation of Article 6 on the basis of the length of the main proceedings, while an applicant need not have resorted to enforcement proceedings in order to satisfy the requirements of Article 35 (in relation to the exhaustion of domestic remedies), if resort had indeed been made to enforcement proceedings to obtain execution of a sentence, the length and effectiveness of the enforcement proceedings will be taken into consideration by the Court, either as part of the entire trial, or even independently if necessary. In LISEYTSEVA AND MASLOV, as held previously in YURIY NIKOLAYEVICH IVANOV,[99] the Court held that the failure to enforce a binding court decision amounts to a violation of ECHR Articles 6, 13 and Article 1 of Protocol No. 1.

In YURIY NIKOLAYEVICH IVANOV the Court recalled that a lack of funds is not considered a valid excuse for the non-enforcement of a valid judgment, and that as long as the obstacles to such enforcement are within the control of the authorities, the state remains liable. The Court accepted that certain reasonable procedural steps may be required for the execution of a judgment, such as the production of bank details, but that this should not go beyond what is 'strictly necessary' and 'does not relieve the authorities of their obligation under the Convention to take timely action of their own motion'.[100] It is clear therefore, that the burden to ensure enforcement of a final court judgment is incumbent upon the state.[101]

In GADZHIKHANOV AND SAUKOV the Court noted that the practical application of the principles regarding the enforcement of judgments has led the Court to hold the respondent state responsible for circumstances such as the erroneous transmission of the writ of execution by one authority to another, or the successive transmissions of the writ of execution to various state authorities after fruitless attempts to secure the respondent's voluntary compliance with the judgment.[102]

What does the Court consider to be unreasonable delay in the enforcement of decisions? A delay of one year and four months for some applicants, and two years and six months for the others in the enforcement of a monetary award against a body of the state has been found by the Court to be excessive in ZUBKO AND OTHERS.[103] In relation to the enforcement of judgments which themselves award compensation for unreasonable procedural delay, however, the Court has set down a six month time limit for enforcement.[104]

2.1.3 Guidance on the length of proceedings for constitutional remedies

The Court has today gone beyond holding that constitutional proceedings will only be considered as part of the period assessed by the Court if the result of those proceedings is capable of affecting the outcome of a dispute before the ordinary courts,[105] to holding that the reasonable time requirement applies equally to constitutional proceedings where these involve the determination of civil rights or obligations or of any criminal charge.[106]

Before the ordinary courts, since all cases which fall within the remit of Article 6 should be heard within a reasonable time, cases should generally be heard in a rotating fashion according to the date of filing of the application, saving matters of urgency, and in accordance with principles for the proper administration of justice. The Court has always stressed however, that different considerations may apply to the hearing of cases before courts of constitutional jurisdiction, where cases of greater social and political importance may require precedence.[107] In a partly dissenting opinion in SÜSSMANN, Judge Jambrek and Judge Pettiti commented that the disregard of chronological order for the hearing of cases must nevertheless respect the:

> Basic obligation of the Constitutional Court to hear also the case moved further down the list within a reasonable time-limit, set by the European Convention. ... all the cases on the list should be treated on equal terms when their nature and their importance in political and social terms is considered as a criterion of priority.[108]

Indeed in the case of OLUJIC the Court noted that notwithstanding the need for the Court to prioritise cases of social and political importance, a period of six years for the determination of a constitutional issue relating to dismissal of the applicant from the National Judicial Council on grounds of inappropriate behaviour could not be considered reasonable. In ORŠUŠ, a period of four years, one month and eighteen days was held to be unreasonable where the subject matter of the case before the constitutional court concerned the applicants' allegations of infringement of their right not to be discriminated against in the sphere of education, their right to education and their right not to be subjected to inhuman and degrading treatment.

Chapter 2 – Section 2 – Article 13: General Observations

2.2.1 Violations of Article 13 shed valuable light on the forms of redress which the Convention requires states to provide

In a length-of-proceedings context, a violation of Article 13 will result where the state has not provided an effective remedy for the violation emanating from Article 6; it therefore implies a structural deficiency rather than a failure to acknowledge a violation of rights in a particular case. Article 13 is also the basis for the continuing scrutiny which the Strasbourg Court exercises over remedies which have acquired sufficient certainty to be in need of exhaustion for the purposes of Article 35. Such a finding could take place where, for instance, a court consistently awards compensation, in length-of-proceedings cases, which is 'manifestly unreasonable'[109] in the light of the Court's case law, or where there is a widespread practice of delays in or outright non-enforcement of compensation awards. Article 13 has been used in this latter sense consistently,[110] and constitutes an essential tool in ensuring that a state not only provides effective structures to remedy violations, but ensures that these remedies continue to be effective.

The Court has set out the following general criteria to assess the effectiveness of a compensatory remedy (as well as of non-enforcement cases):

(i) an action for compensation must be heard within a reasonable time …;
(ii) the compensation must be paid promptly and generally no later than six months from the date on which the decision awarding compensation becomes enforceable …;
(iii) the procedural rules governing an action for compensation must conform to the principle of fairness guaranteed by Article 6 of the Convention …;
(iv) the rules regarding legal costs must not place an excessive burden on litigants where their action is justified …;
(v) the level of compensation must not be unreasonable in comparison with the awards made by the Court in similar cases. …[111]

All the considerations relevant to remedies in need of exhaustion for the purposes of Article 35 and which we examined in Chapter 1, Section 1, apply to the examination of whether there has been a violation of Article 13.[112] Article 13 requires that the effective remedy be exercised before a 'national authority'. The Court has held that this need not necessarily be a judicial authority, 'but if it is not, its powers and the guarantees which it affords are relevant in determining whether the remedy before it is effective.'[113] In NUVOLI[114] the Court held that the faculty of petitioning the president of the court, who was under no obligation to give reasons for his decision and had a wide measure of discretion, to anticipate the date of the hearing could not be considered an effective remedy within the meaning of Article 13.

SÜRMELI concerned three failed attempts, at a domestic level, to obtain a remedy for undue delay. The Court found a violation of Articles 6 and 13. Among the considerations enlisted by the Court when assessing the effectiveness of the array of domestic remedies proposed by the government, it noted that the possibility of an action for damages was not an effective remedy in terms of Article 13 as:

> Even if the relevant courts were to conclude that there had been a breach of judicial duties on account of delays rendering proceedings excessively long, they would not be able to make any award in respect of non-pecuniary damage, whereas, as the Court has previously observed, in cases concerning the length of civil proceedings the applicants above all sustain damage under that head.[115]

It follows, therefore, that if a compensatory remedy is to be considered effective, the Court must have the power to award non-pecuniary damages for delay incurred.[116]

Similarly, and in regard to the constitutional complaint, the Court found the remedy ineffective due to the lack of power of the domestic court to actually set any time frames for the lower court to act, and since such court was limited to declaring the length of proceedings unconstitutional and to requesting increased efficiency. It emerges clearly from this case that states should enable the judicial organs to *effectively remedy* the delays complained of by the parties, if these remedies are to really be considered to be effective. The Court in SÜRMELI also noted that for a remedy to be proved to be effective in practice, proof of a single judicial decision in this regard, moreover given at first instance, did not suffice.[117]

2.2.2 The interplay between Article 13 and the right of access to court under Article 6

The fact that a violation of Article 13 often means the inexistence of a structural avenue of redress implies that issues falling to be examined under Article 13 in regard to the length of proceedings are often intimately tied to the issue of access to court, as the violation would be founded on the fact that an applicant would have no right of action at a domestic level. One such case is F.L. V ITALY where the length of the proceedings in question affected the applicant, who was not a party to the case, but who was precluded from bringing his claim before the courts until the end of a set of liquidation proceedings, being effectively precluded from enforcing his credit which had been outstanding for sixteen years. A violation of Article 13 was found, without any separate examination conducted under Article 6.

Chapter 2 – Section 3 – Case Study Based on the Legal System of Italy: The Scordino-Type Cases[118]

2.3.1 Background and relevance

The Pinto Laws in Italy were introduced in order to provide a domestic mechanism to compensate victims of procedural delay in litigation. The Court had accepted that the remedy was effective in practice in terms of Article 13, and therefore in need of exhaustion for the purposes of Article 35.[119] In a subsequent set of Grand Chamber judgments, however, which we refer to in this study as the Scordino-Type Cases,[120] the Pinto remedies were subjected to scrutiny, failing to satisfy the test of effectiveness *in practice*; the findings hinged on the issues of the insufficient quantum of compensation, which ranged from 8–27 per cent of what the Court itself would have awarded pursuant to the facts at the basis of the domestic proceedings, coupled with excessive delays in the enforcement of such awards.[121]

In the Scordino-Type Cases, the applicants were held not to have lost their victim status as the redress afforded did not constitute adequate state acknowledgement of the breach. Indeed, having afforded the state an opportunity to redress the violation, the fact that an extra set of proceedings was incurred which did not suffice to cause the applicants to lose their victim status was considered by the Court to constitute an aggravating circumstance in regard to the breach of Article 6(1). The Court underlined the importance of ensuring adequate budgetary resources to back a remedy up, in order for it to be effective. Under Article 46 the Court invited the respondent state to bring the decisions of its courts into compliance with its case law, stressing the importance of the principle of subsidiarity.

In awarding compensation, the Court calculated the amount it would itself have awarded in the particular case, calculated what percentage of it had been awarded in the Pinto-law based proceedings, and awarded a compensatory median amount, namely:

> The difference between the amount obtained from the court of appeal and an amount that would not have been regarded as manifestly unreasonable compared with the amount awarded by the Court if it had been awarded by the court of appeal and paid speedily.[122]

It also awarded additional sums for the added frustration occasioned by delay in enforcement of the domestic awards.

The decision of the Court in this set of cases to award not the difference between what it would have awarded and what was actually awarded in domestic compensation proceedings, but a 'compensatory median amount', is worthy of some comment. If one were to add the amount of compensation awarded at a domestic level to the quantum of compensation awarded by the Court as a 'compensatory median amount', the aggregate sum constitutes 46 per cent[123] of what the Court would have awarded according to its calculations.[124] The author cannot but subscribe in full to the arguments adduced by Judge Bonello in a concurring opinion entered in ZARB and CENTRAL MEDITERRANEAN DEVELOPMENT CORPORATION LIMITED. As we have observed above, the Convention is geared towards encouraging states to make adequate provision for Convention violations at a domestic level, in line with the principle of subsidiarity and as guaranteed by the mechanisms of ECHR Articles 35 and 13. Through this manner of affording redress, however, not only will an applicant who has resorted to domestic proceedings – and is obliged by the Convention mechanism to do so – be penalised, but by failing to award the difference between what the Court would have awarded and the amount awarded at a domestic level, the Court is creating a system whereby a state may be incentivised to limit the compensation which can be awarded at a domestic level and never have to award the full amount, even if an application to the European Court of Human Rights is filed.

If the rationale behind the awarding of this median amount is to reward a state for having introduced a remedy at a domestic level, this is clearly being done to the detriment of the individual applicant whose rights were violated and who incurred the extra burden of the domestic proceedings only to be awarded, in the end, less than half of what would have been received, had there been no domestic remedy. From an individualist perspective, and the Convention is, after all, geared to protect above all the fundamental human rights of the individual, any argument attempting to support such a measure would be decidedly untenable.

2.3.2 *Guidance given by the Strasbourg Court in the Scordino-Type Cases*[125]

'The best solution in absolute terms is indisputably, as in many spheres, prevention.'[126] One can hardly overstress this point. Under Article 6 states have a 'duty to organise their judicial systems in such a way that their courts can meet each of its requirements, including the obligation to hear cases within a reasonable time.'[127] Under ECHR Article 46, the duty of a state is not only to implement the individual judgment, but to put an end to the domestic situation giving rise to the violation. Bearing the difficulty of the achievement of this ideal in mind, the Court has given specific guidelines to states as to what domestic solutions are compatible with the Convention, and which are preferable.

A remedy to expedite procedures

This is seen by the Court as constituting the most effective solution to prevent delay, but such a remedy cannot stand alone, as it will not suffice in cases which have already been determined, or where there has already been unreasonable delay *pendente lite*. For such a remedy to be effective, it must *actually be capable of hastening* the main proceedings.[128]

A compensatory remedy

We have examined how a compensatory remedy constitutes the only form of remedy accepted by the Court as effective in respect of delay and violations which have already been incurred, but how this will only be held to be an effective remedy insofar as it satisfies the criteria enlisted in Chapter 2.2.1. Would the introduction of a compensatory remedy alone suffice for the purposes of Article 13? The Court in SCORDINO noted that this was the remedy adopted by the Italian state, and went on to affirm that while a remedy to expedite procedures is not sufficient without being accompanied by a compensatory remedy, the latter can stand alone without being declared ineffective.[129]

It is the opinion of the author, nevertheless, that where there is no remedy to expedite proceedings, a violation of Article 13 should still be found where a party seeks to prevent or put an end to unreasonable delay *pendente lite*. Under Article 13, and in the light of KUDŁA, a party has a right to an effective remedy for the protection of his rights under the Convention, and if there is no remedy to prevent a violation which is likely to occur or is already occurring, the protection purportedly afforded would be rendered illusory.

Miscellaneous redress

In Section 1.1.4 we examined the varied forms through which a state may provide redress, and which the Court has considered effective remedies in need of exhaustion for the purposes of ECHR Article 35.

A desirable combination of remedies

The Court made reference in the Scordino-Type Cases to the practices adopted in some states which introduced a composite range of remedies which parties can avail themselves of at different stages of the proceedings.[130] It must be recalled however that at any one stage, the applicant should not be obliged to make recourse to more than one remedy to obtain redress.[131]

Chapter 2 – Section 4 – How does the European Court Calculate the Quantum of Compensation under Article 41?

2.4.1 Can a fixed formula for the calculation of compensation be arrived at, by studying case law?

'It is in fact an extremely difficult matter to identify with precision the prejudice suffered as a result of the undue length of the domestic proceedings.'[132] The Court has held that in regard to pecuniary compensation, domestic courts are in a much better position to rightly assess whether this is due, and to what extent,[133] but:

> The situation is, however, different with regard to non-pecuniary damage. There exists a strong but rebuttable presumption that excessively long proceedings will occasion non-pecuniary damage[134] ... The Court considers this presumption to be particularly strong in the event of excessive delay in enforcement by the State of a judgment delivered against it, given the inevitable frustration arising from the State's disregard for its obligation to honour its debt and the fact that the applicant has already gone through judicial proceedings and obtained success.[135]

This presumption should therefore constitute the starting point for the calculation of non-pecuniary damage. Indeed, when assessing the sufficiency of the amount of compensation awarded by a domestic court in the Grand Chamber ruling of SCORDINO, the Court held that where non-pecuniary compensation is not awarded notwithstanding that the 'period to be considered' is held to be unreasonable, a court should firmly buttress its decision by giving the reasons for its conclusions.[136]

The aim of awarding non-pecuniary compensation in this context is to make reparation for the frustration, anxiety and inconvenience suffered, and a court must take account of the prejudice sustained in its assessment of the quantum of compensation.[137] It stands to reason that assessments of non-pecuniary compensation in this field of rights cannot be directly tied to the production of evidence, and it has been noted that while '... some forms of non-pecuniary damage, including emotional distress, by their very nature cannot always be the object of concrete proof ... This does not prevent the Court from making an award if it considers that it is reasonable to assume that an applicant has suffered injury requiring financial compensation ...'[138]

The Court has developed a number of criteria which will influence the quantum of non-pecuniary compensation awarded, once a violation of Article 6 is found. These include:

i   The length of the period concerned
ii The number of instances
iii What was at stake for the applicant in the dispute, including effects on the person of the applicant, and including factors such as the:

- Age of the applicant[139]
- Personal income[140]
- Implications on the health of applicant including anxiety or depression[141]
- Level of frustration, distress, inconvenience, prolonged uncertainty and anxiety[142]: 'The more each applicant's personal interests are at stake in the proceedings, the greater the inconvenience and uncertainty to which they are subjected'.[143] One case which is particularly interesting in this regard is that of STEEL AND MORRIS, where the

non-pecuniary compensation awarded by the Court arose out of somewhat exceptional circumstances which linked the issue of the length of proceedings to the principle of equality of arms. Delay in this case had exacerbated the inequality existing between the resources of the parties, as the plaintiff was a multinational corporation and the defendants two private individuals of modest means. In respect of the violations of ECHR Articles 6 and 10 found, the Court awarded the applicants € 20,000 and € 15,000 in respect of proceedings lasting nine years and six months, due to 'the fact that the applicants had to carry out themselves the bulk of the legal work in these exceptionally long and difficult proceedings to defend their rights to freedom of expression. In these circumstances the applicants suffered anxiety and disruption to their lives far in excess of that experienced by a represented litigant ...'

- Missed opportunities,[144] loss of opportunity[145]
- Damage to reputation[146]
- High financial stakes: applicant's economic existence was at stake[147]
- Enjoyment of other rights, such as circumstances which have an impact on family life or the interests of minor children
- Where what was at stake was civil status or legal capacity
- Where the career of the applicant was at stake[148]

iv Conduct of the applicant: If delay is attributable to the applicant or his representatives, then the rate of compensation will be lower.[149]

v Level of participation in the proceedings: The Court will award less where the applicant participated in the main proceedings as an heir without showing much interest.

vi Aggravating factors: An example of this would be the failure of the state to cause a loss of victim status, where the finding of a violation at a domestic level is followed by a failure to provide adequate redress for that breach. Delay in the enforcement of a domestic judgment awarding compensation can also amount to an aggravating factor, and compensation will be paid for the consequent additional frustration. The Scordino-Type Cases reviewed in Chapter 2, Section 3, exemplify both these circumstances.

vii The number of applicants: The cases of ARVANITAKI-ROBOTI and KAKAMOUKAS involved a large number of applicants complaining of the length of proceedings wherein salary arrears of hospital employees were claimed. The Grand Chamber noted that in assessing the quantum it had to have regard to the manner in which the number of applicants influenced the levels of distress, inconvenience and uncertainty of individual applicants. Some elements militated towards increasing the sum, others towards a reduction. The fact that the objective of the applicants was shared would have alleviated the inconvenience and uncertainty experienced. Additionally, the costs of the case would be lower when only one representative is used, and the grouping together of like cases was advantageous to the expeditious resolution of the issue and the good administration of justice. On the other hand the grouping of cases confers an expectation for the authorities to deal expeditiously with the case, so that if delay is incurred, this would constitute an aggravating factor. In this case diametrically opposed opinions were entered by a number of judges. Judge Bratza and Judge Rozakis entered a concurring opinion in which they noted that the need for proportionality of the total award could justify a substantial reduction of the satisfaction awarded. At the other end of the scale Judges Zupančič and Zagrebelsky felt that the Convention requires the affording of just satisfaction to victims of a violation, and that the award should thus not be reduced simply because the applicant was one of a large number of claimants: the size of the award would simply reflect the number of individual violations incurred.

viii Amounts awarded in similar cases[150]
ix Standard of living in respondent state[151]
x Any redress afforded domestically[152]
xi The length of the enforcement proceedings[153]
xii The number of judgments that failed to be properly enforced or enforced within a reasonable time[154]
xiii Other relevant aspects[155]

While it is impossible to specify with precision what effect each of these considerations will have on the quantum, ultimately, the Court will take all these factors into consideration and assess the amount on an equitable basis.[156] A violation found in a case where, in the referenced proceedings, the stakes for the applicant were high, thereby imposing a duty upon the state to act with special diligence, will not necessarily result in a high award before the Strasbourg Court. In SILČ, for instance, the Court recognised that a case involving the right to practice one's profession should be treated with special diligence; when it came to assessing just satisfaction in respect of the breaches of Articles 6 and 13, however, it awarded a mere € 2,000 by way of non-pecuniary compensation, in respect of a period lasting seven years and eleven months. Little indication is given as to the reasons for such quantification, other than that the court ruled on an equitable basis.

In SCORDINO the Court expressed concern for consistency both in the assessment of what is reasonable, as well as in the awarding of just satisfaction under ECHR Article 41[157] in similar cases. It defined 'similar cases' as:

> Any two sets of proceedings that have lasted for the same number of years, for an identical number of levels of jurisdiction, with stakes of equivalent importance, much the same conduct on the part of the applicant and in respect of the same country.[158]

Harris, O'Boyle and Warbrick note that in regard to length-of-proceedings cases, the Strasbourg Court assesses non-pecuniary compensation by reference to the number of years the proceedings lasted against the number of instances, and that in its decision it is guided by a set of tables which have been prepared within the Court's registry in respect of a number of countries, as a tool to ensure consistency. They note that while such tables are not accessible to the public, it was recommended in the Woolf Report that they be publicised in order to act as a guide for national courts so as to improve consistency in decisions given in respect of such breaches.[159]

In the cases of ERNESTINA ZULLO, APICELLA, COCCHIARELLA, MOSTACCIUOLO (NO. 1 and NO. 2), RICCARDI PIZZATI and MUSCI the Chamber (First Section) attempted an articulation of a general method of calculation, setting down the following guidelines for the awarding of just satisfaction pursuant to ECHR Article 41:

i *Discretion*

'The Court enjoys a certain discretion in the exercise of that power, as the adjective 'just' and the phrase 'if necessary' attest.'[160]

ii *Criteria to be Considered*

- Pecuniary damage, which is there to compensate for the loss actually suffered as a direct result of the alleged violation,[161] and
- Non-pecuniary damage, which is there to compensate for the anxiety, inconvenience and uncertainty caused by the violation, and other non-pecuniary loss[162]

iii *Global Assessment*

If one or more heads of damage cannot be calculated precisely, or if the distinction between pecuniary and non-pecuniary damage proves difficult, the Court may decide to make a global assessment'.[163]

The Chamber then proceeded to enlist criteria specific to non-pecuniary damage. The guidelines were as follows:

i *Base Figure* – A sum varying between € 1,000 and 1,500 per year's duration of the proceedings (and not per year of unjustified delay) is a base figure for the relevant calculation.
ii *Outcome of the Proceedings is Immaterial* – The outcome of the domestic proceedings (whether the applicant loses, wins or ultimately reaches a friendly settlement) is immaterial to the non-pecuniary damage sustained on account of the length of the proceedings.
iii *Stakes at Issue* – The aggregate amount will be increased by € 2,000 if the stakes involved in the dispute are considerable.
iv *Reductions* – The basic award will be reduced in accordance with the:

- Number of instances
- Conduct of the applicant (particularly the number of months or years elapsed due to unjustified adjournments for which the applicant is responsible)

- What is at stake in the dispute (such as where the financial stakes are of little consequence to the applicant)
- Standard of living in respondent state
- Level of interest: A reduction may also be envisaged where the applicant has been only briefly involved in the proceedings, having continued them in his or her capacity as heir.
- Domestic redress: The amount may also be reduced where the applicant has already obtained a finding of a violation in domestic proceedings and compensation in regard thereto.

The Grand Chamber did not sanction the method adopted by the Chamber;[164] nevertheless, its assessment of what it would itself have awarded in the various cases differs significantly from the amounts awarded by the Chamber, and little indication is given of the precise reasons for the discrepancy.

If no claim for just satisfaction is made, the Court will ordinarily refrain from awarding compensation.[165] There are exceptions, however, where notwithstanding the fact that the applicant did not enter any express demand for compensation, the Court deemed it just to award a sum for the violation incurred.[166]

2.4.2 What other forms of just sastisfaction have been deemed acceptable by the European Court, aside from financial compensation?

On a number of occasions, the Court has been petitioned to provide other forms of just satisfaction to applicants, but the Court seems to accede less readily to providing such forms of remedies purely in response to a breach of the reasonable time requirement. In DE CLERCK, in the light of a criminal investigation still ongoing at the time of judgment and which had lasted for over sixteen years and ten months, the Court awarded non-pecuniary compensation, but denied the applicant's request for an order to stop criminal proceedings. It held that length-of-proceedings cases do not fall within the category wherein the Court has deemed it fit to indicate individual measures, as the Court cannot interfere in the workings of an independent judiciary and that, in these cases, once a violation is found, the state enjoys a margin of discretion as to how to execute the Court's conclusions. In YAKIŞAN, where the Court found a breach both of ECHR Article 6(1) and of Article 5(3) in relation to pending criminal proceedings which dated back thirteen years to their inception, the Court awarded € 12,000 by way of non-pecuniary damage and issued an order for the violation to cease either by bringing the trial to an early end or by the release of the applicant. In GEORGIOS PAPAGEORGIOU, in the light of a duplicate breach of Article 6 in regard both to the fairness of proceedings as well as their length, the Court awarded non-pecuniary compensation, but held that it did not have the power to accede to the applicant's request to order the quashing of his conviction and the erasure of his criminal record.

2.4.3 Pecuniary compensation

The Court does not usually find that a causal link sufficient to justify the awarding of pecuniary compensation exists when a breach of Article 6 in respect of the length of proceedings is found.[167] The Court has routinely refused to provide compensation for the possibility that, had the proceedings not been prolonged unreasonably, their upshot may have been different, on the basis that it cannot speculate as to any different result proceedings would have had if conducted within a reasonable time, as any such question would pertain to an examination of the fairness of the trial as a whole.[168]

Notes

1. See Chapter 2, Section 1, *The Strasbourg Court's Method of Examination*.
2. Luzius Wildhaber, 'Annual Report 2002 of the European Court of Human Rights, Council of Europe' <http://www.echr.coe.int> accessed April 2015, p. 7.
3. KUDŁA, BUJ, STYRANOWSKI.
4. ECKLE, DEWEER, WEMHOFF, NEUMEISTER, RINGEISEN, MERIT, FOTI AND OTHERS, CALLEJA, REINHARDT AND SLIMANE-KAÏD.
5. See FRYDLENDER at [27]: 'The Court reiterates that for Article 6 § 1, in its "civil" limb, to be applicable there must be a dispute (contestation) over a "right" that can be said, at least on arguable grounds, to be recognised under domestic law. The dispute must be genuine and serious. It may relate not only to the actual existence of a right but also to its scope and the manner of its exercise. Moreover, the outcome of the proceedings must be directly decisive for the civil right in question.'
6. KANGASLUOMA, BERTIN-MOUROT, MARTINS AND GARCIA ALVES, ETCH-EVESTE AND BIDART, COËME AND OTHERS. In the context of criminal proceedings see KRAVTAS [34]: 'one must begin by ascertaining from which moment the person was "charged"; this may have occurred on a date prior to the case coming before the trial court ... such as the date of arrest, the date when the person concerned was officially notified that he would be prosecuted, or the date when the preliminary investigation was opened ... Whilst "charge", for the purposes of Article 6 § 1, may in general be defined as "the official notification given to an individual by the competent authority of an allegation that he has committed a criminal offence," it may in some instances take the form of other measures which carry the implication of such an allegation and which likewise substantially affect the situation of the suspect ...'.
7. STOIANOVA AND NEDELCU, ŠLEŽEVIČIUS, KUDŁA.
8. BEZZINA WETTINGER AND OTHERS, SCORDINO, M.Ö. V TURKEY, COCCHIARELLA.
9. GELLI, SMIRNOVA, VAYIC, VENTURA, BORISENKO.
10. SILČ, VILHO ESKELINEN AND OTHERS, KIURKCHIAN, MESSOCHORITIS.
11. GRÄSSER, REZETTE, CALLEJA, COMINGERSOLL S.A.
12. Harris, O'Boyle and Warbrick, *Law of the European Convention on Human Rights* (Butterworths, 1995), p. 228.
13. Stephanos Stavros, *The Guarantees for Accused Persons under Article 6 of the European Convention on Human Rights: An Analysis of the Application of the Convention and a Comparison with other Instruments*, (Martinus Nijhoff Publishers, The Netherlands 1993) p.106.

14 See also the dissenting opinion was entered by Judge Pejchal in PODBELŠEK BRAČIČ: 'I am of the opinion that the term "reasonable time" is not the same as "a time without delay". However, I have observed that the case-law of the Court has recently been more inclined to define the meaning of "reasonable time" in terms of "a short time".' In his argument, he also links this issue to the minimum level of severity introduced by Protocol 14 into Article 35(3); see, in this regard, the *Chapter Introduction* to Chapter 1.

15 See Chapter 2, Section 1, *The Strasbourg Court's Method of Examination*, Sub-Section 1, *The framework for an examination of the merits of an alleged violation of Article 6*, under the heading, *iv What was at stake for the applicant*. Regarding enforcement proceedings, see also Chapter 1, Section 2, *Article 34 Loss of Victim Status – Incompatibility* Ratione Personae, Sub-Section 2, *State failure to cause loss of victim status notwithstanding the affording of domestic redress* and Chapter 2, Section 1, *The Strasbourg Court's Method of Examination*, Sub-Section 2, *Guidance on the length of proceedings for the enforcement of judgments*.

16 FRYDLENDER, COMINGERSOLL, ZIMMERMANN AND STEINER, BUCHHOLZ, PEDERSEN AND BAADSGAARD, KRASUSKI, HUMEN, PÉLISSIER AND SASSI, COËME AND OTHERS, CAZENAVE DE LA ROCHE, I.J.L. AND OTHERS V THE UNITED KINGDOM, PHILIS, PORTINGTON, CALLEJA, KEMMACHE, KÖNIG, ESPOSITO, MARPA ZEELAND B.V. AND METAL WELDING B.V., KUDŁA, YAGTZILAR AND OTHERS, RICHARD, DOUSTALY.

17 Harris, O'Boyle and Warbrick, *Law of the European Convention on Human Rights* (2nd edition, Oxford University Press, Oxford 2009) refer to NEUMEISTER at p. 279.

18 Pieter van Dijk, Fried van Hoof, Arjen van Rijn, Leo Zwaak (eds), *Theory and Practice of the European Convention on Human Rights* (4th edition Intersentia, Oxford 2006) refer to LORENZI, BERNARDINI AND GRITTI and KATE KLITSCHE DE LA GRANGE at p. 607.

19 Ibid. The authors refer to TRIGGIANI, WIESINGER, VORRASI, DOBBERTIN and C.P. V FRANCE at p. 607.

20 Pieter van Dijk, Fried van Hoof, Arjen van Rijn, Leo Zwaak (eds) (see n 18 (Chapter 2)) refer to ANGELUCCI at p. 607.

21 SMIRNOVA.

22 Richard Clayton, Hugh Tomlinson, *Fair Trial Rights* (reprinted from *The Law of Human Rights*, Oxford University Press, Oxford 2001) at p. 105 as well as Pieter van Dijk, Fried van Hoof, Arjen van Rijn, Leo Zwaak (eds) (see n 18 (Chapter 2)) refer to MANIERI at p. 607.

23 Harris, O'Boyle and Warbrick, *Law of the European Convention on Human Rights* (2nd edition, Oxford University Press, Oxford 2009) refer to WEMHOFF at p. 279.

24 Ibid. See KRASUSKI. See JEHOVAH'S WITNESSES OF MOSCOW AND OTHERS at [198]: '... the responsibility for a delay caused by expert examinations ultimately rests with the State.'

25 Ibid. See also ECKLE.

26 Ibid. Harris, O'Boyle and Warbrick refer to ANDREUCCI.

27 In regard to the fact that the state will not be held responsible for the delays of another state in supplying evidence, Richard Clayton, Hugh Tomlinson, *Fair Trial Rights* (reprinted from *The Law of Human Rights*, Oxford University Press, Oxford 2001) refer to WEMHOFF at p. 105; Harris, O'Boyle and Warbrick, *Law of the European Convention on Human Rights* (2nd edition, Oxford University Press, Oxford 2009) refer to NEUMEISTER (p. 279). See n 29 below (Chapter 2).

28 Pieter van Dijk, Fried van Hoof, Arjen van Rijn, Leo Zwaak (eds), *Theory and Practice of the European Convention on Human Rights* (4th edition Intersentia, Oxford 2006) refer to

MANZONI (1991) in relation to the need to obtain the file of a trial conducted abroad (p. 607).
29 Delays caused by foreign jurisdictions will not be imputed to the respondent state. This position opens up a lacuna in the protection afforded by Article 6. Stavros is well aware of this problem and discusses possible solutions in *The Guarantees for Accused Persons under Article 6 of the European Convention on Human Rights: An Analysis of the Application of the Convention and a Comparison with Other Instruments* (Martinus Nijhoff Publishers, The Netherlands, 1993).
30 WŁOCH.
31 Pieter van Dijk, Fried van Hoof, Arjen van Rijn, Leo Zwaak (eds), *Theory and Practice of the European Convention on Human Rights* (4th edition Intersentia, Oxford 2006) refer to DIANA at p. 607.
32 Ibid. the authors give the example of RÖSSLHUBER in regard to the creation of a special computer program.
33 UNIÓN ALIMENTARIA SANDERS S.A., ECKLE, KÖNIG, BUCHHOLZ.
34 KALASHNIKOV, DOBBERTIN, CALLEJA, LEDONNE (NO. 1).
35 [35].
36 CALLEJA, LEDONNE (NO. 1), ENCULESCU [78], JGK STATYBA LTD AND GUSELNIKOVAS [78].
37 I.A. V FRANCE.
38 KRASUSKI.
39 CALLEJA [132], LEDONNE (N°1) [25], Also see I.A. V FRANCE, ECKLE.
40 [41] Also MALICKA-WĄSOWSKA.
41 Approximately fourteen years.
42 PEDERSEN AND BAADSGAARD, CAPUANO. See also STAROKADOMSKIY [87]: the Court seemed to indicate that there may be grounds for arguing that delay caused by a legal aid lawyer may be treated differently from that caused by a privately retained lawyer.
43 PISHCHALNIKOV [52].
44 ZIMMERMANN AND STEINER, KÖNIG, BUCHHOLZ.
45 NEUMEISTER, WŁOCH. See n 27 and n 29 (Chapter 2).
46 See Stavros at n 29 (Chapter 2).
47 Pieter van Dijk, Fried van Hoof, Arjen van Rijn, Leo Zwaak (eds), *Theory and Practice of the European Convention on Human Rights* (4th edition Intersentia, Oxford 2006) at p. 608, cited in SAID ET V ATTORNEY GENERAL (App no. 10/2007/1).
48 YAGTZILAR [33] Also VARIPATI.
49 DORAN [47], Also see PHILIS.
50 MUSIAŁ [46].
51 See NEUMEISTER, COËME AND OTHERS, SÜSSMANN, IDALOV.
52 Harris, O'Boyle and Warbrick, *Law of the European Convention on Human Rights* (2nd edition, Oxford University Press, Oxford 2009) make reference to HENTRICH and REZETTE in this vein.
53 HOWARTH (violation found with reference to a two-year period of inactivity at appellate stage).
54 GAST AND POPP, BOCA, PROBSTMEIER.
55 DEBONO, DEUMELAND, GUINCHO, KĘPA, ZIMMERMANN AND STEINER.
56 ZIMMERMANN AND STEINER [29].
57 Pieter van Dijk, Fried van Hoof, Arjen van Rijn, Leo Zwaak (eds), *Theory and Practice of the European Convention on Human Rights* (4th edition Intersentia, Oxford 2006) at p. 608 refer to G. V ITALY. See also BURDOV (NO. 2) and DEBONO.

48 *Guidance Drawn from Judgments of the European Court*

58 See GAGLIANO GIORGI and COCCHIARELLA [99] where the Court noted that the four-month time window prescribed by law for the Pinto-law based proceedings aimed to compensate for delay in judicial proceedings was reasonable, but that, nevertheless, so was the length of a case which breached the same domestic time frame and took nine months at a single instance, and also another which took fourteen months at two instances. On the other hand, a period of two years and eight months at a single instance and up to enforcement of the award, in Pinto law-based proceedings, was held to violate the reasonable time requirement. See text to n 46 (Chapter 1).
59 STOIANOVA AND NEDELCU [24], STÖGMÜLLER [5].
60 One year and seven months and one year and eleven months.
61 Inclusive list. Some categories may overlap.
62 Pieter van Dijk, Fried van Hoof, Arjen van Rijn, Leo Zwaak (eds), *Theory and Practice of the European Convention on Human Rights* (4th edition Intersentia, Oxford 2006) at p. 609 refer *inter alia* to X V FRANCE 1992 and DEWICKA. Harris, O'Boyle and Warbrick, *Law of the European Convention on Human Rights* (2nd edition, Oxford University Press, Oxford 2009) at p. 281 refer to BOCK, GHEORGHE and X V FRANCE 1992.
63 HARTMAN.
64 Harris, O'Boyle and Warbrick, *Law of the European Convention on Human Rights* (2nd edition, Oxford University Press, Oxford 2009) refer to PIENIĄŻEK at p. 281.
65 SIMALDONE.
66 FRYDLENDER.
67 Pieter van Dijk, Fried van Hoof, Arjen van Rijn, Leo Zwaak (eds), *Theory and Practice of the European Convention on Human Rights* (4th edition Intersentia, Oxford 2006) refer to OBERMEIER and VOCATURO at p. 609. Harris, O'Boyle and Warbrick, *Law of the European Convention on Human Rights* (2nd edition, Oxford University Press, Oxford 2009) refer to BUCHHOLZ and EASTAWAY at p. 281. Cf. SARTORY. See also MILIĆ [66].
68 Pieter van Dijk, Fried van Hoof, Arjen van Rijn, Leo Zwaak (eds), *Theory and Practice of the European Convention on Human Rights* (4th edition Intersentia, Oxford 2006) refer to NIBBIO, BORGESE, RUOTOLO and H.T. V GERMANY.
69 SILČ, RUOTOLO, DAVIES.
70 OBERMEIER, BUCHHOLZ, JULIEN.
71 SVETLANA ORLOVA.
72 GRÄSSER.
73 A.P. V ITALY.
74 Harris, O'Boyle and Warbrick, *Law of the European Convention on Human Rights* (2nd edition, Oxford University Press, Oxford 2009) refer to POISS and HENTRICH at p. 281.
75 Ibid. the authors refer to BAGGETTA at p. 281.
76 GORODNITCHEV, PISHCHALNIKOV, IVAN PANCHENKO, KALASHNIKOV, GÖÇMEN, ABDOELLA, SMIRNOVA, SARI, TODOROV.
77 Harris, O'Boyle and Warbrick, *Law of the European Convention on Human Rights* (2nd edition, Oxford University Press, Oxford 2009) refer to HENWORTH at p. 281.
78 Pieter van Dijk, Fried van Hoof, Arjen van Rijn, Leo Zwaak (eds), *Theory and Practice of the European Convention on Human Rights* (4th edition Intersentia, Oxford 2006) refer to MARTINS MOREIRA, SILVA PONTES and SIGNE at p. 609. Cf. SILIH. Harris, O'Boyle and Warbrick, *Law of the European Convention on Human Rights* (2nd edition, Oxford University Press, Oxford 2009) refer to SILVA PONTES at p. 281.

79 One should prescind 'reasonableness' for the purposes of Article 5(3) from the concept of 'reasonable time' found under Article 6; see BAK (violation of Article 6 but not Article 5(3) in relation to criminal proceedings which lasted seven years).
80 SARTORY.
81 Harris, O'Boyle and Warbrick, *Law of the European Convention on Human Rights* (2nd edition, Oxford University Press, Oxford 2009) refer to HOKKANEN and H. V THE U.K. at p. 281. See also NIEDERBÖSTER. Also see BOCA (the Court differentiated between the urgency of the different kinds of proceedings at stake on the basis of the interests of the children involved) and NUUTINEN. See also VEISS at [80]: 'what was ... at stake for the applicant ... required particular diligence and urgency in organising the proceedings in such a manner as to minimise the time the applicant's family situation remained in limbo'. See also TSIKAKIS [66].
82 COVEZZI AND MORSELLI.
83 Harris, O'Boyle and Warbrick, *Law of the European Convention on Human Rights* (2nd edition, Oxford University Press, Oxford 2009) refer to SYLVESTER at p. 281. See also BOCA, MIKULIĆ, BOCK, SIMALDONE and V.K. V CROATIA.
84 Pieter van Dijk, Fried van Hoof, Arjen van Rijn, Leo Zwaak (eds), *Theory and Practice of the European Convention on Human Rights* (4th edition Intersentia, Oxford 2006) refer *inter alia* to BOCK and GANA at p. 609. Also see MIKULIĆ, MATTER, MACIARIELLO and TAIUTI.
85 CALOC, DOUSTALY, DACHAR.
86 HOHOLM at [51] and [52]. See also H. V THE U.K. (adoption proceedings), BOCA, LAINO.
87 VUKELIĆ [97].
88 YAGTZILAR AND OTHERS, RICHARD, DOUSTALY, PEDERSEN AND BAADSGAARD, HUMEN.
89 COËME AND OTHERS, LAINO.
90 NUUTINEN, PRETTO AND OTHERS.
91 BURDOV.
92 See BRONIOWSKI, BURDOV (NO. 2), OLARU AND OTHERS, RUMPF, VASSILIOS ATHANASIOU. See also Rule 61 of the Rules of Court (which was inserted by the Court on the 21st February 2011 and came into force on 1st April 2011). See *Statutes*.
93 See BURDOV (NO. 2) and YURIY NIKOLAYEVICH IVANOV.
94 See for instance: MANUSHAQE PUTO AND OTHERS [8].
95 See, among many others, BENKŐ AND SOOSNE BENKŐ, YAVUZ ET YAYLALI, BARIŠIČ, DANIJEL PEČNIK, YURYEVA AND YURYEV, NISKASAARI AND OTHERS, VASILCHENKO.
96 See Chapter 1, Section 2, *Article 34 Loss of Victim Status – Incompatibility* Ratione Personae, Sub-Section 2, *State failure to cause loss of victim status notwithstanding the affording of domestic redress*.
97 SCORDINO [196].
98 See also BURDOV (NO. 2) [66]. See RAYLYAN.
99 Also SIMALDONE, BURDOV.
100 BURDOV (NO. 2) [69].
101 SCORDINO, BURDOV, DEWICKA, COMINGERSOLL S.A, OROŽIM [27], ŞEVKET KÜRÜM ET AUTRES, LISEYTSEVA AND MASLOV [220], LYUBOV STETSENKO [80], PELIPENKO [49]. See also the concurring opinion of Judge Lemmens in ŞEVKET KÜRÜM ET AUTRES, RIĐIĆ. See also RIĐIĆ [77]: '... the respondent State is responsible for the debts of companies predominantly comprised of

socially/State owned capital, which is why neither the lack of its own funds nor the indigence of the debtor can be cited as a valid excuse for any excessive delays in this particular enforcement context …' However, note VUKELIĆ [96]: '… a failure to enforce a judgment because of the debtor's indigence cannot be held against the State unless and to the extent that it is imputable to the domestic authorities, for example, to their errors or delay in proceeding with the enforcement …' (See also BOUCKE [87]). Also, in PELIPENKO the Court noted at [49] that '… when final judgments are issued against "private" defendants, the State's positive obligation consists of providing a legal arsenal allowing individuals to obtain, from their evading debtors, payment of sums awarded by those judgments … It is obvious that the State's positive obligation is not that of result, but one of means. Authorities have to take reasonably accessible steps to assist the recovery of any judgment debt. Consequently, when it is established that the measures taken by the authorities were adequate and sufficient, the State cannot be held responsible for a failure by a "private" defendant to pay the judgment debt …'.

102 [23].
103 Cited in YURIY NIKOLAYEVICH IVANOV.
104 SCORDINO, BURDOV (NO. 2), WASSERMAN (NO. 2).
105 DEUMELAND, BOCK, RUIZ-MATEOS.
106 SÜSSMANN, KRASKA. See also RINGEISEN and LE COMPTE, VAN LEUVEN AND DE MEYERE.
107 SÜSSMANN.
108 SÜSSMANN: Partly dissenting opinion of Judge Jambrek, joined by Judge Pettiti [8].
109 See SCORDINO and Chapter 1, Section 2, *Article 34 Loss of Victim Status – Incompatibility Ratione Personae.*
110 Cases where Article 13 was used to subject theoretically 'effective' remedies to scrutiny of their practical effectiveness include BELINGER, ANDRÁŠIK AND OTHERS, SLAVIČEK, FERNÁNDEZ-MOLINA GONZÁLEZ AND OTHERS, DORAN, HARTMAN, PAULINO TOMÁS, KORMACHEVA, CHARZYŃSKI and LUKENDA.
111 See WASSERMAN NO. 2 [49] and [51], BURDOV NO. 2 [99], GLYKANTZI [78], VASSILIOS ATHANASIOU ET AUTRES [55]. In FINGER at [131]: 'The Court would further emphasise that, to be truly effective and compliant with the principle of subsidiarity, a compensatory remedy needs to operate retrospectively and provide redress in respect of delays which predate its introduction, both in proceedings which are still pending and in proceedings which have been concluded but in which the litigants have already applied to the Court or may do so.'
112 PAULINO TOMÁS, ZARB, CENTRAL MEDITERRANEAN DEVELOPMENT CORPORATION LIMITED, BURDOV, DE CLERCK, KUDŁA, WASSERMAN, MIFSUD, SCORDINO, SURMELI, ŽUNIČ, SILVER AND OTHERS, CHAHAL, BURDOV (NO. 2), WASSERMAN (NO. 2) V RUSSIA (NO. 2), VILHO ESKELINEN.
113 SILVER AND OTHERS [113], CHAHAL.
114 Pre-Pinto legislation: See Scordino-Type Cases in Chapter 2, Section 3, *Case Study Based on the Legal System of Italy: The Scordino-Type Cases.*
115 [113].
116 Text to footnote n 34 (Chapter 1).
117 REZETTE, MARIËN, GAMA DA COSTA.
118 SCORDINO, COCCHIARELLA, MUSCI, RICCARDI PIZZATI, MOSTACCIUOLO (NO. 1), MOSTACCIUOLO (NO. 2), APICELLA, ERNESTINA ZULLO, GIUSEPPINA AND ORESTINA PROCACCINI, DELLE CAVE AND CORRADO, ESPOSITO, ZARB, CENTRAL MEDITERRANEAN DEVELOPMENT, SIMALDONE.

119 See SCORDINO, BRUSCO, DI SANTE.
120 The Court's reasoning in SCORDINO was applied by the Court to all the other cases following a similar pattern.
121 'Annual Report 2004 of the European Court of Human Rights, Council of Europe' <http://www.echr.coe.int> accessed April 2015.
122 SCORDINO [269].
123 In ERNESTINA ZULLO, this went up to 51 per cent, and in GIUSEPPINA AND ORESTINA PROCACCINI 59 per cent.
124 See ZARB.
125 This hierarchy has been consistently reiterated by the Court in 'Scordino-Type Cases'. The considerations in this Section are made with reference to Strasbourg Jurisprudence generally, and not only in relation to the Scordino-Type Cases.
126 SCORDINO [183].
127 SÜSSMANN, BOTTAZZI.
128 FEHR AND LAUTERBURG, GONZALEZ MARIN, TOMÉ MOTA, HOLZINGER (NO. 1).
129 See also MIFSUD, KUPPINGER, MICHELIOUDAKIS and MÜLLER-HARTBURG.
130 The Court referred to the eclectic solution adopted in Austria, Croatia, Spain, Poland and Slovakia, namely the provision of a combination of remedies to both expedite proceedings and compensate for delays.
131 See Chapter 1, Section 1, *Article 35(1) Exhaustion of (Effective) Domestic Remedies*, Sub-Section 4, *What forms of remedies has the Court considered to be effective and in need of exhaustion for the purposes of Article 35?*
132 KÖNIG [19].
133 BURDOV (NO. 2), YURIY NIKOLAYEVICH IVANOV. See also Chapter 5, *Case Study Based on the Legal System of Malta, Part III: Conclusions* under the heading *The Third Problem – A Theoretical Overlap Yet Practical Inexistence of Effective Remedies Where Delay is Imputable to the State, Causing Both Damages in Tort and a Breach of Rights*.
134 SCORDINO [203–204]. See also ZARB, CENTRAL MEDITERRANEAN DEVELOPMENT CORPORATION LIMITED, MARTINS CASTRO ET ALVES CORREIA DE CASTRO.
135 In BURDOV (NO. 2) the Court noted that a domestic avenue for redress whereby the awarding of non-pecuniary compensation in non-enforcement cases is conditional upon establishment of the respondent authority's fault would not be compatible with the presumption required of domestic authorities, as the prejudice is engendered irrespective of fault and may be due to structural causes, such as inadequate budgetary mechanisms, which the state is answerable for.
136 SCORDINO [204].
137 ARVANITAKI-ROBOTI AND OTHERS, KAKAMOUKAS AND OTHERS, COMINGERSOLL S.A.
138 DAVIES, ABDULAZIZ, CABALES AND BALKANDALI.
139 KÖNIG, BURDOV.
140 BURDOV.
141 BURDOV.
142 KÖNIG, ARVANITAKI-ROBOTI, KAKAMOUKAS, COMINGERSOLL S.A., DAVIES.
143 ARVANITAKI-ROBOTI AND OTHERS, KAKAMOUKAS AND OTHERS.
144 KÖNIG.
145 See Harris, O'Boyle and Warbrick, *Law of the European Convention on Human Rights* (2nd edition, Oxford University Press, Oxford 2009) at p. 860.

146 KÖNIG.
147 GRÄSSER.
148 KÖNIG.
149 See also text to n 42 (Chapter 2).
150 ARVANITAKI-ROBOTI, KAKAMOUKAS AND OTHERS.
151 Ibid.
152 BURDOV.
153 Ibid.
154 Ibid.
155 Ibid.
156 ARVANITAKI-ROBOTI AND OTHERS, KAKAMOUKAS, KÖNIG.
157 [177].
158 [267].
159 Harris O'Boyle and Warbrick, *Law of the European Convention on Human Rights* (2nd edition, Oxford University Press, Oxford 2009) at p. 860 refer to The Woolf Report (The Review of the Working Methods of the European Court of Human Rights, December 2005) p. 41 <http://www.echr.coe.int>.
160 With reference to the discretionary powers of the Court in respect of Convention breaches, as conferred by the wording of ECHR Article 41.
161 COMINGERSOLL [29].
162 COMINGERSOLL [29].
163 COMINGERSOLL [29].
164 COCHIARELLA [68].
165 MATTER, AMAT-G LTD AND MEBAGHISHVILI.
166 Two such cases were DEWICKA (the Court awarded € 3,800 as non-pecuniary compensation in respect of an action in tort that had lasted for five years and nine months, where the applicant was a woman, advanced in age and suffering health issues, who was refused the right to enter into a contract for the installation of telephony services) and JACQUIE AND LEDUN (the applicants were the widow and daughter of a man who had been infected with Hepatitis C as a result of blood transfusions; by the time the case was brought before the Court, the claims for compensation had been pending for seven years).
167 However see text to n 19 to 27 (Chapter 5). Also see Pieter van Dijk, Fried van Hoof, Arjen van Rijn, Leo Zwaak (eds), *Theory and Practice of the European Convention on Human Rights* (4th edition Intersentia, Oxford 2006) p. 261.
168 GRÄSSER, LOUERAT, GEORGIOS PAPAGEORGIOU.

3 Case Study Based on the Legal System of Malta, Part I

Human Rights Remedies for Delay

Chapter Introduction

In the remaining chapters we shall seek to apply the principles and concepts we have observed to actual judgments and actual legal remedies, so as to observe how these principles can be used in practice. When analysing any individual legal system or set of facts against the standards set by the Convention, one must bear in mind that while national courts and legislators have a margin of discretion in the implementation of their obligations under the European Convention, the principles we have observed in the initial chapters are universally applicable *irrespective* of differences between national or legal systems. Familiarity with the concepts and guidance of the Strasbourg Court is therefore useful for the analysis of any given set of individual circumstances, or any given national remedy. At the very least, an understanding of such principles is key to determining whether divergences in the method of determining human rights cases regarding the length of proceedings falls within the margin of appreciation which a state enjoys in the implementation of Convention obligations, or whether the stance taken by the courts on certain legal issues is simply out of line with the minimum standards set by the Strasbourg Court. By understanding this background, one is sufficiently informed to be able to determine various relevant issues, including whether there are grounds for an application to be filed to the Strasbourg Court, whether, in the event of a challenge to a national judgment, the applicant would be found to have lost his victim status or even whether, on the merits, a violation of Article 6 or, possibly, Article 13 of the Convention would be found.

The Republic of Malta became a signatory to the European Convention on Human Rights on the 12th December 1966, and ratified the Convention and its First Protocol on the 23rd January 1967. The right of individual petition was first recognised with effect as of the 1st May 1987 until the 30th April 1992, and, finally, *via* Act XIV of the 19th August 1987, the European Convention Act, Chapter 319 of the Laws of Malta was enacted, incorporating the European Convention into the ordinary law of Malta, including the right of individual petition. As of the 19th August 1987, therefore, the fundamental rights set out in the European Convention became enforceable before the national courts of Malta, and all persons hold the right of individual petition to Strasbourg, if the state fails to offer effective domestic remedies for breaches of the Convention.

Within the time period of our study of the legal system of Malta, which spans from August 1987 to May 2010, five length-of-proceedings cases were brought before the European Court of Human Rights[1] to challenge domestic decisions, all of which successful on the merits, constituting thus 23.81 per cent of all Convention violations found against the Maltese state within that time period.[2] The Strasbourg Court has held that the domestic remedies for procedural delay provided for in the Maltese legal system, namely the possibility of an application to the First Hall Civil Court (Constitutional Jurisdiction) at first instance, with an unlimited right of appeal to the Constitutional Court, whether *via* application or by way of a constitutional reference *pendente lite*, constitute an effective remedy for the purposes of Article 13, and therefore require exhaustion for the purposes of Article 35 of the Convention.[3] At the basis of this ruling lay the fact that the local courts are not restricted in the awarding of compensation for findings of violations in length-of-proceedings cases, so that they are, in terms of their legal empowerments, capable of awarding sufficient compensation for such a breach. The fact that, in ZARB, insufficient compensation had been awarded, did not render the domestic remedies ineffective for the purposes of Article 13; the Court ruled that there had been no violation of that article.

Where the applicant has resorted to these remedies, therefore, any plea regarding the non-exhaustion of domestic remedies will be rejected,[4] as happened in BEZZINA WETTINGER AND OTHERS, where the preliminary plea of the non-exhaustion of domestic remedies was rejected as, albeit with a negative outcome, the applicants had in substance raised the issue before the courts of constitutional jurisdiction complaining about delay in the proceedings, even though these had effectively overlooked the complaint.

Under the law of Malta, the right to the determination of judicial proceedings within a reasonable time derives from the twin bases of Article 6 of Chapter 319[5] and article 39[6] of the Constitution. It is manifest that the more recent judgments of the courts of constitutional jurisdiction in Malta are taking increasing cognizance both of the framework for the analysis of and the criteria employed by the Strasbourg Court in its assessment of length-of-proceedings cases.[7] There remain, however, stark divergences between the manner in which local sentences are assessed and motivated, and the jurisprudence emanating from Strasbourg. Three points of divergence stand out in particular, namely:

i   The weight given to the four different heads of examination utilised by the Strasbourg Court to assess the 'particular circumstances of the case', with particular reference to the conduct of the applicant,
ii The general pattern of approach taken by the courts in the examination of a length-of-proceedings application, and
iii The method utilised for determining the quantum of compensation and, hence, the redress awarded ultimately in respect of a breach.

These and other divergences emerging from a study of the length-of-proceedings jurisprudence in the Maltese legal system are examined hereunder.

Chapter 3 – Section 1 – Analysis of Violations Found by the European Court against Malta Resulting From Divergences in the Interpretation and Application of the Convention

While it is clear that domestic authorities have a margin of discretion as to the manner in which to implement Convention obligations,[8] the domestic approach must be capable of recognising that a breach has occurred and to adequately acknowledge the breach through the provision of adequate remedial measures. If the domestic procedures for redress fall short on either score, a Convention violation would still be found by the Strasbourg Court if an application is filed after domestic proceedings are exhausted, and any plea regarding the non-exhaustion of domestic remedies or loss of victim status of the applicant would be rejected.

In CALLEJA[9] the courts in Malta, at both instances, failed to recognise that a breach of Article 6 had occurred at all. A reading of the motivations which led the domestic courts[10] and, subsequently, the Strasbourg Court to diametrically opposed conclusions brings out a sharp difference in approach. The subject matter of the case were criminal proceedings which had lasted seven years, eight months and seventeen days during which the applicant was held in preventive custody for a period of over four years and ten months,[11] until conviction of some of the charges. In analysing the delays which accounted for the length of proceedings, the local courts placed the accused, the prosecution and the court on the same footing as to their duty to expedite proceedings, thus requiring both applicant and respondent to discharge the same burden of proof of diligence. The Strasbourg Court on the other hand has constantly reiterated that the accused has no obligation to expedite proceedings,[12] and that as long as obstructionist tactics are not used which account for the delays complained of, it is a court's duty to ensure that the right to a fair hearing within a reasonable time is ensured, for all parties. Above all, once the period to be taken into consideration is *prima facie* unreasonably long, a presumption in favour of the applicant arises which the state must rebut, and in this case failed to do so.[13]

In DEBONO, once again, the domestic authorities ultimately failed to recognise that a breach had occurred in regard to the length of appeal proceedings where the relevant period was slightly in excess of two years and nine months. In domestic proceedings, in DEBONO ET V PRINCIPAL REGISTRAR OF THE COURTS OF JUSTICE ET[14] the First Hall had awarded € 1,200 in respect of a breach of Article 6, citing a gross violation of the six-month time frame in the Code of Organisation and Civil Procedure, which resulted from the court's overload, as the reason for delay which was imputable to the authorities. The Constitutional Court quashed this judgment, finding no violation on the merits, and restricted its examination to what it considered to be the kernel of the issue, namely that the mere disregard of a domestic time frame did not *ut sic* render the delay unreasonable. However, by so narrowing its assessment, the Constitutional Court failed to further assess whether the period of delay complained of violated the reasonable time requirement in the light of the four different heads of examination utilised by the Strasbourg Court to assess the 'particular circumstances of the case'. Upon application to the Strasbourg Court, a breach of Article 6 was found and € 1,000 awarded by way of non-pecuniary compensation; as we have seen in Section 1 of Chapter 2, backlog could not be considered a valid justification for unreasonable delay in the determination of a case.

We shall be examining in further detail the manner in which the courts in Malta have dealt with the issue of the applicant's conduct. In BEZZINA WETTINGER AND OTHERS the Strasbourg Court awarded € 6,000 by way of non-pecuniary compensation in respect of expropriation proceedings which had lasted fourteen years and eight months at one level of jurisdiction, notwithstanding the fact that the applicants were found responsible for causing some four years' worth of delays. This underlines the fact that any delay occasioned by the applicants will simply be one of the multiple considerations the Court will weigh, both against each other and independently, when assessing the reasonableness of the length of proceedings. Otherwise stated, the diligence, or lack thereof, of the applicants does not exonerate a court from ensuring that proceedings are conducted expeditiously, and a breach will still be found if, aside from the delay occasioned directly by the applicants, there are further unreasonable delays which cannot be so imputed.[15]

Chapter 3 – Section 2 – Overview of the Length-of-Proceedings Case Law of Malta and the Interpretation and Application of Convention Provisions by the Local Courts

3.2.1 Cases where the national courts adopted an approach proximate to that of the Strasbourg Court as observed in Chapter 2

As opposed to the approach taken to the assessment of Strasbourg Jurisprudence, it is not possible to derive a general approach for the examination of the length-of-proceedings cases delivered in Malta. Notwithstanding the tendency for each judgment to follow a distinct and individual pattern, however, one can identify those cases which take an approach proximate to that which we observed in Chapter 2, Section 1, and those which adopt an approach so divergent as to lead the author to the conclusion that the European Court of Human Rights would have reached a different conclusion on the same facts, had an application been filed before that court. A selection of cases from the former category will be analysed in this section, while in subsequent sub-sections the more divergent cases will be studied and the points of divergence underlined.

In the latter category the main points of divergence can, by and large, all be traced back to the three points enlisted in the *Chapter Introduction*.

In XUEREB V REGISTRAR OF COURTS ET[16] the First Hall, and Constitutional Court after it, found a violation in regard to the length of proceedings requesting the issue of a warrant *in factum* which had lasted seventeen years and three months. The case is particularly interesting as both courts conducted an examination proximate to that used by the Strasbourg Court, but drew different conclusions from the facts of the case under the different heads of examination, in particular from the conduct of the applicant. While the First Hall felt that the applicant had demonstrated a clear interest in expediting the proceedings by ensuring that the case was always reappointed for hearing after having been adjourned *sine die*, the Constitutional Court preferred to subtract an entire period of six years from the period to be considered which it felt were entirely attributable to the fault of the applicant. The applicant had alleged that a particular judge, before whom the case had remained pending for nine years, clearly manifested his wish not to decide the case himself. The First Hall gave little probative value to this assertion, as nothing resulted from the *procès verbal* and underlined that, saving proof to the contrary, of which there was none, a judge is to be presumed to have discharged his professional duties with due diligence.

The courts in Malta have taken different stances on the manner in which to draw conclusions from the *procès verbal*. In BARTOLO V ATTORNEY GENERAL,[17] for instance, and in the face of shortcomings in the record of the proceedings rendering the reasons underlying the multiple adjournments nebulous, the court ruled that the applicant, *qua* accused in the main proceedings, should benefit from the resultant doubt[18] since the delay had been objectively unreasonable.

XUEREB V ATTORNEY GENERAL[19] was a complaint in respect of proceedings for the compilation of evidence before the Court of Magistrates as a Court of Criminal Inquiry, which had lasted eight years and was still ongoing at the time of the ruling. The First Hall found a violation of ECHR Article 6 and article 39 of the Constitution and awarded € 699[20] in relation thereto. The court took note of the higher degree of diligence which criminal cases generally require. Delay had been occasioned by a number of futile *renvoi* procedures, a considerably slowed rate in the presentation of evidence after the initial two years, the failure of witnesses to show up on a large number of occasions and a number of adjournments due to the magistrate being unable to attend. Only six witnesses had been heard over a period of two years. In regard to the complexity of the case, the court took note of the fact that there were multiple co-accused, of the seriousness of the accusations which in this case included wilful homicide and aggravated theft, among others, and of the volume of evidence to be presented. As proceedings were still at the compilation of evidence stage, the unreasonableness of their length in this case was evident. The court noted that backlog, according to Strasbourg Jurisprudence, is no excuse for unreasonable delay in the determination of cases. The attorney general in this case had argued that the constitutional proceedings in question were further delaying the process. The court, drawing on applicable Convention principles, noted that the applicant had on several occasions drawn the attention of the magistrate to the length of the proceedings and eventually resorted to constitutional proceedings; by doing so, he had simply availed himself of rights conferred upon him by law, for which he could not be held to be at fault.

The Court Practice and Procedure and Good Order Rules, Part III Section 12 of the laws of Malta clearly requires the court to keep a tight rein on experts appointed. This is in line with the stance taken by the Strasbourg Court where responsibility for ensuring the timely delivery of reports lies with the court. The courts in Malta have consistently found in favour of applicants where delay was imputable to the experts appointed, except, as in DEBONO V ATTORNEY GENERAL,[21] where the parties positively interfered with the expert's mandate and were thus at fault for the ensuing delay.

SAID ET V ATTORNEY GENERAL[22] dealt with civil proceedings for alleged damage caused to a Granspinat chain by a jeweller. Delay in the main proceedings was largely due to repeated failure of the experts to file the requested reports. The case had lasted thirty three years, thirty of which at first instance, involved glaring periods of delay such as a five-year period during which the court waited for a magistrate to present a report. Eventually the Granspinat chain itself was stolen from the court's safe, and the Registrar of Courts was called into the case to answer for the damage. The report was never presented. Upon appeal, the Constitutional Court reiterated the criteria relevant to the assessment of the reasonableness of the period to be taken into consideration, and ran through the procedural stages of the case and the *procès verbal*, noting that the case was of no particular complexity and that eventually the court had pronounced sentence without the expert report. While the case had taken unreasonably long at first instance, the three years it spent before the Court of Appeal could not be considered unreasonable as this was not a case which, of its nature, demanded any particular priority. The Constitutional Court felt that the kernel of the appeal was not whether there had been unreasonable delay, as this was manifest, but rather whether the applicant had contributed to that delay. It disagreed with the First Hall that the applicant had significantly contributed to the delay, for a failure to appear for eight sittings over a period of thirty years had to be considered insignificant. Neither was it unreasonable, over such a long period of time, for the applicant to have changed his lawyer once. The Constitutional Court underlined the fact that responsibility for ensuring timely delivery of justice lies with the court, and that where experts are appointed, these are to deliver their opinions 'under the court's supervision', and that the court remained responsible for any delays ensuing in the preparation of such reports, drawing on Van Dijk and Van Hoof in this vein.[23] The Constitutional Court also underlined the fact that it rejected the respondent's argument that it was up to the plaintiff to spur the case forward and to ensure that the expert reports were completed:

> Our Code of Organisation and Civil Procedure doesn't enshrine the principle that the parties to a suit have an obligation to take the initiative to spur their case onwards, as may be the case in other jurisdictions. The parties have the obligation to respect the legal time frames laid down by the court, however, the conduct of the proceedings remains in the hands of the court [itself].[24]

Although this view is correct, one must add that *even where the initiative does lie with the parties,* the European Court of Human Rights has held that this does not detract from a court's obligation to ensure that proceedings are conducted with due diligence.[25]

The same stance, in regard to delays in the presentation of expert reports, was taken by the court in ELLUL SULLIVAN ET V COMMISIONER OF POLICE AND ATTORNEY GENERAL[26] where the argument that a lack of resources and available experts could justify the fact that an expert report had not been presented for four and a half years was flatly rejected. The duty to ensure that the forensic expert diligently executed the tasks entrusted to him within a reasonable time was incumbent upon the Court of Magistrates which should have *sua sponte* taken the initiative to substitute an expert who was causing delay, once the prosecution had remained passive in this regard.

ZARB V ATTORNEY GENERAL[27] and SPITERI V ATTORNEY GENERAL[28] were two cases, decided on the same day, which throw interesting light on the common difficulty of delay caused due to the presence of several co-accused in the proceedings. It was precisely this factor, and the manner in which the courts approached the issue, which accounted for the overturning of the judgment upon appeal. At first instance the court ran through the heads of examination established by the Strasbourg Court and underlined that criminal proceedings as a rule require a more expeditious approach than civil ones. It then went on to examine the *iter* of the proceedings, noting that there were eight co-accused and various accusations which rendered the case relatively complex. Proceedings had, in the view of that court, been conducted at a regular and quick pace, and the length of the proceedings was due to the large volume of evidence presented, the occasions on which some of the accused failed to appear and the interruptions to deal with various breaches of bail conditions. Upon appeal, various applications had been filed which delayed delivery of the final sentence. The only delay strictly attributable to the court was a period of nine months during which the judge was unable to hear the case. Therefore, although the proceedings had lasted for eleven years, the court ruled that the authorities had not fallen short of the requisite level of diligence. The argument that much of the evidence and witnesses heard, and which accounted for the length of the proceedings, was not relevant to the applicant's case was rejected, as the offences were related and the proper administration of justice required the cases to be heard together in order to avoid repetition in the presentation of evidence.

The applicant appealed from this sentence and the Constitutional Court arrived at a different conclusion on the merits. The court noted that it was clear that the only stage at which there was material delay was before the appellate court. The applicant's appeal was limited to a contestation of the punishment inflicted. None of the appeals filed were of any particular difficulty, and yet it took the Court of Criminal Appeal six and a half years to deliver judgment. It was accepted that on various occasions, having adjourned the case for delivery of sentence, applications were filed by the co-accused for release from custody or for new evidence to be heard, but of these requests, Zarb had filed the fewest applications, and most had been filed by Spiteri. The Constitutional Court held that:

> This Court is of the belief that the Court of Criminal Appeal, confronted by several appellants, had the obligation to prevent these applications, clearly intended to delay the proceedings, from achieving the scope of prolonging them, and this for the self-evident reason that the person who wishes to delay the procedures does so at the expense of other persons, namely the co-accused (or in this case the [co-] appellants).[29]

It concluded that while in regard to Spiteri there had been no breach of ECHR Article 6 or article 39 of the Constitution, as his conduct had been one of the causes of delay, the same could not be said in regard to Zarb, in regard to whom a violation was found. It therefore quashed the judgment of the First Hall in regard to Zarb, awarding € 233[30] by way of moral compensation.

The Court also differentiated between co-defendants in ELLUL SULLIVAN ET V COMMISSIONER OF POLICE AND ATTORNEY GENERAL,[31] wherein the Constitutional Court upheld the finding of the First Hall that there had been a violation of the applicants' rights, but disagreed that they had in any way contributed to the delay. The court differentiated between the complainants, noting that some of them had showed continued interest in the criminal proceedings. This was subsequently reflected in the assessment of the compensation respectively awarded.

3.2.2 The relevance of 'the conduct of the applicant'

In FRENDO RANDON V COMMISSIONER OF LANDS ET[32] the court drew extensively on the principles emerging from Convention jurisprudence in regard to the weight to be given to the conduct of the different players in judicial proceedings. The respondents unsuccessfully argued that while the applicants had no obligation to cooperate in proving title to the land in question, they could not then complain of a violation on the basis of excessive delay. The Constitutional Court held that it was incumbent on the Commissioner of Lands to prove that he did all he could for the proceedings to be concluded expeditiously. It was not a valid excuse to plead that the plaintiffs did not proffer the information required. Nevertheless, the failure of the applicants to make use of the ordinary remedies available to them over such a long period of time could be taken into account when assessing the quantum of redress due.[33]

It transpires with ample clarity from the examination conducted, that the conduct of the applicants is a factor which a court assessing an alleged breach of the reasonable time requirement should consider both as one of the heads of examination, as well as in its determination of the quantum of due compensation. This is, however, merely one of a plethora of other considerations which such court should utilize in its assessment. We have seen that in examining an alleged breach of Article 6 the Strasbourg Court first establishes the 'period to be considered' and then assesses whether this period, which is *prima facie* reasonable or unreasonable, can be considered unreasonable in the 'particular circumstances of the case', by reference to four heads of examination. The 'conduct of the applicant' is one of these heads, but even where there are periods of delay attributable to the applicant, a violation will still be found if other periods of unreasonable delay can be imputed to the authorities, for the duty to ensure that proceedings are conducted within a reasonable time is incumbent upon the state, and not the individual. The courts of constitutional jurisdiction in Malta have not always taken this approach.

The subject matter of the main proceedings at stake in the case of AZZOPARDI V ATTORNEY GENERAL ET[34] were proceedings for libel which had lasted ten years, six of which at first instance during which three witnesses were heard. During the main libel proceedings, the action had succeeded at first instance, but was then revoked upon appeal. The court referred to the fact that the applicant himself admitted to being the cause of certain delays, and ruled that the evidence given to this end was sufficient for it to conclude that the delay complained of could be attributed to the fault of the applicant. In its assessment, the First Hall took the same line as the attorney general, affirming that the applicant had to prove that he tried all possible procedural remedies to speed up proceedings, and did all he could to help the court to administer justice. The court motivated its conclusion by stating that the reasonableness of the length of proceedings in question was dependent on the particular circumstances of the case, and was not simply to be determined by reference to the length of proceedings themselves.

On a number of occasions the Maltese courts have chosen to analyse whether delay in the proceedings is unreasonable either by general reference to the particular circumstances of the case as a whole[35] or else by focusing on one particular aspect of relevance to the circumstances, such as the conduct of the applicant. This approach is therefore different to that taken by the Strasbourg Court where the 'particular circumstances of the case' are assessed by reference to *all four* heads of examination, and are a method of analysing whether a period which is *prima facie* unreasonable can be justified, or whether a period which is *prima facie* reasonable can be nevertheless held to be unreasonable due to the higher degree of diligence required by the particular circumstances of the case. Therefore, while the 'circumstances of the case' should indeed be taken into consideration by a court in its assessment of what is reasonable, Strasbourg Jurisprudence provides a structured method for assessing such circumstances. In a case where the 'period to be considered' is *prima facie* unreasonable, a violation will be found if the delay cannot be somehow justified by reference to all four heads of examination: a narrow focus on any one of these will render an unsatisfactory picture of the proceedings.

Clearly therefore, the starting point of the court in AZZOPARDI V ATTORNEY GENERAL ET should have been the *prima facie* conclusion that the length of the proceedings was unreasonable, which would then have been analysed in the light of the different heads of examination. The court did not start from the position that it is incumbent upon the court to ensure that the parties' right to have their case determined within a reasonable time is upheld, neither did it look into the entirety of the 'period to be considered' and take all the four heads of examination used by the Strasbourg Court into account before deciding whether the test of reasonableness had been met in the particular case. Finally, it did not assess whether there were other unreasonable delays, not attributable to the applicant, which could amount to a violation. By assessing the case in this manner the court inverted the burden of proof completely, as instantiated by the following extract:

> In a case such as the one at hand, the applicant must also prove that he was diligent when he made use of his procedural rights in accordance with the law, and that he did not make use of delay tactics in the same proceedings. Moreoever, he must also prove that he did all he could to ensure that the proceedings were expedited.[36]

Taking a stance diametrically opposed to that which we observed in Chapter 2, Section 1, in regard to chronic backlog, which has never in itself been held by the Strasbourg Court to constitute a proper justification for setting the rights of the individual applicant aside, the First Hall went on to note that '... in our system the court must hear and decide a high number of cases concurrently and, therefore, some cases may have to wait longer than others to be decided.'[37]

The court sought to further support its decision by reference to the outcome of the libel proceedings. It took up the same line of reasoning as the attorney general, one which cannot be traced back to Strasbourg Jurisprudence, namely that due to the failure of the claim in the main proceedings, the applicant, *qua* plaintiff, did not suffer prejudice or a breach of his rights, and therefore could not demand compensation for having unsuccessfully brought a claim, even if that claim had been afflicted by unreasonable delay. It went on to note that while it was true that the right to have one's case determined within a reasonable time applies irrespective of the outcome of proceedings:

> It must also be taken into consideration, however, that in view of the outcome of the proceedings in question, the applicant did not sustain any

prejudice, and his position would have been the same even if the case had been determined earlier.[38]

This unfortunate reasoning was also espoused by the First Hall in BLASCHEM (MALTA) LIMITED V ATTORNEY GENERAL ET.[39] Were the courts unaware of the repeated pronouncements of the Strasbourg Court that unreasonable delay engenders a presumption of prejudice which is not in need of further proof? Were they unaware that *all* parties to proceedings, irrespective of whether their claim or defence is founded, have a right to have their case determined within a reasonable time?

Commenting *obiter*, the same court espoused another argument entered by the respondents, opining that the awarding of compensation in length-of-proceedings cases is the exception, and not the rule,[40] and reserved to cases where delay is manifest and prejudicial, resulting in an injustice to the applicant. Ultimately, the First Hall ruled that in view of the above considerations, there had been no violation of ECHR Article 6 or of article 39 of the Constitution in libel proceedings that had lasted for ten years.

In DEBONO V ATTORNEY GENERAL[41] no violation was found in respect of a period of ten years, of which eight years and two months at first instance. The First Hall concluded that the length of proceedings was not unreasonable due to the complexity of the case, evident from the expert reports required, as well as due to the fact that the parties had, so as to say, 'hijacked' the proceedings by giving the expert appointed the faculty to hear all the evidence of the proceedings, thus extending the limited task entrusted to him by the court. The parties had themselves determined the pace at which proceedings were conducted, allowing the opposing party to adduce fresh evidence without attempting to speed up the proceedings. They were thus considered to have been at fault for the delay.

In AZZOPARDI V REGISTRAR OF COURTS ET[42] the court refused to find a breach where the applicant's conduct was the very basis of the urgency in question, rendering the entire application frivolous and vexatious. An application for a hearing before the Constitutional Court with urgency had been denied. The request had been made on the basis that the subject matter of the judicial demand in the main proceedings, namely for regulations applicable to a race to be impugned, would be rendered void if the race took place before the demand was heard. The request was denied, as although the race was to take place soon after the application was lodged, the delay in lodging the challenge was entirely the fault of the applicant, as the regulations had entered into force well before the race. The First Hall, in a ruling upheld by the Constitutional Court, declared the applicant's case frivolous and vexatious. The 'urgency' in this case had been 'self-inflicted'. The court held that this conclusion was founded also by reference to Strasbourg Jurisprudence which considers the applicant's own conduct as one of the heads of examination which are to be considered in the assessment of whether the 'period to be considered' was reasonable.

A tendency in the jurisprudence of Malta to give significantly more weight to the issue of the complainant's fault than that which is attributed in the Strasbourg Court's jurisprudence emerges clearly from a reading of length-of-proceedings case law. The Strasbourg Court will readily find a violation of Article 6 if, other than any delay caused by the applicant, there were other periods of unreasonable delay for which the state can be held to account. The domestic position is, possibly, a reflection of a civilian approach where judges are used to adopting a certain manner of assessment in cases for civil damages and where, in a tort-based context, the court requires each party to prove that they exhibited the diligence required of them by law in order to establish fault. Of course the problem with this approach is that this examination is being conducted in a constitutional, human rights context where it is the state which, first and foremost, has the obligation to uphold the fundamental human rights of the individual. Even if a fault-based approach were to be taken, this obligation incumbent upon the state must, at the very least, be recognised and reflected in the court's assessment.

A strong taste of irony therefore emerges from a reading of GASAN ENTERPRISES LIMITED V MALTA ENVIRONMENT AND PLANNING AUTHORITY[43] where the applicant was ultimately considered to have contributed to the delay by submitting several different proposals for consideration to the relevant authority. The First Hall had awarded € 466[44] by way of moral damages, and an unsuccessful appeal was entered, contesting the quantum of compensation. The Constitutional Court held, in regard to the claim that the delay caused 'very severe commercial damages', that a human rights action should not be converted into one for civil damages:[45]

> As the current application is phrased, it is clearly requesting a remedy for a breach of Article 6 of the Convention – and a constitutional case seeking a declaration that a breach of a fundamental human right has occurred should not be converted into a case seeking Aquilian-type damages.

The court held that a violation of Article 6 gives rise, as a rule, to moral damages by way of adequate redress for the violation. It noted that the sums awarded in such cases:

> Would reflect the unjustified delay, and this independently of the nature of the case or the value of the property in question, and without prejudice to the material or real damages which that delay could effectively have caused.[46]

As a reading of Strasbourg Jurisprudence attests, however, these elements are indeed criteria which the Court takes into consideration when assessing the quantum of non-pecuniary damage, as the higher the financial stakes for the applicant, the higher the prejudice caused by delay.[47] This blur between the tools which should be employed by a court in a civil law context and the considerations which should apply in a human rights context is evident in several of the cases we shall be examining in further detail.

3.2.3 Compulsory administrative procedures: part of the 'period to be considered'?

In FRENDO RANDON V COMMISSIONER OF LANDS ET[48] the Constitutional Court did not establish and consider the period from start to end as a whole, but, rather, split the proceedings up into two parts: the period which took place prior to the procedures before the board[49] and the proceedings before the board itself, which were ongoing and in respect of which the complaint was that proceedings were not being heard with the diligence required. In regard to the first period, a violation of Article 6 (but not of article 39 of the Constitution[50]) was found. The 'period to be considered' was held to run from the point in time when the 'contestation' arose, namely, when the Commissioner of Lands was notified by official letter of the refusal of the compensation offered. The court distinguished the right of access to a court from the right to the determination of proceedings within a reasonable time, being two distinct rights both emerging from Article 6 of the Convention.[51] This stance is in line with Strasbourg Jurisprudence where the 'period to be considered' when recourse to the courts is predicated on some form of exhaustion of administrative procedures begins to run before the filing of the judicial demand, and will incorporate the period of time during which the case lay before the administrative authorities.[52]

In regard to the proceedings before the board, *viz.* the second period, the First Hall had held that a length-of-proceedings complaint could not be brought where proceedings are still ongoing.[53] It consequently denied the applicant's claims in regard to the length of proceedings, deciding the issue instead on the basis of a denial of access to a court over an extended period of time. The Constitutional Court overruled the First Hall's position, bringing the case back into line with Strasbourg – and domestic – legal principles. Firstly, it is clear that one may, under the law of Malta, file a human rights complaint even in regard to a violation which is likely to occur.[54] Secondly, Strasbourg Jurisprudence is unequivocal in regard to the fact that there is no need for a case to be decided, in order for a claim on the basis of the unreasonable length of the procedures to be brought. The Constitutional Court distinguished a length-of-proceedings case from a claim where what is at stake is the fairness of the trial as a whole, wherein the proceedings must be looked at in their entirety. On the facts, however, it noted that it was up to the applicants to produce a copy of the record of proceedings before the Land Arbitration Board in order to satisfy the best evidence rule. It therefore denied the claim in relation to the second period, awarding €20,000 in respect of the violation in proceedings preceding the contestation before the Land Arbitration Board.

In this context one must take note of CURMI V COMMISSIONER OF LANDS,[55] delivered by the Constitutional Court one month before FRENDO

RANDON V COMMISSIONER OF LANDS ET. The Constitutional Court held, also in the context of expropriation procedures, that notwithstanding the inactivity of the applicant, there was no justification for the Commissioner of Lands allowing twenty years to elapse without paying the compensation due to the applicants, or even making an offer. The court distinguished between article 39 of the Constitution and Article 6, holding that the delay amounted to a violation of Article 6 due to the deprivation of the right of access to an independent and impartial tribunal, but *not* to a violation of article 39(2) for this only envisages procedures which are pending before a court.[56]

Therefore, while ultimately arriving at the same conclusion, namely a violation of Convention Article 6 but not article 39 of the Constitution of Malta, the reasoning underpinning these two decisions is different. In FRENDO RANDON V COMMISSIONER OF LANDS ET, Article 6 was held to be applicable as the contestation could be held to arise before the filing of the application since the applicant was impeded from doing so before other administrative procedures were exhausted. In CURMI V COMMISSIONER OF LANDS, on the other hand, the Constitutional Court framed the violation in terms of a deprivation of access to court on the basis of Article 6, rather than on the length of or delay in the determination of the civil rights in question.[57]

A number of years earlier, a position similar to that taken by the court in FRENDO RANDON V COMMISSIONER OF LANDS ET formed the basis of another length of expropriation proceedings case, ALLIED NEWSPAPERS LIMITED V ATTORNEY GENERAL ET,[58] where the Commissioner of Lands had not sent a notice to treat to the applicants for a period exceeding ten years. This notice was a legal pre-requisite for the commencement of any challenge *via* judicial proceedings. The Constitutional Court relied on LE COMPTE, VAN LEUVEN AND DE MEYERE holding that Article 6 can be relied on not only by those persons whose dispute is pending before a court but:

> It may also be relied on by anyone who considers that an interference with the exercise of one of his (civil) rights is unlawful and complains that he has not had the possibility of submitting that claim to a tribunal meeting the requirements of Article 6(1).[59]

The court found a violation on the basis of the right to a fair hearing within a reasonable time, rather than a deprivation of access, and ruled that a violation of the reasonable time requirement could be found in terms of Article 6 but not of article 39 of the Constitution, as the latter envisaged procedures which had already been brought before a court or other adjudicating authority.

3.2.4 *The adequacy of redress being provided by the national courts*

Are the courts in Malta fully aware that adequate redress must amount to 'sufficient state acknowledgement of the breach incurred', if a party is to lose his victim status under the Convention? To what extent are they aware that in order for such acknowledgement to cause a loss of victim status, where redress is in the form of non-pecuniary compensation, the quantum of compensation cannot be 'manifestly unreasonable' in the light of the Strasbourg Court's case law? Are judgments being delivered with an awareness of the fact that if 'manifestly unreasonable' compensation is awarded in respect of a Convention breach, upon application to the Strasbourg Court, not only will the victim status of the applicant be upheld, but a further – aggravated – violation of Article 6 found on the merits?

The courts in Malta have adduced a myriad of arguments to justify the awarding of 'symbolic' sums by way of moral compensation, or at times no compensation at all, in respect of breaches found in length-of-proceedings cases,[60] including the domestic tradition of awarding damages,[61] the failure to incorporate ECHR Article 41 into Chapter 319[62] as well as the considerations analysed above in regard to the fact that delay, in and of itself, does not cause damage where the action or defence of the applicant fails in the main proceedings.[63] While, as we have seen, states have a margin of discretion in the implementation of Convention obligations, the Strasbourg Court has on countless occasions reiterated that, ultimately, once a violation of Article 6 has been found, the quantum of non-pecuniary compensation must not be manifestly unreasonable in the light of its case law. Both of the cases in which the Strasbourg Court was called to re-examine the compensation awarded locally resulted in the Court declaring that the applicants had *not* lost their victim status, as the sums awarded domestically were manifestly unreasonable.[64] In the ZARB case, the Strasbourg Court noted that the amount awarded locally amounted to a mere 1.7 per cent of what it awards in similar cases.

In BARTOLO V ATTORNEY GENERAL[65] a declaration that a breach of Article 6 had occurred was considered by both the First Hall and the Constitutional Court to constitute appropriate redress in respect of criminal proceedings which had resulted in an acquittal after over fourteen years and eight months[66] had elapsed from the date on which the accused had been charged. The applicant had spent 662 days out of this period in custody, as a result of the conviction at first instance, and no temporary release had been granted. This conclusion was reached at first instance, and upheld upon appeal, notwithstanding that the applicant was not held responsible for the delay, that the hearing of the case started nine years after the bill of indictment was issued and that over a period of two years at appellate stage, not a single witness had been heard.

In his constitutional application Bartolo had argued that the damage due could be calculated by inverting the rule for the serving of an imprisonment term where a fine remains unpaid, which is calculated at the rate of € 11.65[67] daily. The court rejected the applicant's claim for pecuniary compensation, as it held that this was in respect of the detention he alleged was illegal, noting that he had made no claim for compensation for the delay itself. Bearing in mind the fact that the applicant had never attempted to speed up the proceedings, the First Hall ruled that the finding of a violation was sufficient satisfaction for the breach. The applicant appealed on the basis of the quantum of compensation. The Constitutional Court revised the ruling of the First Hall on a number of points, but upheld the final finding and award.

3.2.5 The considerations the courts of Malta have been prepared to bear in mind when assessing the quantum of compensation

First generally accepted consideration: The awarding of compensation is not the exception but the rule once a violation is found; divergent conclusions drawn from the facts at final instance may lead to a variation of the sum awarded

In XUEREB V REGISTRAR OF COURTS ET[68] the Constitutional Court had confirmed the finding of a violation in regard to procedures requesting the issue of a warrant on the basis of a final judgment. The proceedings had lasted eighteen years, six of which were attributable to delays occasioned by the applicant. The First Hall had awarded € 6,988.[69] Upon appeal the Constitutional Court rightly made note of the fact that, contrary to the assertions of the attorney general, the awarding of moral damages was *not* an exceptional remedy and was common practice in length-of-proceedings cases[70] even though in some cases a declaration may suffice. In this case moral damages were due on the basis of the prolonged uncertainty and anxiety suffered, but the delay occasioned by the applicant's conduct had to be reflected in the quantum. On this basis the sum was reduced to € 1,398.[71]

Second generally accepted consideration: The irrelevance of the outcome (in regard to the applicant) of the main proceedings, but its materiality in regard to the quantum of compensation

The upshot of the main proceedings is irrelevant for the establishment of whether there had been a breach of the reasonable time requirement, but such factor could affect the determination of the quantum of compensation along with other factors. This was the position, confirmed at final instance in XUEREB V REGISTRAR OF COURTS ET[72] where the court noted that:

> Both the Constitution as well as the European Convention guarantee a fair hearing within a reasonable time to 'all persons' without any qualification. Therefore it is irrelevant, for the purposes of the guarantees afforded by the Constitution and Convention, if the complaint is lodged by the plaintiff or the defendant, or if the applicant is the party that has won or lost the case.[73]

This stance has, unfortunately, not always been the position of the local courts[74] and will hopefully be drawn on in future decisions.

Third generally accepted consideration: The effect of delay on the standard of living of the applicant

In SAID ET V ATTORNEY GENERAL[75] the violation found at first instance was confirmed upon appeal, but the motivations backing the judgment and quantum of compensation were altered. The Constitutional Court disagreed with the degree of fault attributed to the applicant, as well as with the assertion that the need for expert reports demonstrated the complexity of the case, noting that, ultimately, sentence had been delivered without these reports. In increasing the compensation due to € 6,000, the Constitutional Court differed from the views of the First Hall in regard to whether the proceedings had affected the quality of life of the applicant, noting that other than the monetary and sentimental value of the object at stake, of which the applicant was deprived for a lengthy period, one had to also consider the numerous times which the applicant attended court sittings over the span of three decades (totalling one hundred and fifty sittings, out of which the applicant had only failed to attend five). One had to also consider the inevitable need for consultation sessions with legal counsel prior to these sessions. In the light of these considerations the Constitutional Court felt that it was not possible to conclude that the proceedings had not had a significant impact on the life of the applicant. It increased the moral compensation due from € 2,000 to € 6,000. If the courts were to routinely bear these considerations in mind when assessing length-of-proceedings breaches, there could be significantly positive developments in case law.

Fourth generally accepted consideration: One of the major factors the courts in Malta have been prepared to bear in mind in such cases is proportionality in respect of other domestically delivered decisions

SAID V ATTORNEY GENERAL[76] concerned criminal proceedings wherein the accused was acquitted after a trial which had lasted for eight years and three months. Of the fifty five sittings held, only nineteen were used for the presentation of evidence. The First Hall awarded € 12,000 by way of moral damages, noting that half the time should have sufficed in this case, and that a declaration should suffice as compensation only where the breach was marginal. No *restitutio in integrum* is possible where a violation occurs as a result of delay and, therefore, the only other possibility is financial compensation, especially when the applicant is acquitted in the main proceedings. The First Hall drew on the cases of BUGEJA V ATTORNEY GENERAL ET[77] and FARRUGIA V ATTORNEY GENERAL,[78] examined further on in this section. Upon appeal, the moral compensation awarded was reduced to € 3,000, as the Constitutional Court disagreed that the reputation of the applicant had in any way been tarnished to a greater degree than what is ordinarily the consequence of being a defendant to criminal proceedings. Other factors which the court enumerated were the need for redress to reflect the moral damage suffered by the applicant due to prolonged uncertainty in regard to the upshot of the pending criminal proceedings, the anxiety which was probably suffered as a result of the incertitude felt by the applicant and his family and the fact that unreasonable delay endangers public confidence in the administration of justice and the rule of law itself. The court also considered the fact that the applicant was responsible for part of the delay, noting that the First Hall had overlooked this point.[79] In reducing the amount of compensation from € 12,000 to € 3,000, proportionality in regard to other judgments was clearly a determining factor.

MANDUCA V THE HON. PRIME MINISTER concerned a breach found in respect of proceedings which had lasted over eleven years before the Rent Regulation Board. The First Hall held that the criteria to be borne in mind when assessing the quantum of compensation included the length of the delays in question, the nature of the case, the suffering incurred, the conduct of the applicant and the outcome of the proceedings in question. The court referred to several recommendations of European Commission of Human Rights and decisions of the Strasbourg Court. The applicant had requested € 23,293[80] to be awarded by way of redress. The court examined the awards in a number of Italian length-of-proceedings cases[81] and noted that the concept of awarding moral damages arises out of the breach of Convention obligations which the state has bound itself to respect, but that in length-of-proceedings cases the assessment of the quantum presented certain difficulties. It is clear that the court felt the need to achieve proportionality in regard to other locally delivered decisions. In ATTARD V THE HON. PRIME MINISTER ET the court had awarded € 1,165.[82] In the present case the court felt that the frustration and anxiety felt by the applicant were greater. It noted that adjournments when a date had already been set for delivery of the sentence are particularly harsh. The court felt that the quantum of compensation should be balanced to take account of the domestic background and judicial tradition of the Maltese legal system, and that the courts in Malta were as yet 'very far' from being in a position to award moral damages to the extents requested by the applicant. The court fixed the moral compensation due in this case at € 3,960.[83]

The defendant appealed from this sentence on the basis *inter alia* of the quantum of compensation awarded, complaining that the First Hall had oversimplified the subject matter of the main proceedings. A cross appeal was filed also on the basis of the quantum, requesting that this be increased. The Constitutional Court, while confirming that the overall length of proceedings was excessive, felt that the First Hall had indeed oversimplified the matter both in attributing the blame to the individual judges in question, as well as in stating that the case could have been decided in under an hour. In view of these two divergences, it reduced the compensation awarded to € 1,631.[84] The court considered the excessive nature of the delay, the fact that issues involving property are usually considered less meritorious than other cases of a more personal nature which have a heavy impact on the individual's life such as compensation for death, accident, or cases concerning civil status or legal capacity and finally that delay in the administration of justice necessarily causes unnecessary frustration, anxiety and suffering. In this case the applicant had not adduced proof of any additional suffering of a more grievous or oppressive nature than that which naturally results from delay, and although he could not be held to be at fault for contributing to the delay, neither could it be said that he undertook any particular initiative to attempt to expedite the proceedings. Indeed, the issue of delay in this case was raised by the judge himself. The applicant had to bear the consequences of delay resulting from his error in having filed a case before an incompetent tribunal.

There are no rules of binding precedent which fetter the courts' powers to remedy human rights violations in Malta, and, yet, irrespective of the divergences between the reasoning of the courts at different instances, the point of departure for their respective considerations remain other domestically delivered decisions, thereby underlining the weight given in practice to achieving proportionality.

Fifth generally accepted consideration: Considerations particular to criminal length-of-proceedings cases

BUGEJA V ATTORNEY GENERAL AND COMMISSIONER OF POLICE[85] has been extensively drawn on in subsequent decisions. The case concerned a violation found in regard to criminal proceedings which had lasted twenty years. The court's starting point was *not* the presumption that unreasonable delay will occasion non-pecuniary damage, but the fact that in several cases a declaration constitutes just satisfaction for a breach of the reasonable time requirement. The court went on to hold that such a declaration did not suffice in this case as the delay was not marginal, but covered a period which was excessively long and unreasonable and which had caused uncertainty and anxiety. It noted that the ideal remedy of *restitutio in integrum* was not possible, and that therefore the only possible alternative was monetary compensation for the anxiety felt by the accused over an extended period. The court considered, on the one hand, the serious impact on the life of the applicant deriving not only from the deprivation of personal liberty, but also from the impending possibility of a significantly long term of imprisonment, the fact that the accused was bound to observe the conditions relating to his release *pendente lite* and that delay in the delivery of judgment necessarily causes a state of unnecessary uncertainty, frustration and anxiety to the accused and his family; on the other hand, the court considered that the applicant had not proved that he incurred any suffering of a more grievous or oppressive nature than that usually associated with delay in the determination of judicial procedures, the lack of initiative on the applicant's part to attempt to expedite proceedings and, finally, the fact that the accused did not seem to have reformed his ways and had, meanwhile, incurred other convictions. Ultimately, the court liquidated the sum of € 6,988[86] *arbitrio boni viri*.

CASSAR V ATTORNEY GENERAL[87] is a final judgment delivered by the First Hall in which a violation was found in relation to criminal proceedings which had lasted sixteen years, around eight of which consisted of thirty nine adjournments for sentence to be delivered. The court found a violation of Article 6 and awarded € 3,500 by way of compensation. The case had been complex, with a large amount of evidence adduced, but there was no justification for the delay once the case had been adjourned for sentence. In assessing the quantum of compensation, the court underlined the fact that this was not a case for damages and that the sum liquidated had to reflect the uncertainty and anxiety suffered by the applicant. Factors militating towards increasing the compensation included the excessive nature of the delay, the fact that the applicant was ultimately acquitted, the criminal nature of the case and the fact that pending the outcome of the case the liberty of the accused was subject to conditions. On the other hand the court felt that several factors militated towards a reduction, namely, the fact that prejudice suffered had been occasioned in the main part by the eight-year period of adjournments for sentence rather than the entirety of proceedings,[88] the lack of any initiative to expedite proceedings on the part of the applicant and the fact that, meanwhile, the applicant had been re-employed and that the suspension had been lifted in his regard so that his income was, in the court's view, not affected pending the outcome of the proceedings. On the basis of the above considerations the court awarded € 3,500 by way of moral damages.

In ELLUL SULLIVAN ET V COMMISSIONER OF POLICE ET[89] the court was faced with a request for the annulment of a sentence of the Court of Criminal Appeal. While rejecting this demand, the court felt that neither could, however, a simple declaration suffice to remedy the violation; financial compensation was therefore deemed to be the only appropriate remedy in the circumstances, 'all the more so in regard to those persons found guilty by the sentence of the Court of Criminal Appeal'. This comment is somewhat strange, as a reading of Strasbourg case law indicates clearly that an acquittal after lengthy procedures will usually result in a higher award.[90] The Constitutional Court differentiated between the four defendants to the principal proceedings, two of whom had been acquitted at both instances and showed little interest in the proceedings, awarding € 2,000 for their anxiety and frustration which, however, 'in all probability was somewhat appeased if not redressed by their acquittal from all accusation or finding of guilt'. In awarding an additional sum, the court noted that pending the determination of the case, permission to suspend the payment of fines had been given, and that five years had passed since then. It issued an order to the effect that in addition to sums for moral damages, no interest was to fall due on the sums owed by way of fines to the government.

Sixth generally accepted consideration: The courts will bear in mind any other redress already afforded by the ordinary courts

Another factor which the courts of constitutional jurisdiction are prepared to bear in mind when assessing compensation is any remedy afforded to the applicant by the ordinary courts in the main proceedings, in a manner somewhat analogous to the Strasbourg Court's concept of the loss of victim status as a result of domestic relief afforded. In FARRUGIA V COMMISSIONER OF POLICE ET[91] the First Hall held that a declaration of the violation of the applicant's rights was sufficient satisfaction, in respect of criminal proceedings which had lasted seventeen years, in view of the mitigated sentence given by the Court of Criminal Appeal; there was no appeal from this sentence. In the referenced proceedings, the Court of Magistrate's sentence had been partially quashed. The accused had been acquitted of some of the accusations and the term of imprisonment reduced from five years to three years and six months. The case had been postponed repeatedly for judgment after the first nine years had elapsed. Relying on BECK, since the Court of Criminal Appeal had taken the length-of-proceedings into consideration in sentencing the accused, the court found that sufficient redress had been afforded within the criminal proceedings themselves. The First Hall noted that it would have granted moral damages, but that in this case the applicant had benefited from a reduction in sentence and subsequently a presidential pardon. The court drew attention to the gravity of the offences of which the applicant had been convicted and the light sentence imposed in relation thereto.

3.2.6 *Alternative forms of redress*[92]

Pursuant to article 4 of Chapter 319[93] and article 46(2)[94] of the Constitution, the courts of constitutional jurisdiction in Malta have wide powers to remedy breaches of fundamental human rights.[95] We shall be examining the response of the Maltese courts to requests for various remedies in the face of violations found in the main proceedings. In RAMESH CHETENRAM SHARMA ET V ATTORNEY GENERAL ET, the court considered that there could be cases where the dismissal of the indictment, *via* an order to issue a *nolle prosequi*, could be given to the attorney general. In practice, however, the courts have elected to award non-pecuniary compensation, rather than to issue such an order, in particular due to the public interest vying with the rights of the accused. In ELLUL SULLIVAN ET V COMMISSIONER OF POLICE ET discussed above, and in refusing to order the annulment of the sentence of the Criminal Court, the following motivation was given for the court's decision:

> This is due to the fact that this Court is satisfied that the finding of guilt was in no manner affected by the unreasonable delay which this Court has established to have afflicted the proceedings before the Court of Criminal Inquiry. Specifically, this Court does not find that in view of the relevant delay, the rights of defence were prejudiced in any manner such as in relation to any exculpating evidence which could have benefited the appellants.[96]

The court thus ruled that rights of the defence had not been prejudiced by the unreasonable delay. *A contrariu sensu*, it seems that if the rights of the defence are indeed prejudiced as a result of delays in the trial, the court might be willing to consider such a measure.

The breadth of the powers to afford redress in constitutional matters was placed under the spotlight in the case of BUGEJA V ATTORNEY GENERAL ET[97] wherein the First Hall had, in the light of excessive delay in criminal proceedings which had lasted twenty years, ordered the immediate release of the applicant, thereby annulling not the actual sentence of the Court of Magistrates, but the effects of it, namely, the term of imprisonment imposed. The appeal was heard with urgency. The Constitutional Court had no hesitation in confirming the violation of the applicant's rights, but disagreed in regard to the appropriate remedy to be afforded in the circumstances. While opting to award compensation in the particular case, the court did not rule out the possibility that, where justice so requires, a measure so drastic could be resorted to by the court:

> The wider the power and discretion conferred, the more prudence and diligence in the use and exercise of the same power and discretion is required. ... the Court is therefore required, in the exercise of its discretion, to maintain a suitable and fair balance between, on the one hand the rights of the person looking to the Court for protection, and, on the other hand, the rights of the other persons who may be involved in the case, as well as the rights of society in general, which this Court has an obligation to protect.[98]

This balancing interest was also evident in the case of BONNICI V ATTORNEY GENERAL,[99] where the proceedings in question had lasted thirteen years, and were still pending at the time of the First Hall's ruling. Eleven years of this period had consisted of repeated adjournments for delivery of the sentence by the Court of Magistrates. Bonnici had been accused of sanitary offences relating to the rearing of animals. The First Hall awarded € 4,659[100] by way of moral compensation, and no appeal was entered. The court referred to the factually identical case of FARRUGIA V ATTORNEY GENERAL[101] where the relevant period exceeded twelve years. In regard to the assessment of the quantum of compensation, the court drew on BUGEJA V ATTORNEY GENERAL but felt that in the particular case an order for criminal procedures against the applicant to be discontinued would be unjustified, as these were offences which affected the public at large. Incidentally, the same amount of compensation had been awarded in FARRUGIA V ATTORNEY GENERAL, although in that case the applicant had actually been acquitted by the time the court delivered judgment.

In the abovementioned case of XUEREB V ATTORNEY GENERAL[102] the applicant had requested, in addition to the finding of a violation and the awarding of appropriate compensation, an order for the bill of indictment, if any, to be issued on the basis of the evidence compiled by the time of the last referral to the attorney general before the point in time of filing of the constitutional application, as well as the affording of any other appropriate remedy. This specific request was denied, and the court instead issued an order to the respondent to issue the bill of indictment as expeditiously as possible, if there was a basis for it.

The remedy provided in POLICE V ELLUL SULLIVAN ET[103] was the setting of a time frame in relation to a period of anticipated delay. The case involved compilation proceedings in respect of several persons eventually accused and convicted of fiscal offences. During the compilation proceedings, and in regard to evidence from foreign witnesses required by means of letters rogatory, constitutional action was brought claiming that such evidence would cause delay in violation of Article 6 and article 39 of the Constitution. The Court of Magistrates referred the question to the First Hall, which dismissed the claim. Upon appeal to the Constitutional Court, judgment was reversed and an order issued to the Commissioner of Police to ensure that if evidence was to be admitted by means of letters rogatory, this procedure had to be concluded within a period of six months, failing which the Commissioner would have to request an extension of the time frame from the court itself. This case was drawn on in ATTARD V ATTORNEY GENERAL[104] where the court quoted with approval from Van Dijk and Van Hoof:

> ... in criminal proceedings the public interest in the prosecution and conviction of the criminal may be so great that the prosecution should not be stopped for the sole reason that the reasonable time has been transgressed; another more appropriate compensation should be awarded to the victim of that transgression.[105]

The court finally noted that the remedy of the dismissal of the indictment could not be accepted in this case, as it was essential that justice be also done in regard to society in general. The court felt that the applicant was somewhat to blame for not having had earlier recourse to the constitutional remedies available. It indicated that it may have found differently if the applicant had resorted to constitutional proceedings at an early stage, and that those proceedings had failed to provide him with a remedy. It therefore confirmed the past and ongoing violation of the complainant's rights and imposed a six-month time limit for the appointment of the trial by jury, awarding € 1,165[106] by way of moral damages.

The reasoning of the court in ATTARD V ATTORNEY GENERAL is reminiscent of that in BARTOLO V ATTORNEY GENERAL[107] examined above, where in upholding the First Hall's conclusion the Constitutional Court noted that prevention through early recourse to constitutional remedies should be the main aim of proceedings for the protection of one's right to a fair hearing within a reasonable time. It sought to buttress this reasoning by stating that, saving circumstances where one was somehow impeded from so doing, one should have recourse to constitutional action as soon as proceedings become afflicted by delay:

> The allegation of the violation of a fundamental human right was never [intended to be] and should never have been reduced to a [mere] procedural

tool to interfere with or be used to spur the conduct of judicial proceedings, and neither used for any financial or other advantage to be obtained from a negative situation which, at the relevant time, the applicant found convenient to favour or accept to bear. ... the person who alleges that his fundamental human rights have been actually violated or threated is himself expected to act in a timely manner for the protection of those rights.[108]

In a civil law context, however, in the case of ALLIED NEWSPAPERS LIMITED V ATTORNEY GENERAL ET[109] examined above, the Constitutional Court took a diametrically opposed stance, holding that the applicants could not be blamed for delay in resorting to constitutional proceedings; a party could not be held to be at fault for not having had earlier resort to proceedings which were not considered to be ordinary remedies.

Chapter 3 – Section 3 – Should the Courts of Constitutional Jurisdiction in Malta Decline Jurisdiction on the Basis that Adequate Means of Redress Exist Under Ordinary Law?

3.3.1 The general approach in length-of-proceedings cases

On the basis of the proviso to article 46(2)[110] of the Constitution of Malta and of article 4(2) of Chapter 319[111] of the laws of Malta, the First Hall has discretion to decline to hear the merits of a constitutional application where ordinary remedies were available to the applicant:

> An application for redress under the Constitution is meant to be 'a measure of last resort', as it is presumed that a citizen can and has protection for his fundamental human rights in the [ordinary] law of the country. ... it is only when the ordinary law of the country does not provide a remedy, that the citizen should be able to resort to extraordinary remedies emanating from the country's Constitution.[112]

Resort to the courts of constitutional jurisdiction alleging a breach of fundamental human rights is understood to provide an extraordinary remedy in the sense that recourse should be made to it only where ordinary law does not provide recourse where it should.[113] In XUEREB V ATTORNEY GENERAL,[114] for instance, in rejecting the attorney general's argument that the applicant had an ordinary remedy available, namely, to petition the court of criminal jurisdiction, before which he would eventually be sentenced, to take the length of proceedings into account when sentencing him, the First Hall held that the applicant must have a remedy also during the pendency of proceedings without having to wait for their outcome.

In exercising its discretion in length-of-proceedings cases, the First Hall has taken the approach that the duty of the state to respect the reasonable time requirement precludes it from declining to exercise its jurisdiction where the state is at fault, even if the parties did not have recourse to ordinary remedies. In the context of expropriation[115] proceedings, for instance, the plea of non-exhaustion of ordinary remedies was rejected, notwithstanding the fact that the applicants allowed almost three decades to elapse before resorting to a court to fix a time frame for the Commissioner to act, as their inactivity could not justify the inactivity of the Commissioner. This failure on behalf of the applicants was nevertheless taken into consideration in the assessment of damages. Again, in FENECH V COMMISSIONER OF LANDS ET[116] the court did not decline jurisdiction, even though it accepted that there was a strong element of contributory negligence on behalf of the applicants who allowed sixteen years to pass before undertaking any action.

Otherwise stated therefore, the concept of the exhaustion of ordinary remedies in a length-of-proceedings context is being removed from the remit of article 46(2) of the Constitution (and thus from the context of the preliminary pleas) and examined as part of the merits of the case under the heading of the 'conduct of the applicant' in assessing the damages due, in light of the fact that the duty to expedite proceedings was incumbent upon the authorities in the first place, and that the failure of the applicants to resort to the ordinary remedies available does not detract from the primary failing of the authorities.

3.3.2 Should the civil court decline constitutional jurisdiction due to the availability of an action for judicial review of administrative action?

In VISUAL AND SOUND COMMUNICATIONS LIMITED V COMMISSIONER OF POLICE ET[117] the First Hall declined to exercise its jurisdiction under articles 46(2) and 4 of the Constitution and European Convention Act respectively, noting that:

> ... the remedy for compensation has many times been the remedy of last resort for the breach of fundamental human rights. ... the action for damages in accordance with the ordinary principles of our Civil Code can be based both on the allegation of a violation of the European Convention (since Chapter 319 is part of the ordinary law of Malta) as well as on the allegation that there have been administrative acts which contravene the law, as provided in article 495A of Chapter 12.[118]

This reasoning had been upheld by the Constitutional Court which considered recourse on the basis of ordinary law to be the correct mode of proceeding, notwithstanding the fact that the facts at the basis of the claim were alleged to amount to a breach of fundamental human rights.

More recently, however, in HALL V DIRECTOR FOR THE DEPARTMENT OF SOCIAL ACCOMMODATION ET,[119] the Constitutional Court clarified that henceforth the First Hall of the Civil Court, exercising its competence as a court of constitutional jurisdiction, is the proper forum to examine allegations that administrative action is 'contrary to law' where the law in question consists of the provisions enshrining fundamental human rights. The First Hall should therefore not refuse to exercise its discretion on the basis of article 46(2) of the Constitution on the basis that an ordinary action under article 469A of Chapter 12 is available to the applicant. The author submits that this is the correct position in the light of SÜRMELI as examined above.[120]

3.3.3 Should the civil court decline constitutional jurisdiction on the basis of the availability of an action for damages in tort?

We shall be examining in some detail the reasons for which the court of first instance in Malta *should not* refuse to exercise its discretion on the basis of article 46(2) of the Constitution on the basis of the availability of ordinary remedies, *as there are no ordinary remedies which would qualify as effective remedies to redress a violation of Article 6 in terms of the jurisprudence of the European Court of Human Rights.* It is not the practice of the ordinary civil courts in Malta to explicitly award moral damages where liability in tort is established; neither is the violation of a fundamental human right generally accepted as the exclusive basis for civil liability. Yet, as we have seen, a length-of-proceedings remedy without the possibility for an award under the head of moral damages is not considered to be an effective remedy for a length-of-proceedings violation.[121]

Notes

1. CALLEJA, ZARB, CENTRAL MEDITERRANEAN DEVELOPMENT, DEBONO, BEZZINA WETTINGER AND OTHERS.
2. See Appendix B.
3. ZARB: however, see *Conclusion*.
4. CALLEJA.
5. See *Statutes*.
6. Ibid.
7. This is evident from a reading of decisions such as FRENDO RANDON V COMMISSIONER OF LANDS (App no. 17/2002/1), BUGEJA V ATTORNEY GENERAL (App no. 29/2002/1), CURMI V COMMISSIONER OF LANDS (App no. 25/2005/1), XUEREB V ATTORNEY GENERAL (App no. 14/2003/1).
8. See HANDYSIDE, SIMALDONE.
9. CALLEJA: The Strasbourg Court awarded € 5,000 in non-pecuniary damages for a violation of Articles 5(3) and 6(1).
10. The FHCC(CJ) and the Constitutional Court both denied any breach of Article 6(1). The Constitutional Court remitted the case in regard to Article 5(3), and upon a second hearing the FHCC(CJ) found a violation of that article.
11. In regard to this period the Strasbourg Court found a violation of Article 5(3).
12. See [132].
13. See [133] and [134].
14. App no. 28/2002/1.
15. See SALIBA (App no. 20287/10).
16. App no. 742/2000/1.

17 App no. 571/96.
18 Provision for this is also made in the Court Practice and Procedure and Good Order rules Part III section 10 (see *Statutes*).
19 App no. 14/2003/1.
20 Lm 300.
21 App no. 40/2006.
22 App no. 10/2007/1; also see pending constitutional action of defendant to civil proceedings: GATT V ATTORNEY GENERAL, (FHCC(CJ): Giannino Caruana Demajo (App no. 52/2007) (Registered 17th October 2007 and adjourned to 25th May 2010).
23 Pieter van Dijk, Fried van Hoof, Arjen van Rijn, Leo Zwaak (eds), *Theory and Practice of the European Convention on Human Rights* (4th edition Intersentia, Oxford 2006) p. 608.
24 P. 18 [22].
25 See Chapter 2, Section 1, *The Strasbourg Court's Method of Examination* n 48 (Chapter 2) and Cf. Richard Clayton, Hugh Tomlinson, *Fair Trial Rights* (reprinted from *The Law of Human Rights*, Oxford University Press, Oxford 2001) p. 105 (SCOPELLITI, UNION ALIMENTARIA SANDERS SA). See also BEGGS [239].
26 App no. 651/1998/1.
27 App no. 6/2002/1.
28 App no. 5/2002/1.
29 P. 19 [5]: App no. 6/2002/1.
30 Lm 100.
31 App no. 651/1998/1.
32 App no. 17/2002/1.
33 In this vein reference was made to FENECH V COMMISSIONER OF LANDS (App no. 31/2007/1).
34 App no. 669/1998/1.
35 FINO NOE V PLANNING AUTHORITY ET (App no. 604/1997/1).
36 P. 8.
37 P. 10.
38 P. 10.
39 (App no. 22/2003/1) Cf. XUEREB V REGISTRAR OF COURTS ET (App no. 742/2000/1).
40 Cf. GEORGE XUEREB V REGISTRAR OF COURTS ET (App no. 742/2000/1).
41 App no. 40/2006.
42 Ref no. Volume 80 (1996) Part no. 1 Section – P. 4.
43 App no. 29/2001/1.
44 Lm 200.
45 See MIFSUD V BONELLO (App no. 176/1987/2) wherein the FHCC(CJ) used the multiplier method for the calculation of *lucrum cessans* for a violation of a fundamental human right, and the Constitutional Court felt bound by the strictures of the Civil Code in awarding pecuniary compensation for the breach; see Chapter 4, Section 2, *Ordinary Remedies are Not Prejudiced by and Do Not Prejudice Constitutional Remedies*.
46 P. 12 [7].
47 See Chapter 2, Section 4, *How does the European Court Calculate the Quantum of Compensation under Article 41?*
48 App no. 17/2002/1.
49 A period of thirty years during which the Commissioner failed to institute proceedings before the Land Arbitration Board.

50 See Chapter 2, Section 2, *Article 13: General Observations*, Sub-Section 2, *The interplay between Article 13 and the right of access to court under Article 6*.
51 Cf. CLAYTON COMMUNICATIONS COMPANY LIMITED V THE HON. PRIME MINISTER ET (App no. 55/2008/1) where in relation to a two-year delay in the appointment of the appeal hearing, the FHCC found no violation of the reasonable time requirement on the facts, but did rule that there had been a violation of the right of access to court. The Constitutional Court overturned this judgment – there was insufficient proof that the rate of interest at 1 per cent per month effectively impaired the essence of the right of access to court.
52 VILHO ESKELINEN AND OTHERS, KIURKCHIAN, MESSOCHORITIS, SILČ.
53 The FHCC's reasoning seems also to have been the basis of LICARI NOE V COMMISSIONER OF LANDS ET (App no. 19/2005).
54 Laws of Malta Ch. 319: Article 4 and Ch. 0: Article 46(1); see *Statutes*.
55 App no. 25/2005/1.
56 Also constitutional reference no. 14/2001 in the case of COMMISSIONER OF LANDS V VIOLET BRIFFA ET, a reference from the Land Arbitration Board to the FHCC(CJ) in the light of a thirty two-year period during which the Commissioner of Lands failed to institute proceedings before the board in the context of expropriation proceedings.
57 This was the same stance taken by the FHCC(CJ) in FRENDO RANDON V COMMISSIONER OF LANDS ET (App no. 17/2002/1).
58 App no. 723/1999/1.
59 P. 14.
60 In the following domestic length-of-proceedings cases a declaration was held to constitute sufficient satisfaction in respect of the violation found. The period in respect of which the violation was found is provided after the case. PULIS V COMMISSIONER OF LANDS ET (App no. 34/2005): 36 months; SCICLUNA V ATTORNEY GENERAL ET (App no. 463/1994/1): 72 months; BARTOLO V ATTORNEY GENERAL (App no. 571/96): 176 months (but 108 months *ratione temporis* under the Convention); CACHIA V ATTORNEY GENERAL (App no. 586/97): 393 months (violation of Article 39(2); no violation found of Article 6 but, *ratione temporis*, the court was competent to award compensation in respect of a period of 175 months).
61 MANDUCA V THE HON. PRIME MINISTER.
62 GASAN ENTERPRISES LTD V MALTA ENVIRONMENT AND PLANNING AUTHORITY.
63 BLASCHEM (MALTA) LTD. V ATTORNEY GENERAL ET (App no. 22/2003/1), AZZOPARDI V ATTORNEY GENERAL ET (App no. 669/1998/1).
64 ZARB, CENTRAL MEDITERRANEAN DEVELOPMENT CORPORATION LIMITED.
65 App no. 571/96.
66 The court was competent, *ratione temporis*, to examine a period of nine years.
67 Lm 5.
68 App no. 742/2000/1.
69 Lm 3,000.
70 The court made reference to ZARB V ATTORNEY GENERAL.
71 Lm 600.
72 App no. 742/2000/1.
73 P. 20 [C].
74 BLASCHEM (MALTA) LTD V ATTORNEY GENERAL ET (App no. 22/2003/1), PACE V ATTORNEY GENERAL (App no. 753/2000/2), AZZOPARDI V ATTORNEY GENERAL ET (App no. 669/1998/1).

75 App no. 10/2007/1.
76 App no. 30/2007/1.
77 App no. 29/02.
78 App no. 16/05.
79 Delays amounted to some six years and nine months, of which one year and eight months attributable to the conduct of the applicant.
80 Lm 10,000.
81 DE MICHELI AND BILLI. See judgment for reference details.
82 Lm 500. Reference is made to ATTARD V THE HON. CHIEF JUSTICE ET delivered on the 29th October 1992 by the Constitutional Court as cited in MANDUCA V ATTORNEY GENERAL delivered on the 23rd January 1995 (Ref no. Volume 79 (1995) Part no. 1 Section 1 P. 1).
83 Lm 1,700.
84 Lm 700.
85 App no. 29/2002/1.
86 Lm 3,000.
87 App no. 64/2006/1.
88 This approach is different to that adopted by the Strasbourg Court which establishes the start and end of the entire 'period to be considered'. Cf. also the reasoning of the court in ATTARD V THE HON. PRIME MINISTER ET p. 122 where such adjournments were considered to be particularly harsh.
89 App no. 651/1998/1.
90 SMIRNOVA, SCHAAL, PALMIGIANO, LEDONNE NO. 1, LEDONNE NO. 2, İLETMİŞ.
91 App no. 30/2002/1.
92 Regarding the possibility of issuing an order to the Attorney General see RAMESH CHETENRAM SHARMA V ATTORNEY GENERAL.
93 See *Statutes*.
94 Ibid.
95 Chapter 319 article 4, Chapter 0 article 46(2): see *Statutes*.
96 P. 32 [41].
97 App no. 29/2002/1.
98 P. 12 [28].
99 App no. 3/2007.
100 Lm 2,000.
101 App no. 16/2005.
102 App no. 14/2003/1.
103 Ref no. 1991 Volume 75 (1991) Part no. 1 Section 1 P. 46.
104 App no. 624/97.
105 Pieter van Dijk, Fried van Hoof, Arjen van Rijn, Leo Zwaak (eds), *Theory and Practice of the European Convention on Human Rights* (4th edition Intersentia, Oxford 2006) p. 611.
106 Lm 500.
107 App no. 571/96.
108 P. 26.
109 App no. 723/1999/1.
110 See *Statutes*.
111 Ibid.
112 MIFSUD BONNICI V TABONE 2002 quoted at both instances in FENECH V COMMISSIONER OF LANDS (App no. 31/2007/1 p. 13).

113 AL SAKALLI V PRIME MINISTER cited in FENECH ET V COMMISSIONER OF LANDS ET (App no. 31/2007/1); also GAFFARENA V COMMISSIONER OF POLICE and MCKAY V COMMISSIONER OF POLICE.
114 App no. 14/2003/1.
115 FRENDO RANDON V COMMISSIONER OF LANDS ET (App no. 17/2002/1); FENECH ET V COMMISSIONER OF LANDS ET (App no. 31/2007/1).
116 App no. 31/2007/1.
117 App no. 34/2001/1.
118 P. 9 (Sentence of the 20th November 2001, confirmed by the Constitutional Court on the 12th December 2002).
119 App no. 1/2003/1.
120 See Chapter 1, Section 2, *Article 34 Loss of Victim Status – Incompatibility* Ratione Personae, Sub-Section 1, *Have the authorities acknowledged the violation, 'either expressly or in substance', and was that acknowledgment adequate?* and text to n 36 (Chapter 1) and 115 (Chapter 2).
121 Ibid. See also n 9 (Chapter 1) regarding exhaustion of remedies geared to remedy Convention violations.

4 Case Study Based on the Legal System of Malta, Part II

Remedies for Delay Within Ordinary Law

Chapter Introduction

We shall now assess the gamut of ordinary (non-constitutional) remedies for delay within the law of Malta, so as to explore whether we can identify effective remedies for delay within the domain of ordinary civil law. This possibility shall be explored both in relation to delay which renders the length of proceedings so unreasonably long as to be in violation of the fundamental human rights of the relevant individual and require an effective remedy as prescribed by the Convention, as well as delay which does not attain that minimum level of severity required for the violation of a right, but nevertheless occasions damage, and, therefore, in respect of which a legal remedy would be desirable.

The relevance of such analysis is the quest to find, within the remit of ordinary civil law, effective recourse within the meaning of Convention jurisprudence, for delay in judicial proceedings. As we observed in the foregoing chapters, an effective remedy need not be constitutional in nature; indeed its effectiveness is predicated upon the fulfilment of the characteristics which were outlined in Chapters 1 and 2, and is independent of the domestic classification of the remedy. In SÜRMELI for instance, the effectiveness of an ordinary action for damages against the state was rejected not on the basis of the nature of the action, but due to the fact that through its use, even if delay in terms of Article 6 were proved, moral damages would not be awarded.

The prospect of liability in tort shall be examined both in relation to private parties as well as in relation to the state for, being no longer within the realm of constitutional matters, it would be artificial to ignore the possibility of recourse against private persons.[1]

In light of these considerations, we shall be making reference to a number of cases where the defendant was held liable in delict due to the damage suffered by the plaintiff as a result of delay imputable to the defendant. With the exception of ATTARD V ATTARD, the other cases must be understood by analogy, transposing the court's analysis of the delay at stake into a context where the same principles could apply to delay in judicial proceedings. In order to assess the possibility of recourse through ordinary law for delay in judicial proceedings, one is obliged to resort to deriving applicable principles through analogical reasoning, due to the paucity of judgments which deal strictly with delay in the context of contentious proceedings.

Chapter 4 – Section 1 – No Redress against Private Parties Can Be Sought Through Constitutional Action

In a length-of-proceedings context, no form of satisfaction can be sought against a private party, acting in their individual capacity, *viz. not qua state agents,* through a human rights action before the courts of constitutional jurisdiction.[2] In XUEREB V REGISTRAR OF COURTS ET[3] the *locus standi* of a co-respondent, being a private individual who was a party to the civil proceedings the length of which were being challenged in a human rights-based action, was upheld simply for the sake of completeness.[4] The court was well aware that it could not condemn such private party, even in the face of a glaring period of nine years attributable in whole to her conduct. The court took note of the fact that the civil court took no measures to counter the delay tactics of the relevant party, and specifically entered a reservation to underline that although it could not condemn such defendant in a human rights action, this was without prejudice to the possibility that the applicant could attempt to have recourse under ordinary law against such private party for any damage he felt he had incurred.[5]

The court observed that a state cannot be held responsible for delay resulting from the conduct of the defendant against whom the claim is brought. We have already seen however that there is both foreign[6] and local jurisprudence[7] with pronouncements to the effect that while the state cannot be held responsible for the conduct of a private party, the positive obligations incumbent upon the state oblige the court to take positive measures to counter such tactics and thereby uphold the rights of the other parties. The ordinary courts themselves may – and should – take measures in order to safeguard the rights of the citizen emerging from the Convention. In BRINCAT V ATTORNEY GENERAL[8] the First Hall noted with approval that in its decree the Court of Magistrates had *sua sponte* assessed whether there had been any violation, in the criminal proceedings, of the provisions of Chapter 319, as part of the ordinary law of Malta:

> And it was right to do so, as the function of the Court is to apply all the law of the country, including the guarantees for the fundamental human rights of the individual declared and protected by the Constitution and the European Convention, and this in a preventive manner before the violation has occurred and in order to prevent it.

The need for all state authorities to act with increased awareness, or rather active consciousness, of the implications of the fundamental human rights of the individual is at the centre of Said Pullicino's concept of a 'human rights culture'.[9]

Chapter 4 – Section 2 – Ordinary Remedies are Not Prejudiced by and Do Not Prejudice Constitutional Remedies

On a number of occasions the courts of constitutional jurisdiction have refrained from taking further measures to redress the situation of the applicant, holding that the ordinary courts were the appropriate fora for such remedies.[10] In FARRUGIA V COMMISSIONER OF LANDS,[11] in assessing the quantum of redress, the Constitutional Court clearly set out that once the application is framed in terms of a demand for just satisfaction for a breach of the Convention, it could not be adapted into an action seeking damages on the basis of ordinary law. The court pointed out that the issue of the determination under ordinary law of the fair compensation due in respect of the property in question remained unprejudiced by the constitutional proceedings.

Nevertheless one must take note of the line taken by the Constitutional Court in MIFSUD V BONELLO.[12] The FHCC(CJ) had liquidated compensation for a breach of article 34 of the Constitution using the multiplier method ordinarily used in tort-based cases. In denying any award under the head of pecuniary damages, the Constitutional Court took note of an ordinary case pending against the respondents to the constitutional proceedings, namely, an action for damages which had failed at first instance on the grounds of prescription, and in respect of which an appeal was pending. The Constitutional Court took the line that pecuniary damages can only be claimed in a constitutional action where it would be possible for these to be awarded in a civil action. If the action for civil damages were time-barred, therefore, a court of constitutional jurisdiction could not make an award under this head either. The court consequently refrained from making an award under this head, allowing the appeal in the civil proceedings to take its course. It liquidated moral damages *arbitrio boni viri* with the only indication of the basis for its calculations being that it took the circumstances of the case into consideration in assessing the quantum. No indication was given of the reason for which the court felt obliged to act within civil law strictures in the awarding of pecuniary compensation for a violation of a fundamental human right protected by the Constitution and Convention.

Chapter 4 – Section 3 – What Ordinary Remedies Exist for Delay in Judicial Proceedings?

At first glance the possibilities are several. The courts of constitutional jurisdiction themselves have drawn the attention of applicants to the existence, within ordinary law, of a number of remedies which could address their grievances both in regard to anticipated delay as well as in regard to delay already incurred. Where what is sought is the avoidance of anticipated delay, then a party should simply request the sitting court to take measures to uphold his rights, and only where such court fails to take counteractive measures should a human rights action be filed against the state.

In SPITERI V THE HON. PRIME MINISTER[13] the court noted that even mere registration of a party's opposition to delay which would be caused by an adjournment or other measure requested had been considered an ordinary remedy on another occasion.[14] In FENECH V COMMISSIONER OF LANDS,[15] which was drawn on in several subsequent judgments, the court made reference to the possibility of having recourse to the ordinary courts to oblige the Commissioner of Lands to act within a time limit to perform the action upon which further steps were predicated, in the context of expropriation proceedings. In XUEREB V REGISTRAR OF COURTS ET[16] the court clearly pointed towards the possibility of an ordinary action for damages in tort as a possible remedy for the delay occasioned by the defendant to the main proceedings. It is this last possibility that we shall be examining hereunder.

Chapter 4 – Section 4 – Ordinary Remedies for Delay in Judicial Proceedings – The Action for Damages in Tort

4.4.1 The legitimate defendant

Any individual can be held responsible for being at fault in causing damage to another individual, whether by act or omission. An action for tortious liability arising out of delay caused in the context of judicial proceedings could therefore be directed against any private individual or even against the state itself or its agents, but could only succeed where damage has been caused through delay occasioned by the defendant who is 'at fault' for such delay. Ultimately, what is relevant is not who was *a party* to the main proceedings, but rather *who can be held responsible for having caused damage to the plaintiff in accordance with the ordinary rules of tortious liability.* As in constitutional cases, where the civil action is directed against the state, the legitimate defendant remains the attorney general, in accordance with the general rules established by article 181B[17] of the Code of Organisation and Civil Procedure.[18]

4.4.2 The subject matter of the judicial demand

The test of whether there has been 'unreasonable' delay as construed for the purposes of Article 6 and Article 39 is no longer relevant in the same way in the context of a tort-based action. While the question as to whether the delay incurred was sufficiently excessive as to amount to a violation of the plaintiff's rights under the Convention or Constitution may be of relevance,[19] the court will apply the ordinary rules relating to the establishment of liability in tort which are independent of the violation or otherwise of the plaintiff's fundamental human rights. Otherwise stated, liability in tort may still be found for delay in judicial proceedings where the delay was not so unreasonable as to cause a violation of the applicant's rights.

Where there is no such actual or anticipated violation therefore, it is clear that the only avenue available for damage incurred by a party *is* an action for damages in tort. A tort-based action is also the only remedy where the delay in question, albeit sufficiently excessive to amount to a violation of the applicant's rights, is not imputable to the state, such as where it was occasioned by the opposing party and where the court acted with due diligence by taking positive measures to uphold the rights of the other parties. Where the delay is so extensive, however, as to also amount to a violation of the applicant's fundamental human rights, and such delay *is* attributable to the state, then issues relating to the interplay between civil and constitutional remedies will arise. We shall be exploring this latter possibility in some detail.

In a human rights context, in BLASCHEM (MALTA) LIMITED V ATTORNEY GENERAL ET the court distinguished ordinary delay from a more serious form of delay which would amount to a breach of the reasonable time requirement prescribed by Article 6, holding that in matters of the transcription of evidence which were not completed within the provided time frame, even if delay were proved, since in this case the delay involved a few days or weeks, this sort of delay could *never* result in a breach of Article 6. This reasoning seems also to lie at the basis of the case of VELLA V THE HON. PRIME MINISTER ET[20] where the delay complained of was a single ten month-long adjournment. It is unfortunate, even in light of the fact that only unreasonable delays of a minimum level of severity will cause a breach of the applicant's fundamental human rights, that the court couched its words in such absolute terms.[21]

In a tort law context on the other hand, whether the delay caused was of a few days, a few months or longer yet, this can never be said to be below what is 'reasonable', as in civil law there is no threshold of reasonableness,[22] neither any minimum level of severity which need be attained. While the author respectfully submits that even in a human rights context there may be cases where the urgency of the subject matter renders even an otherwise expeditious hearing unreasonable in the circumstances, this is likely to be the exceptional case, rather than the rule. In a tort law context however, where the exigencies of commerce may require the quick resolution of a dispute, where creditors may require urgent action to safeguard their interests through the issue of precautionary warrants, where defendants themselves may require expeditious review pursuant to a demand for the issue of a counter warrant, where the court of voluntary jurisdiction may be urgently required to rule on a matter where any delay may result in a *de facto* resolution of the dispute in family law matters, as well as countless other scenarios which one may envisage, it seems reasonable to conclude that where a private party uses delay tactics or where the state is responsible for delay which causes damage to an individual, even if this would not be sufficiently grave (or rather, so 'unreasonable') as to amount to a violation of the applicant's rights under article 39 of the Constitution or Article 6 of the Convention, the entity responsible for such delay may be found liable in tort. Delay which is not 'unreasonable' may still cause damage and engender liability if it is in breach of the level of diligence required of the defendant by law.

Ultimately therefore, the questions which must be asked in a tort law context are the following:

i   Did the delay in the proceedings cause damage?
ii Was the delay imputable to the acts or omissions of the defendant?
iii Was the defendant at fault (in breach of the level of diligence imposed by law on the defendant) and/or in breach of a duty imposed by law?

4.4.3 The legal basis

The proper legal basis for a tortious action for damages on the basis of the Civil Code is predicated on whether the defendant to the action is the state or a private party. In addition to the legal bases which shall be examined in relation to private parties, which are also applicable where the state is cited as defendant, where the defendant is the state there exist other applicable bases in the Civil Code out of which the liability of a private citizen could not arise. This is simply due to the fact that while every entity, including the state, is liable for damage occurring through fault, the state is subject to specific and additional legal obligations including the duty to uphold the fundamental human rights of the citizen. A private party therefore has a different level of diligence incumbent upon them and the concept of 'fault' cannot be construed in the same way in regard to a private parties as it can in regard to the state.

Where the defendant is the state

> Any person who, with or without intent to injure, voluntarily or through negligence, imprudence, or want of attention, is guilty of any act or omission constituting a breach of the duty imposed by law, shall be liable for any damage resulting therefrom.
> – Civil Code of the laws of Malta, article 1033

> The Human Rights and Fundamental Freedoms shall be, and be enforceable as, part of the Law of Malta.
> – Ch 319 of the laws of Malta, article 3(1)

If the European Convention is, *via* Chapter 319, part of, and enforceable as part of, the law of Malta, then a breach of Article 6, which imposes a duty on the state to safeguard the rights therein enshrined, falls within the wording of the phrase 'a breach of the duty imposed by law' and the state would be liable for any damage resulting therefrom pursuant to article 1033 of the Civil Code. We must recall however that this action alone is *not* an effective remedy for the purposes of redressing a violation of Article 6, as the courts in Malta have never expressly liquidated moral damages in respect of the finding of liability in tort.[23] The implications of this emerge clearly from a reading of SÜRMELI,[24] wherein the Strasbourg Court dismissed the state's preliminary objection of non-exhaustion of domestic remedies which was founded, *inter alia*, on the fact that the applicants had not had recourse to a civil action for damages. The Grand Chamber noted in this regard that such a remedy was not effective for the purposes of Article 13, since the court would not have been able to make an award in respect of non-pecuniary damage as the courts of constitutional jurisdiction could, and that in length-of-proceedings cases, damages are likely to arise mainly under this head. From a formal perspective, one must also bear in mind that the only court competent to take cognisance of an alleged breach of a fundamental human right (whether incurred, ongoing or likely to occur) is the First Hall in its constitutional competence.

Where the defendant is either a private party or the state

It would appear that a private party cannot be found liable for failing to exercise diligence in upholding the fundamental human rights of another private party on the basis of article 1033[25] of the Civil Code, as a private party has no duty to actively safeguard the right of other parties to a hearing without unreasonable delay. Action may however be taken against such party on the basis of the general rules regulating tortious liability set out in the sections of the Civil Code. A claim against a private party could be based on abuse of procedural rights[26] arising out of an interpretation *a contrariu sensu* of article 1030,[27] or even on the basis of article 1031, which sets out the general principle whereby liability ensues from damage occurring through fault.[28]

Clearly, where obstructionist or temporising tactics are used, issues relating to abuse of procedural rights could arise, while where a plaintiff institutes a case and fails to conduct the proceedings with due diligence to the detriment of the defendant, this may well fall within the definition of fault provided in article 1032(1) whereby: 'a person shall be deemed to be in fault if, in his own acts, he does not use the prudence, diligence, and attention of a bonus paterfamilias.'

It must be recalled that the state may equally be found to have caused damage through fault on the basis of these provisions. However, additional considerations apply where the defendant is the state, such as the level of diligence applicable which may be higher than that required of a private party, even aside from considerations on the basis of Chapter 319. Qualifying the general rule set out in article 1032(1), section 1032(2) provides that: 'No person shall, in the absence of an express provision of the law, be liable for any damage caused by want of prudence, diligence, or attention in a higher degree.' One such provision of law which imposes a higher degree of diligence is section 9 of The Court Practice and Procedure and Good Order Rules[29] which imposes a duty on the Registrar, Civil Court and Tribunals, in creating the list according to article 194 of the Code of Organisation and Civil Procedure, to 'ensure that, *as far as possible*' cases are heard and decided in chronological order according to the date of filing of the application initiating the case, to ensure that only as many cases are inserted into the list as a judge or magistrate considers he can deal with in any particular sitting and, finally, to give priority to cases of retrial, spoliation suits, contempt of court, appeals from decisions of the First Hall Civil Court (Family Section), cases dealing with recognition and enforcement of foreign judgments, arbitration cases and cases which of their nature require to be treated with greater expeditiousness. It would seem that the phrase 'as far as possible' imposes a higher degree of diligence than that required by section 1032(1).

4.4.4 Principles emerging from select tort-based cases involving damage occasioned by delay and imputable to the defendant

FIORINO D'ORO V DIRETTUR TAT-TOROQ[30]

In FIORINO D'ORO V DIRETTUR TAT-TOROQ the government's responsibility in tort arose out of the concept of abuse of rights resulting from a reading *a contrariu sensu* of section 1030 coupled with damage ensuing from fault on the basis of article 1031 of the Civil Code. While acknowledging that a private citizen may be subjected to certain measures in the public interest, the state had to answer for the lack of diligence in carrying out the roadworks in question, which were causing 'more prejudice that is reasonably required' due to the ensuing delay. One could argue by analogy that where the government has undertaken legal action against a private person, that person must not be subjected to more prejudice than is reasonably to be expected by allowing the proceedings to be unduly protracted.[31]

In the context of abuse of procedural rights therefore, what is 'reasonable' may be relevant in order to establish where ordinary use ends and abuse starts. Clearly, this test cannot be identified with the concept of 'reasonableness' under Article 6, for that concept refers to the length of the proceedings and not whether the conduct of a party can be considered 'reasonable'. Otherwise stated, a short period of delay could constitute an abuse of rights (as it is not reasonable in terms of tort law) without causing a violation of the rights of the applicant, as the overall length of proceedings would still be 'reasonable' (in terms of human rights law). Conversely, the rights of the applicant may have been violated due to the unreasonable length of proceedings without any abuse of rights (or unreasonable use of rights) having occurred.

Where a contractual relationship exists between the parties, the test may be simplified if the defendant was bound to act within a specified time limit and failed to do so, as in the case of BUSUTTIL V XUEREB AND AX CONSTRUCTION LIMITED[32] where a private contractor was found responsible for the delay ensuing from roadworks, or ZAMMIT V BORG BARTHET NOE[33] in the context of a delay of ninety nine days exceeding the deadline stipulated in the contract. In the context of judicial proceedings, a party may have been obliged under contract to perform within a specific time limit, but instead instituted a case, vexatiously and without a well-founded basis, simply to defer performance. In such a case, clearly, the delay which occasions the damage does so irrespective of whether the overall length of proceedings was 'reasonable' in Convention terms. What renders the delay 'unreasonable' is the deadline specified in the contract.

ATTARD V ATTARD[34]

The concept of abuse of rights under the law of Malta is sufficiently broad to encompass abuse of procedural rights of litigation, as demonstrated in ATTARD V ATTARD which involved a finding of liability in respect of legal action taken arbitrarily, causing delay in the payment of the sums due to the plaintiff. The abuse hinged not on the decision to contest but, rather, on the fact that a valid court judgment was being contested without any founded basis for such action, which was exclusively aimed at delaying its enforcement. The First Hall awarded damages for deprivation of the use of one's money, on the basis of article 1047[35] of the Civil Code, interpreting 'malicious' not as awareness of the harmful consequences of the act, but as requiring proof of the *animus nocendi*. The court liquidated damages as interest at the rate of 8 per cent from the date on which the plaintiffs had sent a judicial intimation to the defendants.

Had a court, in the context of delay attributable to abuse of procedural rights of litigation causing damage to a plaintiff, to embrace the alternate wording of section 1047(2) which requires proof that the 'party causing the damage ... had particularly the intention of causing him such other damage, *or* if such damage is the immediate and direct consequence of the injured party having been so deprived of the use of his own money', then the damages due could extend to include 'compensation for any other damage sustained by him, including every loss of earnings'. Even as interpreted by the court pursuant to ATTARD V ATTARD, however, it is clear that abuse of procedural rights, even if not 'malicious' in the sense intended by the court, *viz.* without any *animus nocendi*, can entail tortious liability.

BALDACCHINO V COMMISSIONER OF LANDS[36]

Abuse of rights arising out of delay in expropriation procedures, which were ultimately abandoned altogether, lay at the basis of the liability incurred by the Commissioner of Lands and Enemalta Corporation in BALDACCHINO V COMMISSIONER OF LANDS. This judgment perfectly instantiates the increasing overlap and interaction between ordinary and 'extraordinary human rights' actions, for the Court of Appeal confirmed that the violation of a fundamental human right constitutes well-founded grounds for an aggravation of fault found against the state in a tort-based action.

The Court of Appeal did not go so far as to say that the violation of a fundamental human right, in and of itself, constituted a basis for the awarding of damages in tort, although it *did* accept plaintiff's argument that as a breach of Chapter 319 had been found in the same circumstances in MINTOFF ET,[37] that this should be considered in the awarding of damages in tort. The court preferred to take the stance that such a breach could amount to an *aggravation* of the liability incurred through fault, so that the usual method for the establishment of responsibility in tort should be relied on, but where those acts also amount to a violation of the fundamental human rights of the individual, then this factor would amount to an aggravation:

> Insofar as one limits himself to the point that the actions of the respondents may have breached the fundamental human rights of the plaintiff, and that, therefore, this may serve as an additional reason for qualifying the respondent's actions as 'illegal and abusive', this reasoning is well-founded.[38]

The court would perhaps have more readily accepted the argument that as Chapter 319 was incorporated as part of the ordinary law of Malta, the breach of an obligation therein contained could give rise to damage arising through a breach of a duty imposed by law, as per section 1033.

Notes

1. Cf. MIFSUD V BONELLO (App no. 176/1987/2).
2. The discussion of the horizontal effects of human rights *ut sic* would go beyond the scope of this study, but see MIFSUD V BONELLO (App no. 176/1987/2) and CONSIGLIO V AIR SUPPLIES AND CATERING COMPANY LIMITED (App no. 526/95).
3. App no. 742/2000/1.
4. 'In regard to the position of the respondent Dorothy Xuereb in these Constitutional procedures, this person is there merely for the formal completeness of the proceedings, and for any eventual interest she may have, as in proceedings such as the ones at hand, it is only the state which is responsible for the country's institutions, and not the private individual.' p. 14.
5. 'And although it is evident that the respondent contributed substantially to the delay in question, and that the court took no action against her to prevent her from doing so, nor any other action which it deemed fit to take to ensure that there would not be such delay, the respondent cannot be found responsible for a violation of Article 39(2) of the Constitution of Malta or of Article 6 of the European Convention, as these two Articles bind only the state. *If at all, and if the case so merits, it is up to the applicant to seek damages against the respondent, if he feels that he may have a right to do so. Nevertheless, this Court cannot take any provision against the respondent.*' (emphasis added) p. 14.
6. See Chapter 2, Section 1, *The Strasbourg Court's Method of Examination*, Sub-Section 1, *The framework for an examination of the merits of an alleged violation of Article 6*.
7. ZARB V ATTORNEY GENERAL (App no. 6/2002/1), SPITERI V ATTORNEY GENERAL (App no. 5/2002/1).
8. Ref no. Volume 80 (1996) Part no. 1 Section P. 17.
9. Joseph Said Pullicino, 'The Ombudsman: His Role in Human Rights Promotion and Protection' in David E. Zammit (ed.), *Maltese Perspectives on Human Rights* (University of Malta, Malta 2008) pp. 118–146.
10. XUEREB V ATTORNEY GENERAL (App no. 742/2000/1), VISUAL AND SOUND COMMUNCATIONS LIMITED V COMMISSIONER OF POLICE AND ATTORNEY GENERAL.
11. App no. 59/2005/1.

Case Study Based on the Legal System of Malta, Part II 93

12 App no. 176/1987/2.
13 Referred to in SCICLUNA V ATTORNEY GENERAL ET (App no. 463/1994/1).
14 This would not, however, qualify as an effective remedy for the purposes of Article 13, See Chapter 1, *Preliminary Pleas and Fundamental Concepts Relevant to Length-of-Proceedings Cases Brought Before the European Court of Human Rights*.
15 App no. 31/2007/1.
16 App no. 742/2000/1.
17 See *Statutes*.
18 It is settled law that the legitimate defendant in length-of-proceedings cases, whether criminal or civil, in Malta, is the Attorney General, *vide*, amongst many other authorities: in regard to civil proceedings: BLASCHEM (MALTA) LIMITED V ATTORNEY GENERAL ET (App no. 22/2003/1), SAID ET V ATTORNEY GENERAL (App no. 10/2007/1) and in regard to criminal proceedings: XUEREB V ATTORNEY GENERAL (App no. 742/2000/1). Pursuant to ACT XXIV of 1995 the issue is today regulated specifically by Article 181B of Chapter 12 which vests all residual representative standing in matters where a head of department does not exist, in the Attorney General. See FENECH ET V COMMISSIONER OF LANDS ET (App no. 31/2007/1): the state must answer for violations committed by its judicial branch, and the state, according to law, is represented by the Attorney General: '... the Court considers that the question of who needs to respond for an allegation of the breach of a fundamental human right is tied to both the nature of the breach as well as the appropriate remedy which could be given in respect of that breach' (LAY LAY CO. LTD. V MALTA ENVIRONMENT AND PLANNING AUTHORITY ET (App no. 30/2004/1). Even pre-1995, the Constitutional Court had clarified that in constitutional matters there are several types of legitimate defendants, namely, those who are directly responsible for the breach, those who, albeit not being directly responsible, can be made to answer for it, and finally those parties called in as defendants as they are in some manner involved. The Attorney General falls within the second category of defendants. There may, depending on the subject matter of the main proceedings, be other legitimate defendants whose *locus standi* will be upheld. See G. Mifsud Bonnici *Constitutional Procedure Relative to Fundamental Rights and Freedoms 1964–2000*.
19 See, for instance, the position taken by the court in BALDACCHINO V COMMISSIONER OF LANDS ET (App no. 273/1993/2) where the violation of a fundamental human right was held to aggravate the damages due following the finding of liability established in the first place using the general rules applicable to a tort-based action.
20 Ref no. Volume 74 (1990) Part no. 1 Section P. 159.
21 See, for instance, X V FRANCE (1992) where the urgency of proceedings was dictated by the life expectancy of the applicant.
22 Although in the context of abuse of procedural rights, what is 'reasonable' may be relevant in order to establish where ordinary use ends and the abuse starts; see Chapter 4, *Ordinary Remedies for Delay in Judicial Proceedings – The Action for Damages in Tort*, Sub-Section 4, *Principles emerging from select tort-based cases involving damage occasioned by delay and imputable to the defendant*.
23 In this regard see analysis of case law in Chapter 4, Section 4, *Ordinary Remedies for Delay in Judicial Proceedings – The Action for Damages in Tort*, Sub-Section 3, *The legal basis*; see also Claude Micallef Grimaud, *The Rationale for Excluding Moral Damages from the Maltese Civil Code: A Historical and Legal Investigation*.
24 Text to n 36 (Chapter 1) and 115 (Chapter 2).
25 Nevertheless one must take note of the interesting debate which stems from the position of the FHCC(CJ) and Constitutional Court in CONSIGLIO V AIR SUPPLIES AND

CATERING COMPANY LIMITED in regard to the scenario where a private party (such as an employer through disciplinary proceedings) actually 'determines' the civil rights and obligations of another private party. On what basis could the determination of rights within a reasonable time be upheld in such a case? The Constitution only requires that 'the case shall be given a fair hearing within a reasonable time' where such case is held before a 'court or other adjudicating authority prescribed by law'. It would seem therefore that any right of recourse would fall within the realm of ordinary law.

26 See ATTARD V ATTARD (App no. 214/2000).
27 Civil Code, article 1030: 'Any person who makes use, within the proper limits, of a right competent to him, shall not be liable for any damage which may result therefrom.'
28 'Every person, however, shall be liable for the damage which occurs through his fault.'
29 S.L. 12.09: see *Statutes*.
30 App no. 1781/2001/1.
31 This is reminiscent of the concept of a 'disproportionate burden' developed by the Strasbourg Court in a human rights context, see for instance STEEL AND MORRIS.
32 App no. 1728/1995/1.
33 App no. 1768/1993/1.
34 App no. 214/2000.
35 Civil Code article 1047. See *Statutes*.
36 App no. 273/1993/2.
37 App no. 470/1994/2.
38 P. 50 [22].

5 Case Study Based on the Legal System of Malta, Part III
Conclusions

The considerations discussed in Chapters 3 and 4, derived from our study of how Convention principles have been put to work in practice in order to provide redress for delay in judicial proceedings, have led the author to postulate a number of areas of concern for the legal system of Malta which merit individual consideration.

The First Problem – Difficulties in the Awarding of Damages in Tortious Liability Cases Where a Person resorts to the Ordinary Courts for Redress

It is significantly harder to speak meaningfully about compensation where personal emotions, pain, frustration and anxiety are at stake. Neither is it easy, by any means, to quantify loss of opportunity where delay has prevented a person from freely pursuing their activities without being shackled while awaiting judgment. It is, on the other hand, somewhat easier to quantify pecuniary damage in commercial contexts, where one can make projections by reference to historical performance or draw on readily available data regarding the relevant activity. The difficulty in quantification, nevertheless, does not in any manner detract from the reality of the loss suffered. While the author hopes that more targeted and creative methods for the prevention and remedying of delay will, in time, be developed by adjudicators,[1] if we merely rely on the guidance issued to date by the European Court of Human Rights, it is irrefutable that in the context of the length of proceedings, attempting to compensate for delay without resorting to a mixture of both pecuniary and non-pecuniary damage renders a perverse picture of what is being compensated for.

Clearly, even in regard to the quantification of pecuniary compensation, a mathematical calculation is not always possible, as there are cases where damage incurred cannot be assessed by reference to company accounts, as in FIORINO D'ORO V DIRECTOR OF ROADS, nor by reference to expert evaluations, as in BALDACCHINO V COMMISSIONER OF LANDS. It is clear that while the above questions are relatively simple to apply to delays which have occasioned pecuniary damage in a commercial or property rights context, in particular where a penalty clause for delay may have been specified,[2] there are innumerable other forms of damage which simply cannot be compensated for without resorting to the concept of moral damages. Indeed, even in the context of commercial losses occasioned by delay, the courts have at times preferred to award compensation *arbitrio boni viri* due to dissatisfaction with the evidence adduced to support the calculations proffered by the plaintiff.[3]

The Court of Appeal noted in BALDACCHINO V COMMISSIONER OF LANDS:

> In the case at hand, the injustice stemming from the fact that the plaintiff was left in a state of uncertainty ('in limbo') and the resultant frustration, are present. To the Court, all of this, even aside from considerations of a purely Constitution or Convention-based nature, amounts to abusive action in terms of our ordinary civil law.[4]

The sections of the Civil Code of Malta have been interpreted in such a way that where delay in the execution of an otherwise legitimate activity renders the action abusive in terms of law or renders the defendant liable through fault, then the damages to be awarded should reflect the 'actual loss', whether of earnings or of property value, across the span of the period in question. The parameters for this calculation are set out in section 1045. In the context of delay in judicial proceedings, the questions asked by the courts would be the general guidelines for establishing *damnum emergens* and *lucrum cessans*:

i   What actual loss has been caused by the delay?
ii What (additional) expense has the plaintiff been compelled to incur in consequence of the delay?
iii What loss of actual wages or other earnings were occasioned by the delay?
iv Did the delay cause any future loss arising from permanent incapacity, total or partial?[5] The court will look to the nature and degree of the incapacity and the condition of the injured party.

The question which one must ask, however, is whether alternate kinds of losses arising out of delay can be compensated for effectively, independently of patrimonial damage. In the context of a civil action where the courts routinely refuse to award moral compensation, the answer is clearly in the negative, even aside from the difficulties in the quantification of pecuniary compensation where delay is at stake.

The Second Problem – No Single Effective Domestic Remedy for Violations of the Reasonable Time Requirement under Article 6

Simply stated, in Malta, the courts of constitutional jurisdiction do not award pecuniary damages, and the civil courts do not award moral damages,[6] in length-of-proceedings cases. Furthermore, the courts of constitutional jurisdiction have, in the overwhelming majority of length-of-proceedings cases, failed to award sufficient non-pecuniary compensation when the sufficiency of the redress awarded is assessed in the light of the case law of the European Court of Human Rights.[7] If such cases and awards had to be challenged before the Strasbourg Court, the victim status of the applicant would be upheld, and an aggravated violation of Article 6 found on the merits.

The situation in Malta in regard to the awarding of insufficient non-pecuniary or moral compensation is somewhat analogous to the facts out of which the violations found against Italy in the Scordino-Type Cases arose. In those cases, the Pinto remedies aimed to provide a domestic compensatory remedy for length-of-proceedings cases. The European Court of Human Rights found such remedies to be effective for the purposes of ECHR Article 13, and, therefore, in need of exhaustion for the purposes of ECHR Article 35, as it did in relation to the remedies found in the Maltese legal system in ZARB. A series of violations of Article 6 were subsequently found, in the Scordino-Type Cases, due to the fact that the Italian state failed, *in practice*, to provide sufficient compensation in respect of breaches and to effectively enforce those findings within reasonable time periods. The Court stressed, in those cases, that while the state has discretion in the awarding of non-pecuniary compensation, the ultimate quantum of redress must not be 'manifestly unreasonable' when assessed by reference to its own case law, on pain of a finding of an aggravated violation.

It is submitted that the First Hall of the Civil Court of Malta in its constitutional competence should not decline to exercise its jurisdiction on the basis of the existence at ordinary law of effective remedies which the applicant could have resorted to in respect of an alleged breach of Article 6 due to the unreasonable length of proceedings, as there is no remedy within the ordinary law of Malta which, both in theory and in practice, awards adequate non-pecuniary damages in respect of the pain and suffering occasioned by delay.[8] Furthermore, an individual who has lodged a human rights-based complaint to the First Hall of the Civil Court in its constitutional competence would still be obliged to resort to the ordinary civil courts in order to obtain redress for pecuniary loss incurred as a result of delay, and has been directed to do so on a number of instances by the courts of constitutional jurisdiction.[9]

Therefore, if one has regard to the principles that:

i *In regard to the provision of adequate state acknowledgement for a breach of Article 6 in length-of-proceedings cases:* While a state has a margin of appreciation as to how to award non-pecuniary compensation in respect of a breach, the sum ultimately awarded must not be 'manifestly unreasonable' by reference to Strasbourg Jurisprudence.[10]

ii *In regard to the requirements of an 'effective remedy' for the purposes of Articles 13 and 35 of the Convention:*

- A remedy is not effective for the purposes of Article 13 if moral damages cannot be awarded when resort is made to it.[11]

- Requiring applicants to have recourse to more than one avenue of redress at a single stage of the proceedings has been held not to satisfy the requirements of Article 13.[12]
- A remedy must be certain both in theory and in practice and this practical effectiveness is usually assessed by reference to other domestically delivered decisions.[13]

One is obliged to conclude that, in Malta, as the courts of constitutional jurisdiction consistently award sums of non-pecuniary compensation which are manifestly unreasonable by reference to the Strasbourg Court's case law and refer plaintiffs to ordinary remedies to recoup any pecuniary damages incurred as a result of the delay, and the ordinary civil courts do not award moral damages in practice, there is in the legal system, no single effective compensatory remedy which satisfies Convention requirements, a situation which amounts to a structural failure in terms of Article 13 of the Convention. This is being said in full knowledge of the fact that the Strasbourg Court has held[14] that the constitutional redress which can be sought in Malta for a violation of the reasonable time requirement of Article 6 of the Convention satisfies the requirements of Article 13 as, although insufficient in the particular case, there is no legal limitation on the quantum or nature of the compensation which can be awarded by the First Hall or Constitutional Court.

The Third Problem – A Theoretical Overlap Yet Practical Inexistence of Effective Remedies Where Delay is Imputable to the State, Causing Both Damages in Tort and a Breach of Rights

There is, clearly, a theoretical overlap in the possible damages, both non-pecuniary (or moral) and pecuniary which can be awarded where the state is at fault for delay in judicial proceedings and that delay amounts to a violation of a fundamental human right. This theoretical overlap attests to the confusion that exists currently between the relationship of the so-called 'extraordinary' constitutional, human-rights actions and ordinary civil law remedies.

It would seem that the overlap is more likely to occur, in practice, in regard to pecuniary damages, for the courts in Malta, both of constitutional[15] and of civil[16] jurisdiction, have already accepted that in ordinary tort cases pecuniary damages may be awarded for the damage incurred as a result of delay in judicial proceedings. One could argue that any moral damages due pursuant to a finding of a breach of a fundamental human right and any moral damages which could fall due by way of damages in tort have a different underlying cause, and that there is therefore no overlap. While that position is arguable in regard to non-pecuniary damage, it is clear that in regard to pecuniary damage, by which what would be compensated is financial loss incurred as a result of delay, any redress afforded by the courts of constitutional jurisdiction would cover the very same loss as the damages awarded by the ordinary civil courts in a tort-based action.

An attempt to provide a solution was given by the court in MISFUD V BONELLO, where the Constitutional Court ruled that pecuniary damages for a breach of a fundamental human right could only be given where they could be awarded on the basis of ordinary law, but there is actually nothing in the law which renders the rules regulating civil damages applicable to the 'adequate redress' which the courts of constitutional jurisdiction can provide. Besides, if an application is filed to the Strasbourg Court, should that court also take cognizance of the domestic rules regulating the awarding of civil damages in assessing whether any pecuniary compensation is due in respect of a breach? Clearly not.

The Strasbourg Court has already envisaged this possibility in the awarding of pecuniary compensation. In the case of AZZOPARDI, where the length of proceedings aspect of the case was imbricated with a breach of the right to peaceful enjoyment of possessions under Article 1 of Protocol 1 due to delay in expropriation proceedings, the Court decided to award pecuniary compensation itself, noting that the proceedings had been pending for forty years and that delaying this payment any further by awaiting the outcome of such proceedings would be itself unreasonable. With regard to the possibility of an overlap with any future award of a domestic court, it held that: 'There is no risk that the applicant will receive pecuniary compensation twice, as the national jurisdictions would inevitably take note of this Court's award when deciding the case'.[17]

The possibility of such an award being made by the European Court of Human Rights in a purely length-of-proceedings context merits some further consideration. Under the heading of 'just satisfaction', pursuant to ECHR Article 41, the Strasbourg Court is capable of awarding, and does award, both moral and pecuniary compensation in respect of Convention breaches. When is pecuniary compensation awarded by the Strasbourg Court? Harris, O'Boyle and Warbrick note that:

> For an award of pecuniary damage to be made the applicant must demonstrate, to the Court's satisfaction, that there is causal link between the violation and any financial loss alleged. This is seen as a matter of proof rather than speculation. It is easily established when there had been a taking of property but significantly more difficult in other contexts. ... The Court has been prepared to compensate for lost earnings ... where there have been lost earnings flowing from the Convention breach. Claims for pecuniary damage will normally arise in cases involving property under Article 1 of Protocol 1.[18]

Van Dijk and Van Hoof note that:

> Injury pursuant to Article 41 can be made good, as far as it was 'incurred by the applicants in order to try to prevent the violation found by the Court or to obtain redress therefore' and only if, in particular, three

criteria are fulfilled: costs and expenses susceptible of satisfaction must have been (1) 'actually incurred' (2) 'necessarily incurred' and (3) 'reasonable as to quantum'. These criteria apply to costs described as material damage as well as to costs referable to proceedings.[19]

Reference to cases such as AZZOPARDI and SCHEMBRI AND OTHERS also renders a clear picture of the criteria which the Court has established for the calculation of pecuniary compensation in cases where property has been expropriated, and where time has exacerbated the loss incurred by the applicants.[20] It is clear that the basis for the calculation of pecuniary compensation is substantially proximate to the exercise carried out by the ordinary courts in a tort-based case to quantify the damages due.

While it is not usual for the Strasbourg Court to award pecuniary compensation in length-of-proceedings cases,[21] for prejudice is held mostly to arise in respect of the frustration, suffering and anxiety occasioned by delay under the head of non-pecuniary damages, clearly such an award is possible and has, on occasion, been given. In LAINE[22] for instance, both pecuniary and non-pecuniary damages were awarded in respect of delays resulting from compulsory liquidation proceedings brought against the applicant's company.[23] The applicant had demanded pecuniary damages for car stocks which were scrapped and sold as scrap *pendente lite* as well as compensation for profits lost, aside from moral damages. On the basis of the documents available to it, including receipts of the cars scrapped, it awarded to the applicant the sums claimed for failure to realise the assets[24] and an additional sum for profits not recovered.[25] It did not award any damages for loss of profits, as it agreed with the government that the applicant could have had recourse to domestic remedies in this regard by requesting the domestic tribunal to continue trading. In addition to costs and provision for interest to fall due until execution, the Court therefore awarded a total of € 50,155 by way of pecuniary damages and € 7,500 by way of moral damages.

In LECHNER AND HESS[26] a global assessment was made in respect of non-pecuniary damage *as well as* pecuniary damages reflecting a 'loss of real opportunities' in the context of delay in civil proceedings, pending which the property at stake in the civil action was sold to satisfy creditor claims, thus depriving the applicants of the possibility of returning such property to the vendors who were defendants to the civil action. The Commission had held that:

> The auction deprived the applicants of any chance of winning their case and thus of avoiding having to pay court costs and lawyers' fees. In any event, part of these latter expenses could have been eliminated if the relevant tribunals had acted with proper expedition.[27]

This reasoning was upheld by the Strasbourg Court, which felt that while compliance with the reasonable time requirement would not necessarily have prevented the auctioning of the property in question, 'the applicants did suffer, on account of the consequences of the length of the proceedings, some loss of real opportunities which justifies an award of just satisfaction in the present case'.[28] It is clear that the second limb of the Commission's reasoning, namely the awarding of pecuniary compensation for the additional court costs and lawyer's fees sustained as a result of delay, could justify the awarding of pecuniary compensation in any case where a violation of the reasonable time requirement is found.

Other categories of cases where violations in length-of-proceedings cases are likely to translate into pecuniary damages include delays in commercial contexts, or where property rights are involved, such as where the unreasonable delay occurs in enforcement proceedings, a situation which has been held by the Strasbourg Court to also occasion a violation of the right to the protection of property under Article 1 of the Convention's First Protocol.[29]

Strictly speaking, nothing in the positive law of the legal system of Malta bars the courts, whether of civil or constitutional jurisdiction, from awarding both kinds of damages,[30] as in a tort law context 'actual loss'[31] is not defined in the Civil Code, while the Constitution and Convention give unfettered powers to the courts to redress human rights violations.[32] As we have observed, however, in practice, in length-of-proceedings cases the courts of constitutional jurisdiction award moral damages only, and the ordinary courts award only pecuniary damages for *damnum emergens* and *lucrum cessans*. The actual situation, therefore, is one where there are *multiple remedies which are theoretically capable of providing effective redress, but not a single one which effectively does so in practice.*

Killing Three Problematic Birds with One Effective Stone: A Proposed Solution

As the law of Malta stands, the First Hall in its constitutional competence has exclusive jurisdiction to take cognisance of alleged Convention violations[33] and is the proper forum where a breach of rights is alleged in a length-of-proceedings context, whether already incurred, ongoing or likely to be incurred. All three problems envisaged above could be resolved effectively, in regard to delay which occasions a breach of Article 6, if the First Hall were to award *adequate* pecuniary *and* non-pecuniary damages. This would satisfy the requirements of Article 13, as the victim of a violation of the reasonable time requirement protected by Article 6 would have a single remedy, effective and certain both in theory and practice, to which recourse can be had and pursuant to which damages under both heads can be claimed.

If one were to accept that the state can be found liable in tort for having failed to uphold an individual's rights under the Convention pursuant to article 1033 of the Civil Code of Malta,[34] then it would be artificial to distinguish the consequences which would emanate from such a finding from the same finding in respect of the same facts, under the alternate label of a breach of rights, by the same court, exercising jurisdiction under a different competence. Yet, since the First Hall in its constitutional competence has exclusive jurisdiction in regard to alleged Convention violations, it seems that the most economical solution, compatible with the legislation of Malta as it stands today, would be for the First Hall in its constitutional competence, to award pecuniary damages, in addition to adequate moral damages, once a violation of Article 6 is found[35] rather than referring an applicant to the ordinary courts to recoup such damages.

Said Pullicino[36] refers to the compartmentalised approach which provides the parameters, or rather distinct competences, within which the First Hall is obliged to deal with breaches of fundamental rights as the 'straight jacket *iter* that the right of individual petition has to follow before specialised Courts with exclusive jurisdiction, constitutionally determined'. He is of the persuasion that this 'has led to the erroneous notion that the identification of a violation of a fundamental human right or its threat and its redress were exceptional circumstances that require an exceptional remedy.'

A multitude of persuasive arguments could be adduced to bear pressure on ordinary civil courts to award moral damages in cases where delay has occasioned very 'real' losses which can only be compensated by recourse to such a concept. Yet, one cannot discuss this issue within the same parameters as those applicable to identifying what adequate redress is due in respect of delay in judicial proceedings which occasions a breach of the European Convention on Human Rights. In such latter case, the case law of the European Court already unequivocally requires the provision of effective remedies for anticipated breaches, and requires states to compensate adequately for breaches already incurred. This obligation is incumbent upon states pursuant to their positive obligations under the Convention, which requires them to be active, and not passive, agents in regard to the prevention of anticipated violations, and the remedying of breaches in the process of being or which have already been incurred.

In regard to delay in judicial proceedings which occasions a breach of the reasonable time requirement protected by Article 6, unless and until the legal system of Malta provides a single remedy which is both capable of providing, and actually provides, adequate non-pecuniary and pecuniary compensation, in a timely manner, there exists within the legal system of Malta a structural failure in terms of Article 13.

Notes

1 See *Conclusion*.
2 ZAMMIT V BORG BARTHET NOE (App no. 1768/1993/1).
3 BUSUTTIL V ANGELO XUEREB ET (App no. 1728/1995/1).
4 P. 50 [22].
5 See MIFSUD V BONELLO (App no. 176/1987/2) in regard to the use of the multiplier method for the calculation of *lucrum cessans* for a violation of a fundamental human

right; See Chapter 4, Section 2, *Ordinary Remedies are Not Prejudiced by and Do Not Prejudice Constitutional Remedies*.
6 In this study 'moral' damages and 'non-pecuniary' damages are used to cover the same form of redress – as per FRANCIS SAID ET V ATTORNEY GENERAL (App no. 10/2007/1).
7 Cf. Chapter 2, Section 2, *Article 13: General Observations* and Section 3, *Case Study Based on the Legal System of Italy: The Scordino-Type Cases*, to Chapter 3, Section 2, *Overview of the Length-of-Proceedings Case Law of Malta and the Interpretation and Application of Convention Provisions by the Local Courts*.
8 See Chapter 1, Section 2, *Article 34 Loss of Victim Status – Incompatibility* Ratione Personae, Sub-Section 1, *Have the authorities acknowledged the violation, 'either expressly or in substance', and was that acknowledgment adequate?*; Text to n 36 (Chapter 1) and 115 (Chapter 2).
9 XUEREB V REGISTRAR OF COURTS ET (App no. 742/2000/1); in a human rights albeit not length-of-proceedings context, MIFSUD V BONELLO.
10 See Chapter 2, Section 3, *Case Study Based on the Legal System of Italy: The Scordino-Type Cases*.
11 See Chapter 1, Section 2, *Article 34 Loss of Victim Status – Incompatibility* Ratione Personae, Sub-Section 1, *Have the authorities acknowledged the violation, 'either expressly or in substance', and was that acknowledgment adequate?*; text to n 36 (Chapter 1) and 115 (Chapter 2).
12 See Chapter 1, Section 1, *Article 35(1) Exhaustion of (Effective) Domestic Remedies*, Sub-Section 4, *What forms of remedies has the Court considered to be effective and in need of exhaustion for the purposes of Article 35?*
13 See Chapter 1, Section 1, *Article 35(1) Exhaustion of (Effective) Domestic Remedies*, Sub-Section 1, *The general rules*.
14 ZARB.
15 See SAID ET V ATTORNEY GENERAL (App no. 10/2007/1) where the Court noted that 'the remedy which the First Hall (as well as this Court) may give as a remedy for delay can vary from a mere declaration to acknowledge a breach, to moral damages or, exceptionally, also to material damages …'
16 See Chapter 4, Section 4, *Ordinary Remedies for Delay in Judicial Proceedings – The Action for Damages in Tort*, Sub-Section 4, *Principles emerging from select tort-based cases involving damage occasioned by delay and imputable to the defendant*.
17 See also FRENDO RANDON AND OTHERS (App no. 2226/10) [77].
18 (Footnotes omitted) *Law of the European Convention on Human Rights* (2nd edition, Oxford University Press, Oxford 2009) at p. 859.
19 (Footnotes omitted) *Theory and Practice of the European Convention on Human Rights* (4th edition Intersentia, Oxford 2006) at p. 265. Reference made to LE COMPTE, VAN LEUVEN AND DE MEYERE [14], DUDGEON [14], PHILIS [76], MEGYERI [34], BARANOWSKI [82], SABEUR BEN ALI [49] and ILIJKOV [124].
20 See SCHEMBRI AND OTHERS at [55]: 'Indeed, according to the Court's standard practice in respect of just satisfaction, the estimated market value of lawfully expropriated land is that at the date of the expropriation. That amount will have to be converted to current value to offset the effects of inflation. Moreover, interest will have to be paid on this amount so as to offset, at least in part, the long period for which an applicant would have been deprived of the land … Only where the expropriation had been unlawful, just satisfaction should be in line with the principle of *restitutio in integrum*, if this is impossible, compensation for the loss of property requires an award of the current value of the land, increased solely by the appreciation brought about by the existence of the buildings …'
21 See Chapter 2, Section 4, *How does the European Court Calculate the Quantum of Compensation under Article 41?* Sub-Section 3, *Pecuniary compensation*.

22 LAINE.
23 The 'period to be considered' was of sixteen years and nine months including unjustified inactivity attributable to the authorities of approximately nine years and four months.
24 € 35,736.
25 € 14,418.
26 The civil proceedings in question had lasted over eight years and three months.
27 [62].
28 [64].
29 See Chapter 1, Section 2, *Article 34 Loss of Victim Status – Incompatibility* Ratione Personae, Sub-Section 2, *State failure to cause loss of victim status notwithstanding the affording of domestic redress* and Chapter 2, Section 1, *The Strasbourg Court's Method of Examination*, Sub-Section 2, *Guidance on the length of proceedings for the enforcement of judgments*.
30 In relation to the ordinary courts see MIFSUD V SUPRETENDENT CARMELO BONELLO ET (App no. 176/1987/2) Chapter 4, Section 2, *Ordinary Remedies are Not Prejudiced by and Do Not Prejudice Constitutional Remedies*: the Constitutional Court denied that the ordinary courts are capable of providing moral redress for pain and suffering, but noted that the courts of constitutional jurisdiction are capable of liquidating both moral compensation as well pecuniary or civil damages. Also see Claude Micallef Grimaud, *The Rationale for Excluding Moral Damages from the Maltese Civil Code: a Historical and Legal Investigation*.
31 Civil Code of Malta, article 1045.
32 See Chapter 3, Section 2, *Overview of the Length-of-Proceedings Case Law of Malta and the Interpretation and Application of Convention Provisions by the Local Courts*, Sub-Section 6, *Alternative forms of redress*.
33 See *Statutes*, Laws of Malta: Constitution, article 46 and Chapter 319, article 4. Cf. Said Pullicino, 'The Ombudsman: His Role in Human Rights Promotion and Protection' in David E. Zammit (ed.), *Maltese Perspectives on Human Rights* (University of Malta, Malta 2008) at p. 128.
34 See Chapter 4, Section 4, *Ordinary Remedies for Delay in Judicial Proceedings – The Action for Damages in Tort*, Sub-Section 2, *The subject matter of the judicial demand*.
35 As opposed to a 'split' action such as the upshot of MIFSUD V BONELLO where the Constitutional Court awarded moral damages but declined to award pecuniary damages in view of an action pending before the ordinary courts: see Chapter 4, Section 2, *Ordinary Remedies are Not Prejudiced by and Do Not Prejudice Constitutional Remedies*.
36 Joseph Said Pullincino, 'The Ombudsman: His Role in Human Rights Promotion and Protection' in David E. Zammit (ed.), *Maltese Perspectives on Human Rights* (University of Malta, Malta 2008) p. 122.

Conclusion

How does one compensate a parent for being unable to be there while their child grows up, having been deprived of custody pending the determination of separation or divorce proceedings? How does one compensate an individual for being unable to have children from a second marriage due to advanced age, where annulment proceedings in respect of the first marriage took excessively long?[1] How does one compensate a defendant to criminal proceedings, acquitted after a long and gruelling process which had profound effects on his life and reputation?[2] How does one compensate a trader for loss of reputation pending the outcome of proceedings, or for the loss of opportunity to operate or expand as resources were consumed in defending the drawn out proceedings? It is not easy to speculate on loss of opportunity, nor to quantify loss when personal relationships and feelings are at stake, yet, surely, a very real loss is incurred.

The pain that is being experienced by individuals that feel *helpless* in the face of intractable delay afflicting court cases in which they are involved is, by and large, being completely overlooked by governments. The programmes the author has seen, to date, to reform judicial systems have been, although perhaps well-intentioned, insufficient to overhaul the system and effectively tackle the issue.

It is interesting to note that, more often than not, a cursory glance at the positive law of the country will render a completely perverse picture of the actual legal reality of how cases are being heard. The author is thus of the persuasion that it is not through the passage of *more* dead letter legal regulations, and the organization of more ineffective committees to study the problem, that this spectre is going to be eradicated effectively and in a way that can help each individual person whose case is afflicted by delay. The solution is, rather, for individuals to realise that they are already empowered to remedy their own situation, for legal advisors to pro-actively advise their clients in relation to the relevant Convention rights, and for courts to raise the issue of their own motion to effectively pre-empt and tackle cases of delay.

This book attempts to shed light on what legal avenues exist to prevent and compensate for delay, as well as the many pitfalls and weaknesses of the remedies which already exist. It seeks to provide guidance for the provision of effective remedies, and to show where courts can go astray in their assessment of applications. *It is through use that these remedies will be honed into increased effectiveness in each national system.*

While the European Court of Human Rights and many national courts face a significant number of challenges and cases based on the length of proceedings, a mere glance at the average lengths of cases immediately demonstrates that these cases are but a fraction of the total number of potential applicants who could institute either a civil or human rights action based on the length of proceedings. In many cases, individuals are discouraged from doing so due to the mere fact that they find resorting to the very system which has caused them so much pain, in order to seek a remedy for delay, to be in itself objectionable. This attitude, however, seems to stem less from the fact that such person would be unwilling to undertake an extra set of procedures, and more from the fact that there is a general lack of appreciation that excessive delay in the context of legal proceedings violates what is already acknowledged as a human right. This lack of appreciation accounts for a general lack of confidence in individuals that anything can be done about delay in the delivery of justice.

This study also seeks to show that all those persons who have *locus standi* in countries that are parties to the European Convention on Human Rights, can take action whether or not the individual country's laws provide a domestic remedy. As of that point in time when the state becomes responsible for the determination of any person's civil rights and obligations, or of any criminal charge against that person, and in regard to delay which may ensue in such proceedings, unless and until the legal system in question provides remedies which are capable of preventing anticipated or further delay, and providing, in relation to unreasonable delay which has already occurred, adequate non-pecuniary and pecuniary compensation, in a timely manner, there exists within that system a structural failure in terms of Article 13 of the European Convention on Human Rights. Both the failure to effectively remedy, as well as the failure to provide a remedy, are actionable directly before the European Court of Human Rights. Any given legal system, and any individual case of delay, can be analysed and challenged against the standards set by the European Convention on Human Rights.

It is also envisageable that if this right becomes more widely acknowledged and respected, and the case law and guidance of the European Court of Human Rights more understood, that adjudicators faced with an application for effective relief based on a complaint regarding the length of proceedings or, perhaps, even of their own initiative in cases which come to be afflicted by delay, will be more willing to be the ones to deliver the required effective relief and to take more courageous steps to remedy anticipated or actual violations, in the knowledge that they are fully empowered (and obliged) to remedy such violations with effectiveness. It would be a most welcome development if judges were to avail themselves of the power they hold to take broad measures to uphold the fundamental human rights of individuals *to develop new, targeted and effective remedies in response to each individual case of delay.*

It would also be a welcome development if compensation in cases of a breach of the reasonable time requirement protected by Article 6 were to be delivered by adjudicators bearing an additional criterion in mind, in addition to the ones we have studied with reference to Strasbourg Jurisprudence, namely, *the message to be sent to the state that has violated the individual's rights*. Even if national courts were to follow the guidance of the Strasbourg Court in the awarding of compensation, the author is not persuaded that the awards delivered against individual states would be of sufficient impact to jolt the relevant state into actively taking steps to prevent further violations. There is no amount of pecuniary or non-pecuniary compensation that can actually compensate for the pain and suffering which delay can cause, and the awards delivered and remedies provided in each case, as in each case where a violation of a fundamental human right is acknowledged, should endure in a state's memory as would any suitable disciplining of a dog that has bitten the sheep it was meant to protect. It is an undeniable fact that awards delivered and measures taken in response to the finding of a violation are not being delivered with this criterion in mind.

While it is therefore desirable for governments themselves to institute further reforms and mechanisms to both prevent and tackle systemic and individual cases of delay, the fact remains that there already exist mechanisms within the legal systems of each state that is a party to the European Convention of Human Rights, which permit all persons to seek effective relief for unreasonable delay in the delivery of justice. The author is of the persuasion that if individuals suffering due to delay know that something can be done about their situation, and are advised that this suffering amounts to a violation of a fundamental right the state has already committed itself to protect, they will be immensely empowered. If it is more widely understood that we can speak of remedies for delay within a human rights context, individuals will be armed with the confidence to refuse what, effectively, amounts to *a de facto denial of justice*, and to actually ask the single essential question which could get the ball of change rolling, namely: 'If I have *a right* to justice within a reasonable time, how do I enforce it?'

Notes

1 The interplay of Article 6 and various other rights under the Convention has traditionally been a bone of contention. The debate is perfectly instantiated by V.K. V CROATIA, when the Court for the first time ruled that the length of divorce proceedings had occasioned a breach not only of Article 6, but also of the right to marry under Article 12 due to the fact that 'although a right to divorce cannot be derived from Article 12 of the Convention ... if national legislation allows divorce, it secures for divorced persons the right to remarry without unreasonable restrictions ... the applicant was left in a state of prolonged uncertainty which amounted to an unreasonable restriction of his right to marry ...' see [99] and [106]. In a dissenting opinion, on the other hand, Judge Berro-Lefèvre opined that the finding of such a violation provoked the question of whether '... all violations of Article 6 for unreasonable length of proceedings entail, *ipso facto*, a violation of Article 12 if the applicant can demonstrate that he or she has found another soul mate and

is contemplating a fresh attempt at matrimony?' The elements which he considered that the Court had based its decision on, namely, 'the parties' agreement to divorce, a possibility of rendering a partial decision and the urgent nature of the proceedings under domestic law' were to be considered 'elements which are clearly to be taken into account in assessing the length of proceedings, but which cannot be considered, in and of themselves, as restricting or reducing the right in question in such a way or to such an extent that the essence of the right is impaired.'

2 See p. 24 of the White Paper 2005, 'Lejn Ġustizzja Aħjar u Eħfef' (White paper 2005) <http://www.mjha.gov.mt> accessed April 2015.

Appendix A
Statistics Demonstrating the Volume of Length-of-Proceedings Violations Found by the Strasbourg Court, Expressed as a Percentage of Total Convention Violations

The Convention provision which, since 1999, has provided fertile ground for the greatest number of applications, as well as findings of violations, is Article 6, with applications claiming violations of the right to a fair hearing within a reasonable time ranking second after applications based generally on the fairness of proceedings as a whole.[1]

2008
Total no. of length-of-proceedings violations: 456[2]
% of total violations: 29.51%[3]

2007
Total no. of length-of-proceedings violations: 384[4]
% of total violations: 25.55%[5]

2006
Total no. of length-of-proceedings violations: 567[6]
% of total violations: 36.35%[7]

2005
Total no. of length-of-proceedings violations: 311[8]
% of total violations: 28.14%[9]
% of total cases:[10] 25%[11]

2004
Total no. of length-of-proceedings violations: 257[12]
% of total violations: 35.79%[13]
% of total cases: 34.49%[14]

2003
Total no. of length-of-proceedings violations: 210[15]
% of total violations: 29.87%[16]
% of total cases: 33.43%[17]

110 *Appendix A*

2002

Total no. of length-of-proceedings violations: no data
% of total violations: no data
No. of length-of-proceedings cases:[18] 471, of which 299 against Italy[19]
% of total cases: Over 50%[20]

2001

Total no. of length-of-proceedings violations: no data
% of total violations: no data
No. of length-of-proceedings cases:[21] 479, of which 357 against Italy
% of total cases: Over 50%[22]

Notes

1 Basis for calculations: 'Annual Report 2008 of the European Court of Human Rights, Council of Europe', <http://www.echr.coe.int> accessed January 2015.
2 From chart: Violations by Article and by Respondent State (2008) in the 'Annual Report 2008 of the European Court of Human Rights, Council of Europe'.
3 See n 1 (Appendix A).
4 From chart entitled 'Violations by Article and by Country (2007)' in the 'Annual Report 2007 of the European Court of Human Rights, Council of Europe', <http://www.echr.coe.int> accessed January 2015.
5 Ibid.
6 From chart entitled 'Violations by Article and by Country (2006)' in the 'Annual Report 2006 of the European Court of Human Rights, Council of Europe', <http://www.echr.coe.int> accessed January 2015.
7 Ibid.
8 From chart entitled 'Violations by Article and by Country (2005)' in the 'Annual Report 2005 of the European Court of Human Rights, Council of Europe', <http://www.echr.coe.int> accessed January 2015.
9 Ibid.
10 Number of length-of-proceedings cases (whether violation found or not) expressed as a percentage of total caseload (all cases whether violation found or not).
11 'Annual Report 2005 of the European Court of Human Rights, Council of Europe', <http:\\www.echr.coe.int> accessed January 2015.
12 From chart entitled 'Violations by Article and by Country (2004)' in the 'Annual Report 2004 of the European Court of Human Rights, Council of Europe', <http://www.echr.coe.int> accessed January 2015.
13 Ibid.
14 Annual Report 2005 of the European Court of Human Rights, Council of Europe (see n 11 (Appendix A)).
15 From chart entitled 'Violations by Article and by Country (2003)' in the 'Annual Report 2003 of the European Court of Human Rights, Council of Europe', <http://www.echr.coe.int> accessed January 2015.
16 Ibid.
17 Annual Report 2005 of the European Court of Human Rights, Council of Europe (see n 8 (Appendix A)).

18 Including those where no violation was found.
19 'Annual Report 2002 of the European Court of Human Rights, Council of Europe', <http://www.echr.coe.int> accessed January 2015.
20 Ibid.
21 Including those where no violation was found.
22 See n 19 (Appendix A).

Appendix B
Length-of-Proceedings Violations Expressed as a Percentage of Overall Violations per State, 1999–2008[1]

Country	Total Human Rights Violations 1999–2008	Length-of-proceedings Violations	% of Total Violations Found
Albania	11	2	18.18%
Andorra	4	0	0.00%
Armenia	11	0	0.00%
Austria	178	60	33.71%
Azerbaijan	19	2	10.53%
Belgium	96	52	54.17%
Bosnia Herzegovina	7	0	0.00%
Bulgaria	229	89	38.86%
Croatia	151	66	43.71%
Cyprus	51	30	58.82%
Czech Rep	144	76	52.78%
Denmark	24	4	16.67%
Estonia	17	3	17.65%
Finland	99	29	29.29%
France	623	252	40.45%
Georgia	24	3	12.50%
Germany	98	33	33.67%
Greece	440	272	61.82%
Hungary	160	136	85.00%
Iceland	8	0	0.00%
Ireland	12	4	33.33%
Italy	1797	999	55.59%
Latvia	34	6	17.65%
Liechtenstein	4	1	25.00%
Lithuania	48	9	18.75%
Luxembourg	25	13	52.00%
Malta	21	5	23.81%

Moldova	138	7	5.07%
Monaco	0	0	0.00%
Montenegro	0	0	0.00%
Netherlands	71	5	7.04%
Norway	20	2	10.00%
Poland	630	308	48.89%
Portugal	153	60	39.22%
Romania	478	46	9.62%
Russia	643	78	12.13%
San Marino	11	2	18.18%
Serbia	24	11	45.83%
Slovakia	166	108	65.06%
Slovenia	219	205	93.61%
Spain	40	6	15.00%
Sweden	44	10	22.73%
Switzerland	45	4	8.89%
FYROM	46	30	65.22%
Turkey	1905	258	13.54%
Ukraine	482	98	20.33%
UK	292	19	6.51%
Cases Per Country Total	*9742*	*3403*	*34.93%*
Total Number of Cases	**9736**	**3403**	**34.95%**

KEY	
0–10%	
10–40%	
40–80%	
80% and over	

Please note:

The discrepancy between the Cases Per Country Total and the Total Number of Cases allows for six judgments which were directed against two respondent states contemporaneously.

Source of data in first two numeric columns: chart entitled 'Violations by Article and by respondent State (1 November 1998–31 December 2008)' from the 'Annual Report 2008 of the European Court of Human Rights, Council of Europe'.

Discrepancies between the figures relating to the 'length-of-proceedings cases' and the number of cases in which violations were found are due to:

i   The cases in which violations were not found, and
ii The number of 'length-of-proceedings cases' includes both cases under Article 6 and under Article 13 regarding the availability of remedies.[2]

Notes

1 European Court of Human Rights – data compiled from tables found in the Annual Reports.
2 Note of this is made in the 'Annual Report 2005 of the European Court of Human Rights, Council of Europe' (see n 8 (Appendix A)).

Bibliography

Authored Books and Theses

Alastair Mowbray, *Cases and Materials on the European Convention on Human Rights* (2nd edition, Oxford University Press, Oxford 2007)

Claude Micallef Grimaud, *The Rationale for Excluding Moral Damages from the Maltese Civil Code: A Historic and Legal Investigation*, (LL.D. Dissertation, University of Malta, Malta 2008)

Dennis James Galligan, *Due Process and Fair Procedures: A Study of Administrative Procedures* (Oxford University Press, Oxford 1996)

G. Mifsud Bonnici, *Constitutional Procedure relative to Fundamental Rights and Freedoms 1964–2000* (Midsea Books Ltd., Malta 2004)

Harris, O'Boyle and Warbrick, *Law of the European Convention on Human Rights* (2nd edition, Oxford University Press, Oxford 2009)

Harris, O'Boyle and Warbrick, *Law of the European Convention on Human Rights* (Butterworths, 1995)

Hugh W. Harding, B.A., LL.D., F.S.A., F.R.Hist.S., *Maltese Legal History Under British Rule (1801–1836)* (University Press, Malta 1980)

Hurst Hannum, *Guide to International Human Rights Practice* (Edited for the Procedural Aspects of International Law Institute, 4th edition, Transnational Publishers, Lc. Ardsley, New York 2004)

J.J. Cremona, *The Maltese Constitution and Constitutional History Since 1813* (2nd edition, Publishers Enterprises Group (PEG) Ltd, Malta 1997)

John Henry Merryman, *The Civil Law Tradition* (2nd edition, Stanford University Press, Stanford 1985)

Paula Loughlin, Stephen M. Gerlis, *Civil Procedure* (2nd edition, Routledge Cavendish Press, London 2004)

Pieter van Dijk, Fried van Hoof, Arjen van Rijn, Leo Zwaak (eds), *Theory and Practice of the European Convention on Human Rights* (4th edition Intersentia, Oxford 2006)

Richard Clayton, Hugh Tomlinson, *Fair Trial Rights* (reprinted from *The Law of Human Rights*, Oxford University Press, Oxford 2001)

Stephanos Stavros, *The Guarantees for Accused Persons under Article 6 of the European Convention on Human Rights: an Analysis of the Application of the Convention and a Comparison with Other Instruments* (Martinus Nijhoff Publishers, The Netherlands 1993)

Contributions to Books

Guido Alpa, 'The Constitutionalisation of Private Law in Italy' in *Mediterranean Journal of Human Rights* (Volume 3 Number 1, Faculty of Laws University of Malta, Malta 1999)

Joseph A. Filletti, 'The Right to an Effective Remedy: on Sustained Action to Secure the Execution of Judgments of the European Court of Human Rights' in David E. Zammit (ed.), *Maltese Perspectives on Human Rights* (University of Malta, Malta 2008)

Joseph M. Ganado, 'Malta: A Microcosm of International Influences in Studies' in E. Örücü, *Legal Systems: Mixed and Mixing* (Kluwer Law International, London 1996)

Joseph Said Pullincino, 'The Ombudsman: His Role in Human Rights Promotion and Protection' in David E. Zammit (ed.), *Maltese Perspectives on Human Rights* (University of Malta, Malta 2008)

Ugo Mifsud Bonnici, 'Human Rights in Maltese Legislation' in David E. Zammit (ed.), *Maltese Perspectives on Human Rights* (University of Malta, Malta 2008)

Electronic Journals

David Nelken, 'Using the Concept of Legal Culture', (Australian Journal of Legal Philosophy 2004) <http://www.law.berkeley.edu/institutes/csls/nelken%20paper.pdf> accessed January 2015

Elizabetta Grande, 'Italian Criminal Justice: Borrowing and Resistance', (2000) Vol. XLVLLL Amer. J. of Comparative law <http://www.jstor.org/pss/840971> accessed January 2015

Vernon Valentine Palmer, 'The Fate of the General Clause in a Cross-Cultural Setting: The Tort Experience of Louisiana' <http://www.ejcl.org/52/art52–1.html#N_1_> accessed January 2015

Official Reports

'Annual Report 2008 of the European Court of Human Rights, Council of Europe', <http://www.echr.coe.int/echr/en/header/reports+and+statistics/reports/annual+reports/> accessed January 2015

'Annual Report 2007 of the European Court of Human Rights, Council of Europe' <http://www.echr.coe.int/echr/en/header/reports+and+statistics/reports/annual+reports/> accessed January 2015

'Annual Report 2006 of the European Court of Human Rights, Council of Europe' <http://www.echr.coe.int/echr/en/header/reports+and+statistics/reports/annual+reports/> accessed January 2015

'Annual Report 2005 of the European Court of Human Rights, Council of Europe' <http://www.echr.coe.int/echr/en/header/reports+and+statistics/reports/annual+reports/> accessed January 2015

'Annual Report 2004 of the European Court of Human Rights, Council of Europe' <http://www.echr.coe.int/echr/en/header/reports+and+statistics/reports/annual+reports/> accessed January 2015

'Annual Report 2003 of the European Court of Human Rights, Council of Europe' <http://www.echr.coe.int/echr/en/header/reports+and+statistics/reports/annual+reports/> accessed January 2015

'Annual Report 2002 of the European Court of Human Rights, Council of Europe' <http://www.echr.coe.int/echr/en/header/reports+and+statistics/reports/annual+reports/> accessed January 2015

'Annual Report 2001 of the European Court of Human Rights, Council of Europe' <http://www.echr.coe.int/echr/en/header/reports+and+statistics/reports/annual+reports/> accessed January 2015

Lord Woolf, 'Access to Justice: Final Report to the Lord Chancellor on the Civil Justice System in England and Wales' (Published by HMSO, 1996) <http://www.dca.gov.uk/civil/interfr/contents.htm> accessed December 2010

Lord Woolf, 'Access to Justice: Interim Report' (June 1995) <http://www.dca.gov.uk/civil/interfr/contents.htm> accessed December 2010

Lord Woolf, 'The Review of the Working Methods of the European Court of Human Rights, (December 2005)' <http://www.echr.coe.int> accessed January 2015

White Papers

'Lejn Ġustizzja Aħjar u Eħfef' (White paper 2005) <http://www.mjha.gov.mt/downloads/documents/gustizzja_wp.pdf> accessed January 2015

Other Websites and Online Articles of Interest

<http://hudoc.echr.coe.int> accessed January 2015
<http://conventions.coe.int/treaty/en/treaties/html/005-1-bis.htm> accessed January 2015
<http://www.mjha.gov.mt/home.html> accessed January 2015
<http://www.justiceservices.gov.mt/courtservices/Judgements/> accessed January 2015
<http://www.echr.coe.int/Pages/home.aspx?p=home> accessed January 2015

Dr Vincent Degaetano (Diskors Fl-Okkazjoni Tal-Bidu Tas-Sena Forensi 2009–2010) <www.judiciarymalta.gov.mt> accessed December 2009

Dr Vincent Degaetano (Diskors Fl-Okkazjoni Tal-Bidu Tas-Sena Forensi 2008–2009) <www.judiciarymalta.gov.mt> accessed December 2009

Dr Vincent Degaetano (Diskors Fl-Okkazjoni Tal-Bidu Tas-Sena Forensi 2007–2008) <www.judiciarymalta.gov.mt> accessed December 2009

Dr Vincent Degaetano (Diskors Fl-Okkazjoni Tal-Bidu Tas-Sena Forensi 2006) <www.judiciarymalta.gov.mt> accessed December 2009

Dr Vincent Degaetano (Diskors Fl-Okkazjoni Tal-Bidu Tas-Sena Forensi 2004) <www.judiciarymalta.gov.mt> accessed December 2009

Dr Vincent Degaetano (Diskors Fl-Okkazjoni Tal-Bidu Tas-Sena Forensi 2003) <www.judiciarymalta.gov.mt> accessed December 2009

Prof. Dr Luzius Wildhaber, (Address delivered at the Old University, Aula Magna, Valletta, Malta, 16 January 2003) <www.judiciarymalta.gov.mt> accessed December 2009

Dr Said Pullicino (Diskors Fl-Okkazjoni Tal-Bidu Tas-Sena Forensi 2001) <www.judiciarymalta.gov.mt> accessed December 2009

Dr Said Pullicino (Diskors Fl-Okkazjoni Tal-Bidu Tas-Sena Forensi 2000) <www.judiciarymalta.gov.mt> accessed December 2009

Mr Justice Joseph D. Camilleri (Address delivered on the occasion of the commemoration of the Third Anniversary of the official launching of the Judicial Studies Committee Vassalli Hall Mediterranean Conference Centre Valletta Malta 22nd January 2007) <www.judiciarymalta.gov.mt> accessed December 2009

Dr Tonio Borg, 'Siltiet mid-diskors tal-Viċi Prim Ministru u Ministru tal-Ġustizzja u l-Intern Dr Tonio Borg waqt l-għoti ta' warrants lil avukati ġodda' <http://www.mjha.govmt/news/pressreleases/pdf2006/03march/avukatigodda_20060302.pdf> accessed January 2015

Dr Marse-Ann Farrugia, 'Pending magisterial inquiries', Sunday, 13th July 2008 <www.judiciarymalta.gov.mt> accessed January 2015 <www.publiclawproject.org.uk> accessed January 2015

'Id-deċiżjonijiet tal-Qorti tal-Appelli Krimininali għandu jsir fl'iqsar żmien – Imħallef Joseph Galea Debono' <http://www.il-gensillum.com/news> accessed January 2015

'Three year appellate proceedings pending which accused remained in custody resulting in acquittal' <http://www.timesofmalta.com/articles/view/20091102/local/appeals-court-revokes-25-year-jail-term> accessed January 2015
Vanessa Macdonald, 'The quest for expeditious justice – Chief Justice Vincent de Gaetano at the recent opening of the forensic year at the law courts' <www.judiciarymalta.gov.mt> accessed December 2009
Steve Mallia, 'Judging the judges', Sunday, 7th September 2008 <http://www.timesofmalta.com> accessed January 2015

Statistical Information

Miscellaneous

Council of Europe: Data published by the European Commission for the Efficiency of Justice (CEPEJ)
European Judicial Systems edition 2006 (2004 data) European Commission for the Efficiency of Justice (CEPEJ) <www.coe.int/cepej/> accessed December 2009

Malta

MITTS Ltd, Published Statistics <http://www.justice.gov.mt/statistics/default.asp?lng=ENG STATISTICS 2000–2009> accessed December 2009

France

Annuaire statistique de la Justice (edition 2008) Secrétariat Général Service support et moyens du ministère <www.justice.gouv.fr> accessed 9 Oct 2009
Annuaire statistique de la Justice (edition 2007) Secrétariat Général Direction de l'Administration générale et de l'Équipement <www.justice.gouvfr> accessed 9 Oct 2009
Annuaire statistique de la Justice (edition 2006) Secrétariat Général Direction de l'Administration générale et de l'Équipement <www.justice.gouv.fr> accessed 9 Oct 2009
Zakia Belmokhtar, 'Les victimes face à la justice: le sentiment de satisfaction sur la réponse judiciaire', Infostat Justice 98 Décembre 2007 Numéro 98 Bulletin d'information statistique Ministère de La Justice

United Kingdom

The Human Rights Act: the DCA and Home Office Reviews © Crown Copyright 2007 <www.dca.gov.uk> accessed 2nd October 2009
Delivering Simple, Speedy, Summary Justice – An evaluation of the magistrates' courts tests <frontline.cjsonline.gov.uk/_ ... /CJSSS_in_the_Magistrates_Courts_Test_Site_Evaluation_22.02.07.pdf> accessed October 2009
Ministry of Justice: Judicial and Court Statistics 2008, September 2009 © Crown Copyright 2009
<www.official-documents.gov.uk/> accessed January 2015
<www.justice.gov.uk/publications/docs/judicial-court-statistics-2008-intro.pdf> accessed January 2015

Disclaimer

This work is provided and published for academic purposes.

Nothing stated therein should be construed as legal advice or as a recommendation.

Readers should always consult the latest versions of and updates or additions to all legal instruments, statistics, information and bodies of case law cited in the text.

Additional considerations and legal instruments, aside from those considered in this text, may be material to any claim which may arise relating to the subject matter of this work.

Index

abbreviations xlvi
access to justice, *see* link, nexus between Article 6, 13 and 35 and other ECHR articles
acknowledgement of violation, *see* inadmissibility of application to ECHR, preliminary pleas ...; loss of victim status
action for damages in tort li, 15, 36, 64, 78, 83–92, 95–104; *see also* compensation, proceedings for and calculation
adequacy of redress, *see* inadmissibility of application to ECHR, preliminary pleas; loss of victim status, incompatibility *ratione personae; see also* compensation, proceedings for and calculation
administrative proceedings pre-requisite for filing court action, *see* compulsory administrative proceedings
AKDIVAR AND OTHERS 20
AKSOY 20
ALLIED NEWSPAPERS LIMITED V ATTORNEY GENERAL ET 66, 76
alternative forms of redress, *see* remedies for length-of-proceedings violations
analysis of cases and remedies, outline of approach 4
ANDRÁŠIK 20, 50
APICELLA 20, 21, 43, 50
applicants: conduct of (*see* method of examination); eligibility (*see* inadmissibility of application to ECHR, preliminary pleas); issues at stake for (*see* method of examination); *and* nature of proceedings 29–32
Articles: ECHR articles (*see* European Convention on Human Rights, articles under other legal instruments); guide to capitalisation xlvi; statutes x
ARVANITAKI-ROBOTI 41, 51, 52

ATTARD V ATTARD 83, 91, 94
ATTARD V ATTORNEY GENERAL 75
ATTARD V THE HON. PRIME MINISTER ET 70, 81
audi alteram partem, right of 26
AZZOPARDI 99, 100
AZZOPARDI V ATTORNEY GENERAL ET 61, 62, 80
AZZOPARDI V REGISTRAR OF COURTS ET 63

BAKO 15
BALDACCHINO V COMMISSIONER OF LANDS 91–2, 95, 96
BARANOWSKI 103
BARIŠIČ 32, 49
BARTOLO V ATTORNEY GENERAL 57, 67–8, 75, 80
BECK 21, 73
BELINGER 21, 50
BELPERIO ET CIARMOLI 18
BEZZINA WETTINGER AND OTHERS 20, 45, 54, 56, 78
BLASCHEM (MALTA) LIMITED V ATTORNEY GENERAL ET 63, 80, 87, 93
Bonello, Giovanni, European Court of Human Rights li, lii, 38
BONNICI V ATTORNEY GENERAL 74
BOTTAZZI 7, 51
BRINCAT V ATTORNEY GENERAL 84
BUGEJA V ATTORNEY GENERAL AND COMMISSIONER OF POLICE 69, 71, 74, 78
burden of proof, *see* exhaustion of (effective) domestic remedies
BURDOV 17, 21, 47, 49–52
BUSUTTIL V XUEREB AND AX CONSTRUCTION LIMITED 90, 102

Index

CALDAS RAMIREZ DE ARRELLANO 20
CALLEJA 20, 21, 45–7, 55, 78
career: impact of delay on (*see* nature of proceedings; stakes, urgency due to nature of proceedings); *see also* pecuniary and non-pecuniary damage and compensation; prevention; remedies for length-of-proceedings violations
CASSAR V ATTORNEY GENERAL 72
CENTRAL MEDITERRANEAN DEVELOPMENT CORPORATION LIMITED 21, 38, 50, 51, 78, 80
CERIN 20
CHAHAL 21, 50
children, *see* minors
civil code of Malta: article 1033 88–102; article 1045 96, 104
civil proceedings, applicability of Article 6 ECHR 2, 23
civil status: legal capacity (*see* nature of proceedings); *also see* stakes, urgency due to nature of proceedings; *and* pecuniary and non-pecuniary damage and compensation; *and* prevention; *and* remedies for length-of-proceedings violations
COCCHIARELLA 7, 20, 21, 43, 45, 48, 50
compensation, proceedings for and calculation: *a posteriori* examination of local compensation awarded 4, 12, 16, 31; discontinuance of delayed proceedings as compensation 17; enforcement of compensation, delay in 19, 34; general Article 41 ECHR, calculation of quantum, effectiveness of compensatory remedy 14–19, 35, 39–45; inflation, compensation for 17; interest as compensation 16; length of compensation proceedings 13; length of enforcement of compensation 19, 34; local courts, case studies (*see* Pinto law in Italian Republic; Scordino-Type Cases); *see also* Malta, legal system of the Republic of; loss of victim status, compensation and (*see* inadmissibility of application to ECHR); manifestly unreasonable, what is 14–19, 35–8, 66–8, 97–8; pecuniary and non-pecuniary (moral) damage (*see* pecuniary and non-pecuniary damage and compensation); prevention instead of compensation 2; reduction in length of sentence as compensation 17; *see also* nature of proceedings, stakes, urgency due to nature of proceedings: criminal, civil, industrial, labour, employment, pension, the right to practice one's profession, high financial stakes, commercial and professional matters, property disputes, title to land, actions of retrial, actions for compensation for human rights and Convention violations, enforcement proceedings, combination of several factors for assessing reasonableness of length of proceedings: for assessing reasonableness of length of proceedings 3, 24, 29–31, 48 (*see also* method of examination); for determining the quantum of compensation 40–4, 64, 69 (*see also* pecuniary and non-pecuniary damage and compensation)
competent authorities, conduct of 27–9
complexity of the factual or legal issues *see* method of examination
compliance of national legal remedies with ECHR standards 2
compulsory administrative procedures: general 24; in Malta 65–6
conduct of the applicant *see* method of examination
conduct of the competent authorities *see* method of examination
constitutional proceedings: applicability of Article 6 ECHR 3, 34–5; guidance on length of 34–5; powers of court to remedy breaches of Convention, what is required 36; ordinary law versus extraordinary (constitutional) proceedings: general xlix, li, 9–14; in Malta 76–8, 85
Convention *see* European Convention on Human Rights
cost, excessive burden 16, 35
criminal proceedings: applicability of Article 6 ECHR 1–3, 22, 23; co-defendants, delay caused by 27; imprisonment, delayed detention, unjustified detainment 17, 30, 67, 71, 73, 74; method of examination: complexity of the factual or legal issues of the case 25; conduct of the applicant, absconding pending proceedings 26; conduct of the competent authorities 27–8; stakes for assessing reasonableness of length of proceedings 3, 24–5, 29–31, 49 (*see also* method of examination); stakes for determining the quantum of compensation 40–4, 64, 69 (*see also* pecuniary and non-pecuniary damage

and compensation); stakes, what was at stake for the applicant 29–32; *see also* method of examination; period to be considered 23, 24, 45; reasonableness, Article 5(3) versus Article 6 49; *see* European Convention on Human Rights (Convention), Article 13; remedies for length-of-proceedings violations: different types of remedies, effective remedies 15–17, 35–6, 38–9, 44; pecuniary and non-pecuniary damage and compensation: alternatives 16, 17, 44; special diligence 29–30, 31
CURMI V COMMISSIONER OF LANDS 65–6, 78

DALIA 20
damages *see* pecuniary and non-pecuniary damage and compensation
damnum emergens, establishment of 96
DEBONO 21, 24, 47, 55, 78
DEBONO ET V PRINCIPAL REGISTRAR OF THE COURTS OF JUSTICE ET 55–6
DEBONO V ATTORNEY GENERAL 58, 63
DE CLERCK 30, 44, 50
defences of respondent state: defences on the merits (*see* method of examination); preliminary pleas (*see* inadmissibility of application to ECHR, preliminary pleas)
defendant: constitutional vs ordinary law remedies 83; private party, state, as defendants within domestic law of Malta 83–92
DEGUARA CARUANA GATTO AND OTHERS 21
delay of court proceedings: cases filed for 106; compensation for pain due to 105–7
DELLE CAVE AND CORRADO 18, 20–1, 50
DI COLA 20
DIMITROV AND HAMANOV 21
DI SANTE 20, 51
divorce proceedings, length of 105, 107–8
domestic remedies *see* subsidiarity; *see also* exhaustion of (effective) domestic remedies
DUDGEON 103

ECHR (European Court of Human Rights) 1, 5
ECKLE 21, 45, 46, 47

effectiveness of remedies *see* exhaustion of (effective) domestic remedies
ELLUL SULLIVAN ET V COMMISSIONER OF POLICE AND ATTORNEY GENERAL 59, 60, 72, 73
enforcement proceedings, enforcement of judgments: criteria for effectiveness 35; delay in enforcement of compensation 19, 34; general 33–4; interest as compensation for delay in enforcement 16; lack of funds 33, 50; positive obligations of state relating to enforcement proceedings 50; preliminary pleas 13, 16; requirement to bring 13; systematic practice of non-enforcement 35; *see also* exhaustion of (effective) domestic remedies; Scordino-Type Cases
enforcement proceedings, length of: as factor for determining compensation 42; as a factor in assessing the period to be considered 24; general 33–4, 47; as material factor for the stakes of the case 30–1; reasonable length for enforcement of compensation for delay 15–16
enforcement proceedings, moral damages: aggravation of moral damages due to delay in enforcement 40, 41; inversion of burden of proof regarding state fault 51
equality of arms, delay and 40–1
erga omnes effect, judgments of Strasbourg Court 5
ERNESTINA ZULLO 20, 21, 43, 50–1
ESPOSITO 18, 46, 50
European Convention on Human Rights (Convention), Article 6: applicability 3, 10, 22–5, 45; duty of states pursuant to Article 6 5; equality of arms and reasonable time 40–1; foreign jurisdictions, delays caused by foreign legal systems 47; foreword, text and guide to use of capitalisation xii, xxvi, xlviii, 1–3, 22; general 16–19; 22–35; link to other articles (*see* link, nexus between Article 6, 13 and 35 and other ECHR articles); *locus classicus* for complaints 23; remedies, redress under (*see* remedies for length-of-proceedings violations); use in Italy (*see* Scordino-Type Cases); use in Malta (*see* Malta, legal system of the Republic of, length-of-proceedings case law)
European Convention on Human Rights (Convention), Article 13: foreword, text and guide to use of capitalisation xiii,

xxvi, 3, 22; general 10–14, 18–19, 23, 31, 35–9, 50; link to other articles (*see* link, nexus between Article 6, 13 and 35 and other ECHR articles); remedies for violations of (*see* pecuniary and non-pecuniary damage and compensation; remedies for length-of-proceedings violations; pilot judgments); separate examination under, conducted by court of own motion 31; stakes for the applicant 30; systemic, structural failure 18–19; use in Italy; Scordino-Type Cases 37–9; use in Malta (*see* Malta, legal system of the Republic of, length-of-proceedings case law)
European Convention on Human Rights (Convention), Article 34 xiii–xiv, 8, 14–20
European Convention on Human Rights (Convention), Article 35 xiii–xiv, 8–14, 20, 33, 35, 37, 39, 54, 97
European Convention on Human Rights (Convention), Article 41, 'just satisfaction' under xiv, 32, 39–45, 52, 67, 99
European Convention on Human Rights (Convention), Article 46, pilot judgment xiv, 31, 37, 38
European Convention on Human Rights (Convention), Articles: temporal application 24; interpretation of 1–2; Italy and (*see* Italian Republic); Malta and (*see* Malta, legal system of the Republic of); subsidiary nature of 6; text of various articles x; *see also* Protocol to the European Convention on Human Rights *and* Rules of Court
European Court of Human Rights (European Court or Strasbourg Court): case study (*see* Scordino-Type Cases); framework for assessment: for preliminary pleas *see* inadmissibility of application to ECHR, preliminary pleas, for merits *see* method of examination; general 1, 5, 105–7; overview of 22–3; pilot judgments *see* pilot judgments
exhaustion of (effective) domestic remedies: burden of proof 11–12, 51; court acknowledgement of own delay 16, 19; dismissal of plea 14; effective forms of remedies 13–16; enforcement proceedings (*see* enforcement proceedings); general rules 8, 9, 10–14, 35; powers of court to remedy breaches of Convention 36; relation to finding of a violation on the merits 14; second national complaint for delay in compensation proceedings 13; subsidiarity and 5–6, 14, 38; sufficiently certain status, ongoing scrutiny 12; *see also* loss of victim status, incompatibility *ratione personae*
expropriation 56, 66, 77, 80, 86, 91, 99, 103

failure to cause loss of victim status, *see* inadmissibility of application to ECHR, preliminary pleas
fair trial rights, *see* European Convention on Human Rights: Article 6
family life, compensation for interference with private rights, *see* pecuniary and non-pecuniary damage and compensation; *see also* stakes, urgency due to nature of proceedings
FARRUGIA V ATTORNEY GENERAL 69–70, 74
FARRUGIA V COMMISSIONER OF LANDS 85
FARRUGIA V COMMISSIONER OF POLICE ET 73
FENECH V COMMISSIONER OF LANDS ET 77, 79, 81–2, 86, 93
FHCC(CJ), FHCC(GJ) xlviii
FIORINO D'ORO V DIRECTOR OF ROADS 90–1, 95
F.L. V ITALY 36
FOLDES AND FOLDESNE HAJLIK 17
foreign jurisdictions, delays caused by foreign legal systems 47
framework for examination, Strasbourg Court, *see* method of examination
FRENDO RANDON AND OTHERS 80, 103
FRENDO RANDON V COMMISSIONER OF LANDS ET 60, 65–6, 78, 80, 82, 115
FRYDLENDER 32, 45–6, 48

GADZHIKHANOV AND SAUKOV 34
GAGLIANO GIORGI 9, 21, 48
GASAN ENTERPRISES LIMITED V MALTA ENVIRONMENT AND PLANNING AUTHORITY 64, 80
GEORGIOS PAPAGEORGIOU 44, 52
GIUMMARRA AND OTHERS 20
GIUSEPPINA AND ORESTINA PROCACCINI 20, 21, 50, 51
GIUSTI 20
goodwill, loss of, *see* nature of proceedings

GOUVEIA DA SILVA TORRADO 20
GRÄSSER 21, 45, 48, 52
GRZINČIČ 21

HADJIKOSTOVA 29
HALL V DIRECTOR FOR THE
  DEPARTMENT OF SOCIAL
  ACCOMMODATION ET 77–8
Harris, O'Boyle, Warbrick 24, 28, 42, 45,
  46, 48, 51, 99
HARTMAN 21, 48, 50
HOHOLM 30, 49
HOLZINGER (NO. 1) 21, 51
horizontal application of human rights,
  redress against private parties 84, 92,
  83–107
HORVAT 10, 20
human rights remedies for delay in Malta,
  see Malta, legal system of the Republic
  of, length-of-proceedings case law
HUMEN 27, 46, 49
H. V THE U.K. 30, 49

ILIJKOV 103
imprisonment, see criminal proceedings
inadmissibility of application to
  ECHR, preliminary pleas: abuse of
  the right of individual application
  8–9; loss of victim status (see loss of
  victim status, incompatibility ratione
  personae); manifestly unfounded 8–9;
  no significant disadvantage 8–9, 46;
  other pleas 8; overview 8–9; see also
  exhaustion of (effective) domestic
  remedies
individuals, empowerment of 107
interplay between different ECHR articles
  (see link, nexus between Article 6, 13
  and 35 and other ECHR articles)
interpretation in the light of ECHR articles
  6 and 13 2, 22
intervention, by state, by judge, see positive
  obligations
Italian Republic, Republic of Italy: case
  study, legal system 37–9; civilian nature
  of legal system of 2; Pinto Laws in 15,
  18, 37, 97; Scordino-Type Cases 12, 18,
  37–9, 97

JENSEN 17
judges' obligations, see positive obligations
Judgments 4
just satisfaction under Article 41 32, 39–44,
  45, 99

KAIĆ AND OTHERS 13
KAKAMOUKAS 41, 51–2
KALAJZIC 19, 21
KHASHIYEV AND AKAYEVA 20
KINCSES 32
KOZLICA 18
KRASUSKI 20, 46, 47
KUDŁA 7, 13, 14, 20, 23, 31, 39, 45–6, 50
KUPPINGER 20, 51

LAINE 100, 104
laws, requirements of national legal
  systems 22
LECHNER AND HESS 100
LE COMPTE, VAN LEUVEN AND DE
  MEYERE 50, 66, 103
LEDONNE (NO. 1 and NO. 2) 29, 47, 81
legal basis for tortious action for damages
  88–90
legal systems: common law, civil law,
  hybrid jurisdictions 2; differences in
  interpretation of the ECHR, margin of
  discretion 2
legal tradition, differences in interpretation,
  margin of appreciation/discretion 2
length-of-proceedings violations, volume
  of: as percentage of overall violations
  per state 112–13; as percentage of total
  Convention violations 109–10
liability in tort 83, 86–92
LIADIS 26–7
link, nexus between Article 6, 13 and 35
  and other ECHR articles 10–11, 13, 14,
  16, 22, 18, 19, 33, 35, 36–7, 107; property
  rights, failure to enforce a binding
  court decision amounts to a violation of
  Articles 6, 13 and Protocol 1 Article 1 33
LISEYTSEVA AND MASLOV 33, 49
LIZANETS 21
ŁOBARZEWSKI 26
loss of revenues, see nature of proceedings
loss of victim status, incompatibility ratione
  personae: acknowledgement of violation
  14–17; awarding compensation that is
  'manifestly unreasonable' 18; cumulative
  nature of requirements 19; delay in
  enforcement of compensation 19; delay
  in remedial proceedings 18; failure
  to cause loss of victim status as an
  aggravation 19; failure to recognise
  the breach 18; overview 8–9, 14–19;
  reservation of assessment of loss of
  victim status to merits 19; state failure to
  cause loss of victim status 17–19; see also

inadmissibility of application before ECHR, preliminary pleas
lucrum cessans, establishment of 96, 103
LUKENDA 14, 20, 21, 50

MAJOR PETER MANDUCA V THE HON. PRIME MINISTER 70, 80, 81
Malta, legal system of the Republic of: laws of x; length-of-proceedings case law and legal remedies for delay within legal system of Malta: adequacy of redress 66–8; alternative forms of redress 73–6; competent courts 76–8; compulsory administrative procedures 65–6; conclusions to case study 95–104; conduct of the applicant 54–5, 60–5; damages, courts' ability to award 54; *damnum emergens*, establishment of 96; defendant, legitimate, in constitutional and ordinary law remedies (private parties and the state, as defendants) 83–92; divergences from Strasbourg case law 54–5; effective remedies 83, 95–102; enforcement proceedings 90, 91, 101; expropriation, calculation of compensation 103; ordinary remedies for delay in 83–92; ordinary versus constitutional remedies 76–8, 86–7; overlap of remedies 98–101; overview 53–5; quantum of compensation considerations 68–73; remedies, redress of legal system of Malta: adequacy of 66–8; alternative forms of 73–6; solutions proposed 101–2; violations found against 55–6
margin of appreciation/discretion, national implementation of Convention 2, 15, 16, 38
MARTINS AND GARCIA ALVES 45
MARTINS CASTRO ET ALVES CORREIA DE CASTRO 21, 51
MARTINS MOREIRA 48
MEGYERI 103
MERIT 11, 45
Merryman, J. 7
METAXAS 21
method of examination, framework approach, Strasbourg Court 22–32; heads of examination, particular circumstances of the case: overview 24–32; complexity of the factual or legal issues 25; conduct of the applicant: for assessing reasonableness of length of proceedings 25–7; for assessing compensation 41; relevance in Malta 60–5; conduct of the competent authorities 27; what was at stake for the applicant: special diligence, exceptional diligence 29, 30; stakes, urgency due to nature of proceedings: criminal, civil, industrial, labour, employment, pension, the right to practice one's profession, high financial stakes, commercial and professional matters, property disputes, title to land, actions of retrial, actions for compensation for human rights and Convention violations, enforcement proceedings, combination of several factors: for assessing reasonableness of length of proceedings (*see also* method of examination) 3, 24, 29–31, 49; for determining the quantum of compensation (*see also* pecuniary and non-pecuniary damage and compensation) 40–4, 64, 69
Micallef Grimaud, C. 93, 104
MIFSUD 20, 50, 51
Mifsud Bonnici, G. 93
Mifsud Bonnici, U. 7, 9, 111
MIFSUD BONNICI V TABONE 81
MIFSUD V BONELLO 79, 85, 92, 99, 102, 103, 104
minimum standards ECHR 2, 22
minors 2; *see also* pecuniary and non-pecuniary damage and compensation; prevention; remedies for length-of-proceedings violations; stakes, urgency due to nature of proceedings
MINTOFF ET 91
moral damages, *see* pecuniary and non-pecuniary damage and compensation
MOSTACCIUOLO (NO. 1 and NO. 2) 20, 21, 43, 50
MUSCI 20, 21, 43, 50

national differences in implementation of ECHR 2
nature of proceedings: civil, common law, hybrid jurisdictions 2; criminal, administrative, civil, constitutional 2, 23; inquisitorial and adversarial 2; number of instances (*see* pecuniary and non-pecuniary damage and compensation); stakes *see* stakes, urgency due to nature of proceedings: criminal, civil, industrial, labour, employment, pension, the right to practice one's profession, high financial stakes,

commercial and professional matters, property disputes, title to land, actions of retrial, actions for compensation for human rights and Convention violations, enforcement proceedings, combination of several factors: for assessing reasonableness of length of proceedings 3, 24–5, 29–31, 49 (*see also* method of examination); stakes for determining the quantum of compensation 40–4, 64, 69 (*see also* pecuniary and non-pecuniary damage and compensation)
number of instances *see* pecuniary and non-pecuniary damage and compensation
NUVOLI 36

OLUJIC 34
ÖNERYILDIZ 21
opportunities, missed, *see* pecuniary and non-pecuniary damage and compensation
ordinary civil remedies, damages and tort: case study 83–104; versus constitutional and extraordinary remedies 9–13, 35–6, 76–82
ORŠUŠ 34
OSCOLA 2006 guidelines xlvii, 4
outline of approach, analysis of cases and remedies 4

PARIZOV 10
particular circumstances of the case, *see* method of examination
PATRIANAKOS 27
PAULINO TOMÁS 20, 21, 50
pecuniary and non-pecuniary damage and compensation: alternatives 16, 17, 44; compensating for frustration, anxiety and inconvenience 40; criteria for determining quantum of non-pecuniary damage 40, 43; evidence and non-pecuniary damages 40; express demand for 44; general 15, 40–5; moral damages, synonym for non-pecuniary damages 103; pecuniary compensation, casual link, speculation 45; power to award moral damages for effectiveness of remedy 36; presumption of moral damage, special cases 40
period to be considered: compulsory administrative proceedings preceding main proceedings 24; criminal proceedings, calculating period to be considered (*see* criminal proceedings); general 23; presumptions, prima facie 24–5; reasonableness of 23–35; *see also* method of examination
personal circumstances, health, age, reputation, other, exceptional diligence, *see* method of examination
PHILIS 46, 47, 103
pilot judgment: Article 46 ECHR xiv, 31, 37, 38
Pinto Laws in Italy 15, 18, 37, 97
PISHCHALNIKOV 26, 27, 47, 48
POLICE V ELLUL SULLIVAN ET 75
positive obligations: state obligations, judicial activism 27, 28, 31, 38, 49–50, 84, 102
powers of court to remedy breaches of Convention, *see* positive obligations
practice incompatible with the Convention, *see* pilot judgment
preliminary pleas, *see* inadmissibility of application to ECHR, preliminary pleas
prevention 3, 10, 13, 38, 39, 75, 95, 102, 106
private parties, redress against, *see* horizontal application of human rights
property rights, failure to enforce a binding court decision amounts to a violation of Articles 6, 13 and Protocol 1 Article 1 33
Protocol to the European Convention on Human Rights, article 1 x

RAMESH CHETENRAM SHARMA ET V ATTORNEY GENERAL 73, 81
reasonable time, what is reasonable? 24, 42, 48
relevance of Articles 6 and 13 to length-of-proceedings cases 22–52
remedies for length-of-proceedings violations: adequacy of remedy and redress (*see* loss of victim status); compensatory remedies 38; at different stages of the proceedings 38; different types of remedies, effective remedies 15–17, 35–6, 38–9, 44; to expedite procedures 38; ordinary remedies for delay in Malta, action for damages in tort (*see* Malta, legal system of Republic of); overview xlix–li, liii, 2–7, 13–14; structural adequacy of remedies (*see* European Convention on Human Rights: Article 13); *see also* exhaustion of (effective) remedies

Republic of Italy, *see* Italian Republic
Republic of Malta, *see* Malta, legal system of Republic of
reputation, damage to, *see* pecuniary and non-pecuniary damage and compensation
research, aims and parameters of 1–4
restitutio in integrum 2
RIBIČ 19
RICCARDI PIZZATI 20, 21, 43, 50
Rules of Court, ECHR, articles 1–10 x

SABEUR BEN ALI 103
SAID ET V ATTORNEY GENERAL 47, 58, 69, 93, 103
Said Pullicino, J. 6, 7, 84, 92, 102, 104, 126–30
SARTORY 19, 21, 48, 49
SCHEMBRI AND OTHERS 100, 103
SCORDINO 7, 20, 21, 39, 40, 42, 45, 49, 50, 51
Scordino-Type Cases xlvi, 12, 21, 37–9, 41, 50–1, 97
SELMOUNI 20
SIERMIŃSKI 20
SILČ 42, 45, 48, 80
SILVER AND OTHERS 21, 50
SIMALDONE 15, 16, 21, 48, 49, 50, 78
similar cases, consistency 2, 18, 32, 35, 42, 67
SLAVIČEK 11, 18, 50
solutions, *see* remedies for length-of-proceedings violations
SPITERI V ATTORNEY GENERAL 59, 92
SPITERI V ONOR. PRIM MINISTRU ET 86
SPROTTE 17
stakes, urgency due to nature of proceedings: criminal, civil, industrial, labour, employment, pension, the right to practice one's profession, high financial stakes, commercial and professional matters, property disputes, title to land, actions of retrial, actions for compensation for human rights and Convention violations, enforcement proceedings, combination of several factors 3, 24, 29–31, 49 (*see also* method of examination); for assessing reasonableness of length of proceedings (*also see* method of examination) 3, 24–5, 29–31, 49; for determining the quantum of compensation 40–4, 64, 69 (*see also* pecuniary and non-pecuniary damage and compensation)
standard of living 15, 19, 42, 44, 69; *see also* nature of proceedings; pecuniary and non-pecuniary damage and compensation; stakes, urgency due to nature of proceedings
states: as defendants 88–90; failure to cause loss of victim status (*see* loss of victim status, incompatibility *ratione personae*); obligations of state (*see* positive obligations); violations of Convention: sending a message to the State 107; statistics per state (*see* statistics); *see also* Italian Republic; Malta, legal system of the Republic of
statistics: volume of length-of-proceedings violations expressed as a percentage of total Convention violations 109; volume of length-of-proceedings violations expressed as a percentage of total Convention violations per State 112–13
Statutes x
Stavros, S. 24, 27, 45, 47
STEEL AND MORRIS 40–1, 94
Strasbourg Court, *see* European Court of Human Rights
structural deficiency: pilot judgments (*see* pilot judgments); significance of Article 13 (*see* European Court of Human Rights, Article 13); state obligation to remedy 38
sua sponte, examination by court of its own motion 31, 106
subsidiarity, principle of I, 5–6, 14, 20, 33, 37, 38, 50
SUKOBLJEVIC xl, 13, 18
SÜRMELI 21, 29, 36, 50, 78, 83, 88–9
SÜSSMANN 7, 34, 47, 50–1

theoretical overlap in possible damages 98–101
threshold for finding of a violation, *see* reasonable, what is reasonable?
tort law, *see* Malta, legal system of the Republic of: ordinary law versus extraordinary (constitutional) proceedings; *see* pecuniary and non-pecuniary damage and compensation
type of proceedings, *see* nature of proceedings
TYRER 6

UNIÓN ALIMENTARIA SANDERS SA 26, 47, 79
universal application of ECHR standards 2

Valentine Palmer, V. lii, 6, 115
Van Dijk, Van Hoof 46, 47, 48, 52, 58–9, 75, 79, 81, 99, 114
VANEY 21
VASSILIOS ATHANASIOU ET AUTRES 20, 49, 50
VELLA V THE HON. PRIME MINISTER ET 87
VERNILLO 20
VIDAS 21
violations: of Article 6 (*see* European Convention on Human Rights, Article 6); of Article 13 (*see* European Convention on Human Rights, Article 13); found by ECHR against Malta 55–6; loss of victim status (*see* loss of victim status, inadmissibility *ratione personae*); Scordino-Type Cases (*see* Scordino-Type Cases); *see also* statistics
VISUAL AND SOUND COMMUNICATIONS LIMITED V COMMISSIONER OF POLICE ET 77, 92
V.K. V CROATIA 49, 107–8

VLADIMIR ROMANOV 20
VUČKOVIĆ AND OTHERS 11, 20

WASSERMAN 21, 50
Woolf Report 43, 52

XUEREB V ATTORNEY GENERAL 57, 74–5, 76, 78, 92, 93
XUEREB V REGISTRAR OF COURTS ET 57, 68, 79, 84, 86, 92, 103
X V FRANCE 30, 48, 93

YAKIŞAN 44
YURIY NIKOLAYEVICH IVANOV 21, 33, 49, 50, 51; failure to enforce a binding court decision amounts to a violation of Articles 6, 13 and Protocol 1 Article 1 33

Zammit, D. E. 7, 20, 92, 104
ZAMMIT V BORG BARTHET NOE 90, 102
ZARB 14, 21, 38, 50, 51, 54, 67, 78, 80, 97, 103
ZARB V ATTORNEY GENERAL 59, 80, 92
ZIMMERMANN AND STEINER 29, 46, 47
ZUBKO AND OTHERS 34